PWoods.
10.9.82

D1437836

REPORT of the
FIFTH INTERNATIONAL
ROCK GARDEN PLANT
CONFERENCE AND SHOW

HELD AT

NOTTINGHAM—ENGLAND

MONDAY 13 APRIL 1981—THURSDAY 16 APRIL 1981

EDITOR

ALFRED EVANS, S.H.M., A.H.R.H.S.

CONFERENCE SPONSORS

ALPINE	SCOTTISH
GARDEN	ROCK GARDEN
SOCIETY	CLUB

JOINT COMMITTEE

ALFRED EVANS (Chairman)
J. A. COLMER (Vice Chairman)
Mrs JILL SLEIGH (Secretary)
F. F. H. CHARLTON (Treasurer)

Mrs K. N. DRYDEN,   Dr J. G. ELLIOTT,   Mrs E. IVEY,
J. H. A. MILNE,   Dr D. M. STEAD,   E. M. UPWARD

Printed in Great Britain by
Thomson Litho Ltd, East Kilbride, Scotland

Contents

List of Illustrations

Monochrome   PLATE

Line Drawings by Vicki Matthews

INTRODUCTION

"Alpines '81" is but a small chapter in the long and interesting story of the cultivation of plants. Gardening or horticulture as a profession, job or hobby has been practised for a very long time. I understand that Adam was a gardener—at least so we have been told—but I doubt if that gentleman would have seen or even been interested in any of the plants that we as rock gardeners class as our own today. No doubt he had other problems to concern him but I feel on firm ground when I say that the idea of nurturing Aretian Androsaces, Petiolarid Primulas, New World Fritillarias or some of the more fascinating plants from the antipodes never crossed his mind. We have progressed somewhat since Adam was a boy, at least in some respects.

As alpine plant enthusiasts we have come a long way but we are all aware that the end of the road so far as plants are concerned is not yet in sight. There are still many questions to be answered but I am sure we all agree that there is an element of expertise among some of our hobby members which would be difficult to surpass. The show held at Nottingham bears witness to that.

The Fifth International Rock Garden Plant Conference, "Alpines '81", was held for no other reason than it was expected that it would happen. After all, four conferences had taken place previously at 10-yearly intervals, apart from the longer gap between the first and the second where a war intervened and interfered with plans. One could almost say that a pattern of arranging rock garden plant conferences is established and it is one which may now be difficult to break. When something is enjoyed as much as the growing of alpine plants and the appreciation of their beauty, then specialised societies which set themselves up as the organisers of topical events, such as meetings and shows, cannot be surprised, although they may view the prospect with some alarm, when the demand for a conference by members becomes pressing. Conferences are great things and they contribute a great deal towards the full enjoyment of our pastime. I cannot speak from complete first hand knowledge of all international conferences, for I did not attend the first one held in 1936 but I have been involved in all the others and enjoyed them thoroughly.

I relate an historical fact and not news when I say that the Fifth International Rock Garden Plant Conference was sponsored jointly by the Alpine Garden Society and the Scottish Rock Garden Club, two societies with the same objectives, namely furthering of interest in alpine plants. Councils are very much the servants of members, or they should be, and as both societies have been involved in these ventures since 1951 it was inevitable that they would again unite in 1981. And so a small joint investigating committee was set up to look first of all into the feasibility of organising a conference at this time and then, when it was accepted by the respective councils that the scheme was possible, the committee was increased in size and asked to plan and run the affair. I was going to use the word control but who could ever hope to control such an enthusiastic group of plantsmen, many having travelled long distances to attend the meetings? Who would want to anyway?

That committee worked as a team and as individuals to make the organisation a success. The aim was to provide the conditions whereby delegates from as many countries as possible could meet, discuss and learn as much as they could about alpine plants, world wide, and the lecture programme was arranged to take account of this. The field was wide and the opportunity was taken to introduce into the programme as many facets as possible that affected our hobby. They were all meant to be talking points and, whilst the fact that certain subjects may not have been the favourite ones of individuals, hopefully, by the end of the lectures, those who may have felt this will have been made more aware of the problems facing the world's flora as well as being better informed on how to manage their alpines. The programme schedule was packed. This was done on purpose for the simple reason that with so many delegates one could not hope to leave gaps to be filled by personal interests. On the other hand there was really ample free time provided it was arranged; one simply need only not attend a lecture to have an hour's freedom. You could gauge quite clearly the amount of Scottish blood in the veins of delegates by the way so few of them missed anything, even although, finally, many said that they could have used up more time chatting.

Nottingham University Sports Centre has a lot to offer. Apart from a large marquee which was erected to house the trade stands and other worthwhile exhibits from public bodies, and was close by, all the conference activities took place under one roof. The large lecture theatre was spacious and its inside perimeter walls were suitably used to display numerous non-competitive exhibits. The large hall in which the Conference Show was held also gave ample room for the 600 plus delegates and others to mill around without feeling crowded out, and from the opening of the show the hall was never free from the type of hubbub present at all flower shows. All these facilities are mentioned at intervals in this report. Accommodation for most delegates was in university student halls of residence. There were four halls involved and these were set at some distance from, but more or less around, the conference centre. A pleasant walk across a mown playing field was the lot of some delegates and fortunately for them, and the organisers, the weather was perfect. Strolling across the campus in the company of friends was an exercise enjoyed by many.

But now for acknowledgements, for a conference, be it large or small, does not run by itself. It requires sponsors, organisers and helpers and, in the end, participants. Early in the arrangements one could not tell how many delegates would be likely to apply to come. You all know the sponsoring bodies who confidently accepted the responsibility and risk. The conference organising committee has been mentioned, their names are listed elsewhere in the report, and it is for you to judge how successful were their efforts. The local group of the Alpine Garden Society and the small Nottingham Rock Garden Society worked like Trojans attending to the multifarious tasks which precede, attend and follow in the wake of a gathering of this sort. The lecturers and the plant exhibitors had certainly done their homework. The university personnel who co-operated in many ways to ensure the smooth running of the domestic side of things and who often must have wondered what this group of flower people would be like, were unstinting with their help. And although not mentioned earlier, Nottingham City Council very kindly laid on a Civic Reception large enough to allow all the overseas delegates to be invited. It was a very generous gesture. Three national bodies which contributed a great deal with material and lecturers were the Royal Horticultural Society, Wisley and the Royal Botanic Gardens of Kew and Edinburgh. The Regius Keeper at Edinburgh deserves special thanks for allowing the facilities of that garden to be available and also for permitting its address to be used for conference business for a period of approximately three years. I am also grateful to Vicki Matthews for the line drawings.

Among the others who deserve our thanks are the plantsmen who produced such high quality specimens and responded to the plea to make this conference show a memorable one; the judges and their helpers; the considerable number of individuals and groups of people who prepared and assembled the many non-competitive displays which were both attractive and instructive and to which delegates returned again and again; the nurserymen and others who filled to capacity the large marquee with mouth-watering rarities and much sought-after species and forms and many other contributors whom it would be difficult to place in one of these categories. And finally, we are indebted to many generous donors who presented valuable and often decorative prizes for the competitive classes and those who provided free facilities, equipment and material.

It is not possible to thank individually the dozens of willing people who were involved with the many aspects of "Alpines '81". To them all we shall be forever grateful. I have purposely avoided using names for there can be no yard-stick by which one can judge the value of single contributions in a project of this size. Co-operation, tolerance, understanding, determination and hard work were the qualities required. They were there in plenty, both at Nottingham and previously, and these I hope will continue, for they are the same attributes needed to produce first-rate rock garden plants.

I hope you enjoy reading this report. I hope it brings back pleasant memories of April days spent in good company and among wonderful plants. Those who were at the conference may be aware of some of the omissions, there are not many I trust, and those who read this report and were not at Nottingham will, I hope, glean much from what is written. The question for the future, however, is where will the 6th International Rock Garden Plant Conference be held? When that is answered I hope the project will receive the same support and encouragement as "Alpines '81".

Alfred Evans

Pre-Conference Tour

MICHAEL UPWARD

To report objectively on an event that one had personally organised is not always easy for the person who is near the centre of things. All those who participated in the tour seemed to enjoy what had been arranged for them and any success that it may have had must be attributed to them. They were in good spirits the whole time and coped with any minor vicissitudes with admirable good humour.

Three coaches started off from London and headed south and east reaching Sissinghurst Castle garden in time for lunch where the café was opened especially for us. Although the intention was simply to stop for lunch, there was just time for a brief visit to the garden. It was perhaps a little too early in the season for most plants but it was the right time to see that strikingly beautiful but curious parasite *Lathraea clandestina* growing on the roots of willow. It was also seen later at Kew.

One coach only made a quick visit to the Birch Farm Nursery at East Grinstead where Will and Paul Ingwersen greeted the visitors, who later departed loaded with plants. One could not help but wonder how many of the overseas delegates would explain their purchases or get them through customs on their arrival home.

The garden at Coldham, Little Chart Forstal, near Ashford has been laid out since the last conference by Jack and Jean Elliott and the entire family were there to greet us, still smiling, notwithstanding the damage caused to the lawn outside by one of the coaches becoming bogged down earlier in the day. Here bulb enthusiasts drooled over *Fritillaria michailovskii*, numerous Calochortus spp. and three forms of *Tecophilea cyanocrocus*.

Not to have included Kew, Windsor or Wisley in the itinerary would have been unthinkable and as it happened the delegates were not disappointed in what they saw. The alpine house at Wisley was as interesting as ever, with the attractive beds down its outside walls where *Sanguinaria canadensis* 'Flore Pleno' caught everyone's attention. The visit to Kew was highlighted by the preview we had of the new alpine house—it was to be opened officially the following Friday—this new concept in growing alpines has yet to stand the test of time and no doubt comparisons will be made in 1991. The Savill Garden at Windsor cannot in truth be classed as alpine, but our interests are wide, the setting was magnificent, and there *Lysichiton americanum* and magnolias were responsible for most of the colour.

Dr Lionel Bacon's garden near Winchester showed delegates how to garden on chalk. The continental beds were educational and Joyce Bacon's alpine house in which she grows the rare bi-generic hybrid ×*Jankaemonda vandedemii (Jankaea heldreichii* × *Ramonda myconi)* evoked great interest. One coach went to Longstock, the garden belonging to the John Lewis Partnership in the nearby Test Valley, to see the waterside planting of moisture-loving subjects.

And then to the Oxford Botanic Garden, the oldest botanic garden in Britain, where the natural order beds and in particular the collection of much-coveted, variegated plants were much admired. The visit to Joe Elliott's nursery and garden at Broadwell led to the coaches being filled with even more plants. His stock of *Paraquilegia grandiflora* attracted much attention as did Lewisias 'Pinkie' and 'Perkie' and a white form of *Primula* 'Linda Pope'.

Two coaches went on to Birmingham to visit the garden of Mr and Mrs Roy Elliott where the tufa cliff holding many attractive alpines is now nicely mature, and bedded out in the alpine house are former show plants living in happy retirement. Not far away is the garden of Mr and Mrs Jim Broadhurst, with a raised bed, protected overhead, in which *Tropaeolum polyphyllum* grows like a weed and where plants from the New Jersey Pine Barrens were growing happily. Those on the third coach had lunch at the National Trust Garden at Hidcote Manor, which we had almost to ourselves. In the afternoon we visited a curious little garden near Alcester called the Pleck Garden and which is worth a visit, if only for its eccentricity.

The finale of the tour was the visit to Boughton House, Kettering, where Sir David and Lady Scott have created a fascinating garden— the woodland garden beyond the stone walls having been started by Sir David earlier in the century and which is now delightfully mature, whilst Lady Scott (Valerie Finnis) has assembled her collection of alpine plants in raised beds along the walls. There we saw a pink form of *Sanguinaria canadensis* and a fine specimen of *Rhodothamnus chamaecistus* amongst hundreds of other treasures.

Obviously one could compile a long catalogue of plants which were seen and discussed during visits to these gardens but perhaps it might be better to leave the arranging in order of preference in the memories of those who joined me during the six days on the run-up to Alpines '81.

A Highland Nursery Garden

JACK DRAKE

Primula griffithii

The title of this article is delightfully vague. It is "A Highland Nursery Garden" and I feel it gives me the opportunity to write about anything I like. And that is what I mean to do.

As this is based on the talk arranged for the Alpines '81 Conference which was probably the last talk I am likely to give I have decided that I shall be completely self-indulgent with no thought at all for my readers.

There are innumerable plants which we grow and greatly admire, and although we may recognise that they are both beautiful and desirable they don't have that particularly something, that ultimate attraction that makes them special. However, I am going to discuss some of the magical plants which, above all others, have a particular appeal for me. These need not be beautiful, rare or difficult to grow. In fact they may be downright ordinary, and yet they have that extra appeal which draws us to them. The lyric of a popular song hit asks, "What's in a kiss? Have you ever wondered just what it is?" What is it then that certain plants have in their make-up which demand this marked attention, almost worship, from us?

I think, therefore, that a sub-title to this article could read "One Man's Loves". While making my selection I often felt that I had set myself an impossible task. There are so many plants which clamour for inclusion, yet space and time to discuss them are limited.

My title refers to the Inshriach Alpine Plant Nursery. I know that some of you reading this will have visited that establishment but I hope you will bear with me if I describe the place very briefly for the benefit of those who have not.

Inshriach Nursery is situated right in the centre of Scotland, in the valley of the River Spey, some 35 miles south of Inverness. The great massif of the Cairngorm Mountains rises to the south-east and the beautiful Monadhliath Mountains to the north-west.

Being so far from the sea and under the influence of these high hills, the climate tends to be very severe. Frost can occur during any month of the year, including June, July and August, while in the winter zero temperatures fahrenheit, 32 degrees of frost, are not uncommon. Although in recent years there has been a run of comparatively mild winters and we have had to wait until April and May for our winter weather, these apparently more temperate conditions have brought disastrous results.

The loam is a light, acid, sandy gravel with a minimum of top soil. This certainly gives perfect drainage but it also means that copious yearly dressings of humus must be applied to keep the soil fertile.

It will be understood, therefore, that only the hardiest plants will survive at Inshriach and in consequence we must be very selective in what we grow.

The garden, quite apart from the nursery proper, covers about $\frac{1}{4}$ of an acre and consists of a rock garden, a wild garden with a burn, a peat garden, various formal terraces and an alpine house.

The exact date when spring arrives at Aviemore is difficult to define but early in that season *Crocus gargaricus* appears. This species is from western Turkey and produces brilliant orange flowers. This is the only orange or yellow coloured Crocus that can be grown for almost invariably the others are destroyed by mice and pheasants. While easy enough to cultivate and it increases fast by stolons, it does not always flower freely. The best clump is flourishing in a root-infested area and is in almost complete shade from late spring onwards. This is a marvellous little Crocus and it is admired several times a day.

The aciphyllas are nearly all from New Zealand and undoubtedly they are an acquired taste. They range in stature from huge giants to midgets and many of them have wicked, needle-like spikes on the tips of their leaves, as I remember to my discomfort when in New Zealand after sitting down on what appeared to be a grassy ledge to eat my lunch. The "grass" turned out to be seedling aciphyllas and it was what I should imagine sitting on a porcupine would be like. The miniature species are much less formidable and appeal to me most. *Aciphylla spedenii* is one of the most attractive, forming rosettes of hard spiky leaves. Unfortunately its blooming is erratic, and although handsome as a foliage plant it is even more decorative when it produces umbels of white flowers. It is not too difficult to cultivate in a gritty well-drained soil.

Aquilegia nivalis grows wild in Kashmir. It is rarely seen in gardens and even where it is grown it is not too easy to coax into flower. When it does condescend to produce its sombre, velvety-purple, dark-centred flowers these are of exceptional beauty.

Bupleurum angulosum is not in the least showy but it holds its own attraction for me. It comes from the Pyrenees and appeals because of the very nature of its astonishing, jade-green flowers. It seems to be very easy to grow in any good soil.

Just after the last war I happened to visit the Royal Botanic Garden, Edinburgh, and was struck by an incredible clump of what appeared to be bright pink buttercups in bud at the bottom of the old scree. This turned out to be *Callianthemum rutifolium* from the Alps. I was so impressed by this little charmer that I scanned the lists for seeds. Eventually I obtained some but the resulting seedlings only produced pure white flowers. They were nice enough but it was the pink one I sought. I persevered until finally I was rewarded, and my pink flowered seedling appeared. I grow it in a pot in the alpine house where I can gloat over it at close quarters. It is a plant of alpine turf in nature and seems to appreciate a fairly rich, well-drained compost.

The Tridentate group of campanulas is native to the Caucasus and Asia Minor. These species are very much alike and are all equally attractive. I consider them to be the most lovable of all campanulas. They tend to be the first of the genus to flower and seem to prefer a very well-drained position in a gritty, but not impoverished soil. The species which does best for me is, I believe, *C. bellidifolia* and it never fails to produce a multitude of gorgeous violet bells.

The cassiopes are dwarf ericaceous shrublets which have a special appeal because of their exquisitely dainty white flowers. The tiny bells are held on hair-like stalks. Cassiopes are aristocrats in the world of miniature shrubs and because of their floriferousness, their whipcord-like stems and the manner in which they effectively carpet the ground they command our admiration. My prime favourite is the little Japanese species, *C. lycopodioides*. This plant forms flat green mats which, in the better forms, may be smothered with the smallest possible white fairy thimbles. Many years ago when Harold Fletcher was Director of Wisley Gardens I lunched with him in a nearby pub. After lunch, in a somewhat hilarious frame of mind, we wandered through the gardens and, while in the frame-yard, I almost tripped over a pot lying on the path. It contained what appeared to be a half-dead, scruffy little shrub but it was in fact *C. selaginoides* L & S 13284. Harold said, "Seeing that you have practically smashed the plant you had better put it in your pocket before anyone sees it". And this is how this superb Cassiope came into my possession. The plant is something of a mystery for, after seeing it in the nursery, neither Ludlow nor Sherriff remembered ever having encountered it in the wild. It is certainly a most outstanding form of *C. selaginoides* with huge pure white flowers. Their texture is solid and the habit of the plant is compact. A well flowered specimen carrying this collector's number received an Award of Merit when displayed at the R.H.S. Halls in 1954. Since being introduced into gardens, cassiopes have produced numerous spontaneously occurring hybrids and one of the first to appear, and one of the finest is *C*. 'Muirhead'. This is considered to be a cross between *C. wardii* and *C. lycopodioides*. This remarkable plant gained a First Class Certificate when shown at Edinburgh. It is an easy plant to cultivate in acid, peaty soil and it makes a glorious specimen for the alpine house.

I am not sure why *Celmisia sessiliflora* (Mount Potts Form) gives me such inordinate pleasure. It has the great asset of always looking the same, summer and winter. Its silvery, spiky rosettes form a hard, satisfactory dome, which increases year by year, occasionally being covered with white, stemless, daisy-like flowers. It comes from the foothills of Mount Potts in the South Island of New Zealand. The type plant is much larger and is equally attractive but for some reason it does not appear to be as hardy as the form from Mount Potts. On my visit to the South Island, although over ten years ago, one day, especially, stands out. I enjoyed a magical walk up Gertrude Valley to Gertrude Saddle in Fiordland where one could look down on Milford Sound. The valley was full of enormous, silver rosettes. They were celmisias but nobody could say for certain what they were and all in the party agreed that they must be hybrids. I managed to get some viable seeds and for the want of a better name the resulting mature plants have become known as the Inshriach Hybrids. They are enormous, opulent and splendid with flowers almost the size of Shasta daisies.

Clintonia borealis is native to some North American forests and is a plant which seems to appeal all the more the longer you have it. Each year I look forward with great anticipation to its flowering. The elegant stems carry delicate little flowers of a subtle chartreuse yellow and give the impression of miniature lilies. It runs about happily in a cool humus-rich, acid soil where eventually it will make mats of vegetation. It is herbaceous.

Codonopsis convolvulacea 'Alba' is an entrancingly lovely plant from the Himalayas and is a garden rarity. The type plant has deep lavender-blue flowers. It is a twiner and in the open requires the association of a dwarf shrub to support it. If grown in a pot it can be trained on pea sticks. The stems emerge from fat, rugged tubers which should be planted about six inches deep. I have the blue species growing through an ancient specimen of *Salix × boydii* where it flowers in late summer and many visitors to the nursery ask for the "shrub with blue flowers".

Before our early winter sets in, our Highland autumn tends to go out in a blaze of glory. We get those wonderful golden days with a touch of frost at night and the birch trees and rowans are aglow. It is at this period that I wait impatiently for the blooming of the colchicums, especially for *C. speciosum* 'Atrorubens'. It is surprising how seldom one sees this outstanding form, for it seems just as easy to grow and increase as the lilac-pink types, and to my mind it is infinitely more desirable. The low autumn sun lights up the great goblets like lanterns. But beware of the huge suppressing leaves which appear in spring; they can so easily overwhelm and destroy any small plant in their vicinity. Perhaps in a position on their own such as under a tree or in a small meadow are the best places for them.

One of the most thrilling plants to come my way in recent years is *Corydalis ambigua* which is native to northern Japan. It has been proved to be of the utmost hardiness, growing well in the peat garden. It is also superb in the alpine house in spring. Stout spikes carry many quite large flowers of a glorious sky-blue and no photograph I have seen does justice to the colour. It is said to vary in shades of blue but our stock seems to be fairly uniform and even those showing a trace of purple in the bud turn blue as they expand. It may come as a surprise to many that I am not including *C. cashmiriana* in my list. Beautiful it certainly is, but for me the rather hard, greeny-blue does not have the attraction of the sky-blue *C. ambigua*. Actually I have a very soft spot for Corydalis and so I include two more in my list. In the alpine house in February the pans of *C. solida* var *densiflora* in full bloom ensure frequent visits daily. What there is about this plant which draws me is difficult to define. The flowers open a soft, purplish-grey and fade to almost pure white. But its lush growth so early in the year and the waxy texture of the flowers seem to have an irresistible appeal. This particular form was collected by Brian Mathew in Turkey in 1965. *Corydalis transsilvanica* is my third choice. What a marvellous plant this is! Its origin seems rather obscure but there is no denying the wonderful brick-pink shade of the flowers in the best forms. It is still very rare in cultivation but, fortunately it has set seed at Inshriach and, in time, I hope a small stock will be assembled. Because of its scarcity it is still treasured and coddled in the alpine house where it seems established.

Daphnes have always had an attraction and again I have chosen three. *Daphne arbuscula* is a gem from the Carpathians and forms attractive, compact clumps on a scree. There it produces its lilac-pink flowers. *Daphne cneorum* 'Alba' is a very rare white form of the "Garland Flower" and is, I believe, only to be found in the Carpathian Mountains. Like many alpines it is very slow growing and, regrettably, it is extremely difficult to propagate. The form of *D. cneorum* listed as 'Pygmaea' was raised from seed collected in the wild at Lauteret in the French Alps. It is a compact little plant with brightly coloured, richly-scented, rose-red flowers. It occasionally sets a few viable seeds here.

Dianthus, being mostly lime-lovers, do not take kindly to the soil at Inshriach or to our conditions generally, but there are exceptions and among them is that true calcicole from the eastern Alps, *D. alpinus*. This is surely one of the finest of all rock garden plants. It forms quite big clumps and the large rose-red, dark-zoned flowers attract enormous attention. *Dianthus neglectus* carries buff-backed, rich pink flowers and these have always appealed to me, but in a plant which appeared here and is offered under the cultivar name of "Inshriach Dazzler" the pink is deep, glowing and intense in colour. It is a very strong grower and I suspect it may have a touch of *D. deltoides* in its make-up. It is certainly a great garden plant and always in demand. An absolutely splendid plant from Greece and one which forms neat, hard hummocks is *D. simulans*. The clumps can be almost hidden beneath the warm, rose-red flowers. I find this plant totally irresistible if only because it has a will to grow in scree, trough or pan.

Dicentra peregrina grows on pumice-stone screes in Japan. This species always fills me with wonder for the quaintly shaped, rose-red "Bleeding Hearts" and dainty silvery-blue filigree leaves hardly seem to be real and could very well have come from one of those pictures of magic, fairy gardens that I remember from childhood days. It has delicacy and grace which are quite breath-taking. It is also a tricky plant to grow well but the reward makes the challenge worthwhile.

Allied to the campanulas is Edraianthus, two of which I find particularly to my liking. They both delight in sunny calcareous scree or tufa rock. They are native to the Balkans and the first, *E. pumilio,* is an absolute joy in the scree, developing tight cushions hidden by blue stemless flowers. The other, *E. serpyllifolius,* has a 'Major' form which is said to have appeared in Reginald Farrer's garden at Ingleborough. This is an absolute winner, the compact clumps disappearing under the wealth of huge bells of imperial purple. Unfortunately it must be propagated vegetatively, the only method available to gardeners if the form is to be retained, but, due to the age of the clone which is now losing vigour, this is becoming more difficult.

Erigeron aureus 'Canarybird' is a marvellous little plant with light yellow flowers which was raised here many years ago from seed of the golden *E. aureus* collected in the vicinity of Mount Rainier in the state of Washington. It would appear to be a hybrid but the collector assured me that no other Erigeron grew in this area. Whatever it is in that respect it is a little gem. It should be grown in a gritty soil in full sun and is ideally suited for trough culture. It sets no seed and so must be propagated from cuttings.

Nearly all erythroniums have a prominent place in my affection, and this applies particularly to those from the North American continent. They seem to possess every quality a plant should have— great beauty of flower and frequently, as an added bonus, elegant leaves. Once they have flowered and the seed pods form they quickly shrivel and, tidily, they die away. In this they are unlike so many other bulbs which leave a messy mass of rotting vegetation behind. Once more I confine my remarks to three although I know you are all aware that there are many more. Some have attractive, descriptive, common names and one "The Avalanche Lily", *E. montanum,* from the slopes of Mount Rainier where it grows by the million, describes perfectly the scene. Most books and periodicals state that this species is difficult or even impossible to grow but I take a special pride in this for here it grows and flowers well. Close by is a colony of *E. oregonum,* a species which varies in colour from white to sulphur. They are descendants of plants collected on Vancouver Island nearly 50 years ago and, when I see them in flower, they bring back happy memories. Finally, *E. revolutum,* a plant almost identical with the last except for the colour of its flowers, is of high merit especially in the better colour forms which can be glorious rose-pink.

I am ashamed to say that my knowledge of snowdrops is almost nil. For me a snowdrop is a snowdrop but I appreciate them all very much. I am especially attracted to those with big, fat, dumpy flowers, many of them being forms of *Galanthus plicatus.* One that is always splendid in February is *G. plicatus* 'Mrs Backhouse', the huge open flowers lasting for weeks, and every time I go out of my back door I selfishly gloat, like a miser, over the increasing large colony.

The late David Wilkie, the authority on gentians, saw a plant in the nursery and pronounced it to be the true *Gentiana alpina.* Wilhelm Schacht of the Munich Botanic Gardens disagreed with him entirely. I have now seen the true *G. alpina* growing in the Pyrenees and am forced to agree with Herr Schacht. Nevertheless, my plant is very fine, dwarf and compact, obviously a form of *G. acaulis.* However it is as *G. alpina* that this clone has been distributed and to my mind it is the most attractive of all, with exceptionally deep-blue flowers. Another plant I find irresistible (this time one of questionable parentage), which grows happily in a trough, is a hybrid between *G. verna* var *angulosa* and *G. pumila. Gentiana pumila* is a *verna*-like plant from eastern Europe. It is not very easy to grow but we have managed to establish it in a trough where, encouragingly, it runs about. It was seed from this colony that produced the hybrid. It is early days to say whether or not it will keep its character but rock gardening is full of promise. The late Mr G. H. Berry used to experiment with crossing various autumn-flowering gentians and one of his best hybrids was *G.* 'Farorna', (*G.*

farreri × *G. ornata*), which did well here for a number of years. We found that it set seed prolifically and it is from this seed that the gentians classified in the catalogue as Drake's Strain were born. We call it a strain because it is raised annually and the seed is saved from specially selected plants. The aim is to try to preserve the vivid Cambridge blue of *G. farreri* and the dumpy bells of *G. ornata*. It is usually the earliest of the autumn-flowering gentians to bloom and from time to time some very attractive creamy-white forms are produced. I feel sure most of you will know the famous hybrid *G.* × *macaulayi*. What is probably not so well known is that several other seedlings were raised from the same pod. Mr Macaulay was a close friend of Dick Trotter who lived not far from me, and he was given the whole set by Mr Macaulay. One day I was looking at them all in flower and felt that amongst them was one outstanding seedling which was worth propagating. Material was kindly given to me and, at the outset, we agreed on the name *G.* × *macaulayi* 'Kingfisher'. In my opinion it is the best all-round autumn-flowering gentian. It is very near to one of its parents, *G. sino-ornata*, but blooms a fortnight earlier (a great asset in cold northern gardens) and is rather more compact and a lighter shade of blue.

The Japanese *Glaucidium palmatum* is a superb plant with huge, lavender, poppy-like flowers but when the selected white form is first seen it is quite breath-taking. The large flowers seem to have a distinctive waxy texture. It is offered as *G. palmatum* 'Album'. Glaucidium is a monotypic genus and is one of those attractive Japanese species which adds to the quality of a garden collection. Fortunately it is not difficult in cultivation provided it is given a cool position in semi-shade.

Of all the whipcord hebes from New Zealand the one I find most fascinating is *H. cheesemanii*. It is also I believe the tiniest, forming charming little compact clumps covered with minute white flowers. It is ideal for troughs and screes and tholes the harsh Inverness-shire climate without adverse effects. So, too, does *Helipterum albicans* and particularly the variety *alpinum*. The velvety white leaves and the glistening white everlasting flowers remain in good condition for weeks. Here it is given full sun and a gritty soil mixture.

Jurinea macrocephala is a member of the thistle family and comes from the Himalaya. I always await the flowering of this curious plant with anticipation. The boss of lurid black flowers, enlivened by the white tipped stamens, sitting in the centre of a rosette of silver-grey leaves is completely fascinating. It appears to prefer a light sandy soil.

Different kinds of lewisias have been raised at Inshriach for a long time but a number of years ago we had a lucky break. An individual seedling raised from seed collected from a pink *L. cotyledon* hybrid produced rather small flowers but of an astonishing colour. It was almost orange-scarlet and we called it 'Comet'. From this plant, with us now long defunct, were raised the first batch of *Lewisia* (Sunset Strain) showing a warmth of colour and including yellow, apricot, orange and peach shades. By careful selection over the years the strain is now greatly improved. Some of the more recent shades are really entrancing and one can spend hours amongst them selecting and re-selecting. We have come a long way from the old wishy-washy, magenta-pink, stripy flowers.

Of all the blue poppies we grow, *Meconopsis grandis* 'Slieve Donard' seems to be the ultimate in size, colour, shape and robust growth. If I were to be restricted to growing just one this would undoubtedly be it. I understand it was selected from among a batch of seedlings raised from wild collected seed in the Slieve Donard Nursery, County Down, alas no longer in business. For a long time it was listed in their catalogue as *M. grandis* 'Prain'. It is a sound perennial, forming large clumps in cool well-drained, humus-rich soil. Also from the area where *M. grandis* grows wild is a plant which associates well with it, *Nomocharis saluenensis*. It is related to Lilium. All Nomocharis are fascinating but the reason why I think this particular species has a special place for me is because of the trusting way in which the lovely rose-pink flowers look up at you. All the rest hang their heads. It is dwarfer than most of the others and revels in the conditions here.

Omphalogrammas are fascinating plants with more or less trumpet-shaped flowers in varying shades of violet and here I have chosen *O. minus,* one of the lesser known species. Its undoubted charm lies in its smallness. By no means so spectacular as its close allies—and perhaps because of this—I like it. All omphalogrammas come from the Himalaya and China and enjoy moist, fertile soil in semi-shade.

Polygala chamaebuxus with yellow and cream pea-shaped flowers is a prostrate shrublet common throughout the mountains of Europe. The form I grow here, however, is *P. chamaebuxus* 'Rhodoptera' where the flowers are yellow and carmine. It is an amazing plant and is rarely out of flower. I am frequently told that 'Rhodoptera' is identical with the forms 'Grandiflora' and 'Purpurea', both of which I have tried, to which I must add that the form I call 'Rhodoptera' is infinitely more free-flowering than either of the others and is one of the most admired plants in the nursery.

Primulas come high on my list of plants for consideration and out of a host of highly desirable species queuing up for inclusion I have chosen a mere six. A large number of primulas enjoy the conditions in the Scottish Highlands. Under the name *P. petiolaris* we grow a most charming little plant which forms tight, compact rosettes filled with Victorian posies of vivid pink primroses in early spring. Whatever its correct name may be, and there is great confusion in the naming of petiolarids, I find this little plant fascinating. It is one of the easiest of this section, being quite happy in a shady position in the peat garden. Another of the same section, *P. edgeworthii* 'Alba', when grown well must surely be one of the loveliest of all primulas. It has frosted-grey leaves and crystalline white flowers. It likes the same treatment as the previously-mentioned species but it is not very long lived. It is necessary to raise it from seeds regularly. *Primula valentiniana* with cherry-red bells belongs to the section Amethystina. Regrettably this darling little Primula is no longer with us and I miss it from my collection. Our plants were raised from seed collected by Ludlow and Sherriff and we grew it successfully for many years. Unfortunately it never set seed and so the plants eventually died out. I wonder if anyone still has this species? Included in the section Soldanelloides is a Primula which exudes real class. It is *P. reidii* and everything about it is exquisite, and when it produces these gorgeous, waxy-white, heavily scented flowers it is impossible to come away from it. Unfortunately it is difficult to keep it true as it crosses only too readily with its variety, *P. reidii* var *williamsii* and so tends to lose its elegance. Neither is it too easy to grow, but with care it can be managed in a semi-shaded position in vegetable soil. The place where it does best is in a shady frame where the resting buds may be covered in winter. The Sik-

Ramonda nathaliae   (*Plate 1*)

Dianthus alpinus   (*Plate 2*)

Edraianthus serpyllifolius 'Major'   (*Plate 3*)

Morisia monantha   (*Plate 4*)

Dicentra peregrina var. pusilla (*Plate 5*)

Viola delphinantha (*Plate 6*)

Rhodothamnus chamaecistus   (*Plate 7*)

Daphne arbuscula   (*Plate 8*)

kimensis section of Primula embraces some coarse species but the Tibetan *P. ioessa* can never be accused of being that. I remember Mrs Dorothy Renton of Branklyn, Perth giving me seed of this and saying that she hoped that I would find it as endearing a plant as she did. I do indeed and at flowering time the large, drooping, lavender bells always give delight. It is the first of its section to flower and it appreciates a moist position. And lastly, although well enough known, *P. chionantha,* with milk-white scented flowers, never fails to stop me in my tracks when it commences blooming, and it is one of my prime favourites. It is one of the easiest of the Nivalis section to manage but although a strong grower it is not very long lived. Luckily it is very easy to raise from its plentifully-produced seed.

The pulsatillas are popular in the garden and I have chosen three which are favourites of mine. *Pulsatilla alpina* is surely one of the most breath-taking of all alpine plants with its huge white chalices. It is perfectly easy to grow in any good garden soil, but watch out for the expanding carroty leaves which develop after flowering. They can smother neighbouring plants. *Pulsatilla aurea,* this absolutely marvellous plant from the Caucasus, is seldom seen in cultivation. It is not easily grown but it is not impossible to do so, and when its huge golden-yellow flowers appear it is much admired. Another species, *P. alba,* not to be confused with *P. vulgaris* 'Alba', is a plant which is little known. I find it hard to understand why, for coming from eastern Europe, and especially from the Tatra Mountains in Czechoslovakia, it has the great advantage of usually blooming twice in a season. The flowers, although not so large as those of *P. alpina,* are equally beautiful and are enhanced by the blue stain on the undersides of the petals. It is perfectly easy to grow and is long lived.

Jim Archibald sent home some plants of *Ramonda nathaliae* from his Macedonian expedition in 1964. They carried the number JCA 686. One of them turned out to be something really special. It is exceptionally free-flowering and has large flowers of a luminous lavender. I have never seen a Ramonda quite like it, so keep it in a pan in the alpine house where I can enjoy looking at it constantly.

What can one say about *Ranunculus lyallii,* known as the "Mountain Lily" in New Zealand, except that it is as tricky to grow as it is beautiful to look at. That it can be grown and grown well is proved at Inshriach, and I get the greatest satisfaction from it when it does produce these heads of huge white buttercup-like flowers. In nature it seems to succeed in a variety of positions from scree to heavy bog, but in cultivation it seems to prefer a deep, very rich soil which is always moist. New Zealand is also known for its vegetable sheep. They form large woolly cushions and the most publicised I suppose is *Raoulia eximia* which really does look like a flock of sheep when seen in quantity growing on a scree. Belonging to this group of plants is one known as *R. × loganii,* a wild-occurring hybrid ? which I find particularly attractive. It forms mounds of silver-grey woolly rosettes and has the advantage of being less difficult to manage than many of the others. There is uncertainty about whether or not this plant is a bi-generic hybrid between the "New Zealand Edelweiss", *Leucogenes grandiceps* and *Raoulia goyenii* or a true species. That need not worry us unduly as it makes a fine specimen for the alpine house where it will grow happily in a well-drained gritty soil. It can be propagated with ease from cuttings.

A near relative of the trilliums, *Scoliopus bigelovii,* which I find entirely captivating, is an oddity from California. Although perfectly hardy it is best grown in a pot in the alpine house because of its small size. There its green and dark-purple flowers can be examined closely, while the spotted leaves add an exotic touch. But you should be prepared to wear a mask for I find the odour emitted quite revolting.

I suppose it is true to say that everyone loves soldanellas. They have an inexplicable charm not least of which is their ability to grow and flower through the snow. Unfortunately they tend to be temperamental in their flowering in cultivation, but now and then a seedling comes along which seems to make up for the shortcomings of its relatives. Such was a form of *S. montana* which appeared here. As a tiny seedling it produced a number of flowering stems and went from strength to strength. Its death knell was tolled when it was awarded an F.C.C. by the R.H.S. Everybody who saw it wanted it and so it was divided and more than divided to try to cope with demand. It never really recovered and eventually died. I wonder if there are any plants still around?

I can never understand why *Trillium ovatum* is always treated as a poor relation of *T. grandiflorum*. It is native to the western states of North America and flowers with us about three weeks ahead of *T. grandiflorum*, thus extending the Trillium season. Certainly it is smaller and more compact but its superb white flowers which turn pink with age, and its neatness and grace are most disarming. It seems easy to grow in any woodland-type soil and is probably best without lime.

Tropaeolum polyphyllum comes from the Chilean Andes and when once established in the garden bids fair to take over large chunks of it. It forms huge running tubers about a foot down in the soil and these emit long streamers which may erupt anywhere. The flowers are of an intense yellow and appear in profusion among the silvery-grey foliage. The plant can be an embarrassment in a nursery as everyone who sees it in bloom wants it and it is by no means easy to propagate in commercial quantities. It is ideally suited to cascading down the face of a terrace wall.

And to end with a blaze but before winter sets in there are two other plants I should like to mention. The spindleberry from China which never fails to take my breath away with its dazzling autumn attire of glowing reddish-pink is *Euonymus alatus*. It is so easy to grow and is compact enough for the smaller garden. It is one of my most favourite autumn-colour shrubs. The other is a Mountain Ash, *Sorbus* 'Joseph Rock'. Our stock originated from the same post-lunch amble round Wisley Gardens with Harold Fletcher which produced the Ludlow and Sherriff *Cassiope selaginoides*. The yellow berries were lying about under the small tree and some went into my pocket. The resulting young trees produced berries in varying shades of red, pink, amber and yellow and the autumn colour presented by the foliage is invariably magnificent.

I have no doubt that not everyone will agree with my list of special "loves" but as my aim is to stimulate and perhaps encourage you to think seriously about your own special favourites, in that, I hope I have been successful.

Modern Vegetative Propagation

PHILIP McMILLAN BROWSE and PETER HUTCHINSON

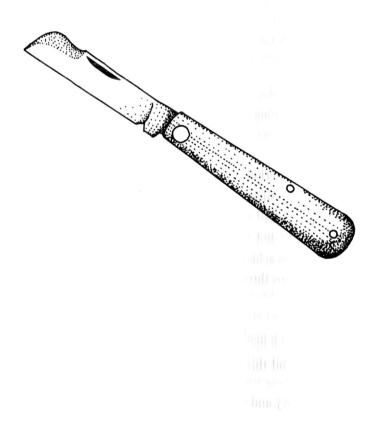

Plant propagation, within the current conceptual limits of conventional macro-methods, has not altered fundamentally in terms of practice over the last hundred and fifty to two hundred years. The same basic methods are still used and no new principles have been discovered. Modern advances have been achieved by refining the techniques of operations using our improved understanding of the underlying scientific principles; and the inexorable advances in technology, which provide the opportunity to allow the more certain application of these principles in practice: and thus allows a greater degree of success to be achieved, albeit still within the framework of these basic methods. In arriving at our present level of capability it should not be ignored that most positive advance has been determined by the application of simple and clear-minded common sense and has been achieved by propagators who were capable of surveying the whole scene, correlating information, discarding the erroneous and unnecessary, and using the relevant and applicable to improve on current practice.

Real progress in the development of plant propagation stems from only a little over thirty years ago when the technological advances, accelerated by the necessities of a World War, became available to a new generation of propagators. Biochemical synthesis provided artificial growth-promoting substances, improving industrial technology supplied more reliable electrical equipment such as soil warming cables and automatic mist systems, and scientific knowledge accelerated the development of pesticides and fungicides.

Prior to this period, propagation technique was much shrouded in magic and mysticism, and was "understood" and practised only by a few who had survived a long apprenticeship; in general, knowledge was not shared, the status quo was maintained and limited progress achieved. Techniques were often complicated and difficult, perhaps through ignorance or because of the necessity to maintain and bolster a position. However the basic methods employed were, and still are, fundamentally the same. Recent advances have been made primarily by the sharing of knowledge and information, and this in turn has shorn much of the unnecessary aspects from these traditional techniques and has reduced them to their elementary and essential components. Thus modern advance is generally concerned with simplification and the reduction of any method to those essential factors which are required for success. Therefore, in general, today's techniques are simpler, more effective and quicker in response.

Present-day advance has not provided any panacea with which the tried systems may be revolutionised or superseded. In the recent past the introduction of growth-regulating substances (rooting hormones etc.), the advent of mist propagating units and, latterly, the technique of chip budding have all been heralded as replacing and/or even eliminating much of previous procedures: but in actual practice they have enjoyed only a brief period of publicity and then slipped back to where they belong—progress certainly, but only as contributions to the overall pattern. It is thus important to maintain a balanced view, so being able to assess any new proposal, determine its usefulness, using it to advantage but in the end incorporating it as part of the total design where its own emphasis and importance can be used to advantage (currently, systems of micro-propagation tend to be the latest fad, although many proponents of these techniques foresee them as eliminating all other methods in the future. That day is yet a long way ahead and for the immediate future it is likely that it will feature only as another component in the pattern of possibilities. Its use will be justified only for those plants which can bear the expense).

The last decade has probably seen the most rapid and successful advances ever made in plant propagation, not necessarily because science or technology has produced anything new but because so much information has become available. It has become possible to correlate and place in perspective so much knowledge that it is now possible to escape from the constraints of traditional approach and view the whole problem in its entirety. This has permitted an almost imperceptible movement away from a slavish concern for dealing with the plant material at "propagation" to a consideration of the basic plant material itself.

In the past much thought has been given to those conditions which affect the performance of the plant material once it has been introduced into a propagating system; and many trials and much observation have been carried out on, for example, the materials and recipes for composts, the varying strengths of rooting hormones, the value of wounding and the control of the environment. All this has been done most often without consideration of the basic plant material under observation—as though all conditions of plant material were the same. Present-day trends have been concerned with determining those treatments to which a plant should be subjected in order to provide conditioned vegetative material which has a high regenerative capacity. In real terms it has become apparent that it is futile to invest much time and effort in attempting to propagate from plant material which has not been suitably prepared and is inherently not capable of performing in the way that it is anticipated it should. Thus current advance is chiefly concerned with determining how to manipulate plant material so that a highly regenerative condition is engendered and subsequent propagation should thus be a formality. When this state is reached it becomes obvious that, provided common sense and practicality in providing suitable environmental conditions are applied the need to use hormones, wounding, etc. disappears.

From the previous emphasis of these notes it is obvious that the most significant modern trend has been in determining "regenerative capacity" but it should then be necessary to define this somewhat nebulous concept. In general terms regenerative capacity can be determined as a function of "juvenility" or "vegetativeness" and this is most realistically achieved by manipulating the plant material required for propagation into a "non-flowering" condition. It should perhaps not come as a surprise that plant material in a flowering condition is concerned with reproduction by seed and therefore will only secondarily be likely to reproduce vegetatively. Whereas plant material which has been manipulated (albeit temporarily) into a non-flowering and therefore vegetative condition will need to show enhanced ability to propagate vegetatively if survival is to be achieved. However for reasons which are not entirely clear the development of regenerative capacity may also exhibit a seasonal response. Despite plant manipulation and the production of material which should exhibit high regenerative capacity there are within the context of a particular method of propagation "best times" to achieve a maximum response.

Having achieved plant material which is basically capable of producing a new plant it is now relevant to consider how the response in achieving greatest performance can be resolved. There are, necessarily, two aspects to completing a satisfactory performance—the survival of the plant material until a new plant is established and the continuing regenerative function.

Thus, initially, environmental conditions should be concerned with adequate aeration (necessarily required with the high level of respiratory activity), a suitable pH of any compost used and the maintenance of the most satisfactory temperatures in the region of regeneration, so that regenerative response occurs as quickly as possible. It would be expected that the maintenance of a normal water status would be a sine qua non of this part of the process but it is relevant to propose that such a condition would primarily be considered as an aspect of survival at a level at which regenerative responses would occur in conjunction with the provision of light (where necessary), the suppression of any growth not immediately connected with the regenerative process (to conserve food supplies) by keeping temperatures down, and the provision of protectants against pests and diseases. Other aspects seem so obvious as to be unnecessary of mention but at least the maintenance of polarity should be emphasised as regeneration will only occur speedily if plant material is maintained in its normal and functional orientation.

Successful propagation depends on maximising response to all these aspects so that regeneration and the rate at which this response is achieved should encourage the speediest resolution, and that the period over which the material is required to survive (prior to the establishment of a new plant) is kept to only the essential minimum.

These notes do not imply that all the questions to vegetative plant propagation have been answered but the present level of knowledge does suggest that the future will allow the problems of many more plants to be resolved as and when time, energies and finance permit.

Flowers of Macedonia

LIONEL BACON

Crocus sieberi

Since there is now no autonomous state or country called
"Macedonia" I must first define the area to which my title relates.

Some three thousand years ago, to the north of what is now
Greece, there emerged from an earlier civilisation a powerful kingdom called Macedonia. Its boundaries were constantly changing,
according to the fortunes of war and conquest, its power and extent
perhaps reaching their peak in the second half of the fourth century
B.C., when Philip II and his son Alexander the Great were the
monarchs. After this it began to disintegrate, and in 146 B.C.
Macedonia became a Roman Province. During the 2000 years from
then until the beginning of the present century it remained, for most
of the time, occupied territory; and for the last 500 years or so of
that period it was a part of the Turkish Empire.

Perhaps it is surprising that even the name "Macedonia" has
survived—but it has, and after the disintegration of the Turkish
Empire around the beginning of this century Macedonia was par-
titioned by treaty and divided between Greece, Jugoslavia and
Bulgaria—and that remains the present position.

It lies in the great Balkan Peninsula, at the junction between its
larger continental part to the north, which is essentially Central
European in its climate and flora, and the southern part of the
peninsula, that is to say mainland Greece, which is essentially
Mediterranean in its climate and flora. It consists of Jugoslavian
Macedonia, which is the southernmost of the six Federal Republics
of Jugoslavia; Greek Macedonia which is the northernmost and
largest of the Departments of Greece; and the southernmost corner
of Bulgaria, where the name "Macedonia" still persists for some
purpose.

The greater part of this area is mountainous, but in the south-east
there is a substantial coastal zone, including the Chalkidiki Peninsula and the island of Thasos. Here the climate and flora tend to be
Mediterranean in type, and although I shall not be writing of this
area I should mention that its influence spreads up the river valleys,
and plants from the lower-lying areas, and even the upland plains
such as that to the north of the Voros Mountains, have to be
suspected of tenderness in British gardens.

The boundaries of Macedonia in the main follow the mountain
chains. The mountains are of no very great height, and have little

permanent snow and no glaciers: Mt. Olympus at 2911 m. is the highest. Most of this account relates to these frontier mountains.

The surface crust of Macedonia is for the most part calcareous; but here and there, as for instance in the Šar Planina, on Smolikas and on Jugoslavian Pelister, acidic formations are exposed.

The climate is very varied. In the north a continental pattern prevails with summer rainfall predominating and cold winters, and hence winter-resting vegetation. In the south Mediterranean conditions are more usual, with mild wet winters and hot dry summers and hence a large component of summer-resting flora. But in many areas conditions are transitional between these two patterns, so that more local and specialised plants are to be found. Thus the Macedonian flora is very extensive and varied. There are a few species which occur only within Macedonia, the greatest part tending to spill over its boundaries, but the majority of the plants here to be considered are Balkan in their distribution, though some have a footing in Italy as well, and some have their headquarters in Asia— an interesting point because in geological terms the Balkan Peninsula was once a part of Asia, separated from Europe. There are at least 150 plants of good garden value from the Balkan flora alone in Macedonia. I must perforce select, and will confine myself to plants which my wife and I have seen in the wild, and so shall say nothing of the Pirin and Rila Mountains of Bulgaria, which we have not visited; but those who have read Mr Gilbert Barrett's contribution on Bulgaria to *Mountain Flower Holidays in Europe* will realise that this too is a rich and exciting area.

Our visits have been made in early May and early June, entering the area from the north, where the Šar Planina range forms the boundary between Serbia and Jugoslavian Macedonia. At its north-eastern end is Mt. Ljuboten, which has been the subject of several reports in the "Bulletin" of the A.G.S. in its early days. Several plants with the epithet '*scardicus*' are named for the Šar Planina. *Crocus scardicus* is a very distinct, beautiful and local plant: *Saxifraga scardica* on the other hand is widespread throughout Macedonia from the Šar Planina to Mt. Olympus. *Edraianthus graminifolius*, an attractive species in this rather confusing genus, has a similar range of distribution: it is a good garden plant, which has proved long-lasting in our Hampshire garden. Most of our

Macedonian plants are grown in a slightly raised bed facing south, in a sunny position: the soil is chalky and rapidly dries out in the summer. Another plant from Ljuboten is *Bruckenthalia spiculifolia*, an ericaceous plant indicating the acid nature of the soil on parts of this mountain, and another calciphobe plant here is pretty little *Androsace hedraeantha. Anemone narcissiflora, Cerastium alpinum, Dryas octopetala* and *Silene acaulis* are examples enough of the typical European alpine flora to serve as a reminder that the Balkan flora here to be considered is but one component of the Macedonian scene.

At its southwest end the Šar Planina is dominated by Mt. Korab, on the Albanian frontier. This is now, alas, an inaccessible area, but there are many interesting plants among the foothills on the Jugoslavian side of the frontier. Here lies the little town of Mavrovo on its lake, now dammed to make a reservoir: the emerging river runs southward along the fine Radika Gorge, and here on the rocks grows *Saxifraga sempervivum*, an Engleria with fine spiky glaucous leaves, very attractive and a good garden plant. A glowing purple patch among the rocks here proved to be *Malcolmia illyrica*, a crucifer reminiscent of a stock—unfortunately an annual. Close to it, growing under some shrubs, was *Campanula versicolor*, a sound perennial nine or ten inches tall, variable but very attractive in the forms we have seen: but with us it has not proved very enduring—I think it is intolerant of our hard frosts after making early spring growth. *Ramonda serbica*, whose headquarters are in Albania, is also reported to grow in the Radika Gorge; and in a valley running up towards Mt. Korab we found a clear yellow form of *Iris reichenbachii*, a large-flowered dwarf bearded Iris.

Travelling southward from Mavrovo one comes at last to Ohrid, on its great, very deep, lake among the hills. This is a warm area, with delightful flowers along the lake-side road. *Verbascum undulatum* is a Balkan endemic attractive in leaf and flower but biennial or short-lived, and with it were *Ajuga chamaepitys* subsp. *chia, Scutellaria orientalis* (a central Asian plant at the western end of its range) and *Crepis rubra*—all three tender or short-lived but all readily propagated by seed and well worth the trouble.

The western side of Lake Ohrid is in Albania. One looks across at the mountains and wishes one could visit them—as did Dr and Mrs

Giuseppi, Dr Roger-Smith and others before the war. They encountered considerable discomfort and some danger, but were assisted and protected from the local banditry by a military guard: now it is the military that will ensure that you don't enter Albania!

The frontier continues across the mountain mass called Galičica to another large lake, Lake Prespa, which is divided between Jugoslavia, Albania and Greece. At the northern end of Galičica is an outlying hill called on one of our maps Goga—a most rewarding hill to visit. By the steep road leading up to it grow beautiful violas in many colours: they are probably *V. elegantula*, but there are a dozen or so pansies in this part of the world and they are hard to name. An outstanding orchid here (among dozens of species, but one of very few that are restricted in their distribution to the Balkans) is *Himantoglossum hircinum* subsp. *calcaratum*, much more attractive than the typical lizard orchid in its rosy coloration and in lacking the offensive smell of the type-plant. Here too is *Erodium guicciardii*, a beautiful storksbill combining the silvery foliage of *E. chrysanthum* with rosy-purple flowers: it has proved a very good garden plant—perhaps a little large for a small rock garden. *Haplophyllum boissierianum*, a charming member of the rue family and a great deal neater than its name, also grows by the roadside on Goga—though we had first met it growing among the ruins of a Roman theatre at Stobi, further east: for five years it grew and flowered in the garden, though with a good deal of die-back each winter, and in the sixth year it did not survive. In the same place was *Lychnis viscaria* subsp. *atropurpurea*, a plum-purple subspecies confined to the Balkans and Romania, and a good garden plant coming true to colour from seed. Yet another distinctive plant on Goga is a neat brilliant blue Anchusa, named for us as *A. macedonica*, though this is given in *Flora Europaea* as annual or biennial whereas the Goga plant is perennial, if short-lived—possibly it is *A. serpentinicola*. *Dianthus gracilis* subsp. *armerioides* on Goga has neat tuffeted leaves and pretty cherry-red yellow-backed flowers, resembling those of *D. pavonius*, but it is a much longer-stemmed plant and grows on calcareous soil.

Goga abounds in monocotyledonous plants, including crocuses (*Cc. pulchellus, sieberi, chrysanthus* and *veluchensis*), a pretty little Fritillaria with very globular flowers (*F. orientalis?*), *Iris sintenisii*, a lovely Ornithogalum with large stemless flowers, and *Colchicum hungaricum*. The rocks at the top are clothed with mats of *Saxifraga marginata*, including some effective pinkish forms.

East of Lake Prespa (where there are acres of glowing rosy-purple *Orchis laxiflora* in the marshy areas by the lake side) is Mt. Pelister (or Perister), wooded on its lower slopes and still snow-capped in early June. It is being developed for ski-ing, and so there is a road part-way up it. By the roadside we found brightly coloured *Geum coccineum*, which seems to do well in damp areas in the garden, *Geranium cinereum* subsp. *subcaulescens*, and *Fritillaria pontica*. In open spaces between the trees were the leaves of *Lilium albanicum*, and higher still among the rocks were *Crocus veluchensis*, *Jovibarba heuffelii*, and a local form subsp. *cymosa* of the mossy saxifrage *S. pedemontana*. As on the Šar Planina there are acid rocks near the summit, and *Bruckenthalia spiculifolia* grows among Vaccinium species.

At the foot of Mt. Pelister lies Bitola, an expanding modern town adjacent to Heraclea, a magnificent Graeco-Romano-Byzantine site; and from Bitola the road runs southward into nearby Greece. But let us first travel north-eastward across the hot Bitola plain and over the hills by Prilep, where marble is mined; for this is an area where the climate and the flora of the Mediterranean spread inland from the Aegean Sea with no significant intervening hills. Lovely *Convolvulus althaeoides* subsp. *tenuissimus* was here, with *C. cantabrica* and *Linum tenuifolium*, all three widespread through southern Europe—so one sees here an intrusion, as it were, of the Mediterranean into the more typically Balkan flora. But the latter is not wanting: *Hypericum rumeliacum* is by the roadside, and the quietly attractive *Stachys iva* with sulphur-yellow flowers and white downy foliage on eight-inch stems. The latter is liable to die in the winter in our garden, but it sets good seed and is worth maintaining. But the most outstanding Macedonian plant we saw in the hills beyond Prilep was *Campanula formanekiana*, growing here in shallow crevices on the vertical face of the limestone cliffs. It was a soft powder-blue, and growing in this situation was very different in appearance from the upright pyramidal white-flowered plant which we commonly see on the show bench. Dr Giuseppi, who re-introduced this plant in 1931, commented that it was white in the

Voros Mountains which separate Jugoslavia from Greece, but blue further north as here near Prilep. It is monocarpic (indeed *Flora Europaea* says biennial) and doubtfully hardy in the open garden.

Still further to the north-east, near Skopje, is the Treska Gorge on the Vardar River, the subject of reports in pre-war Bulletins. The Vardar had been dammed since those days, but the interesting plants are still to be found, of which two are outstanding. One is *Ramonda nathaliae* growing in the shade of alder or other scrub; and the other is *Saxifraga grisebachii*, a well-known garden plant generally in its rather blown-up Wisley form. Both are fine additions to the rock garden, the former in a north-facing crevice and the latter in full sun in limestone.

Leaving Jugoslavia, we went on to visit a few selected spots in the mountains of Grecian Macedonia, which is bounded on the west side by the Pindus Range and on the south is separated from Thessalia by hills which reach no great height except in the massif of Olympus.

Access to the northern Pindus Mountains is in fact from the west (Epirus) side, and is reached by crossing the Katara Pass, which lies just outside Macedonia—so we will cheat a little and trespass a mile or two beyond the Macedonian border. The flowers of the Katara Pass are varied and interesting. They include the lovely red turks-cap lily, *L. chalcedonicum*; the commoner but less attractive asphodels, *Asphodeline liburnica* and *A. lutea*; and in a damp meadow area, among orchids and poet's narcissus, a pretty little white-flowered, sweet-scented Allium which I am tentatively calling *A. breviradium*. The well-known *Daphne blagayana* also is to be found here, growing on the edge of the woodland; showy *Campanula ramosissima* (unfortunately an annual); *Helleborus cyclophyllus*; *Jovibarba heuffelii*; *Sempervivum ciliosum*; *Soldanella pindicola*; and *Tulipa sylvestris*—among many others. There is no question of frost-tenderness among plants from the Katara Pass, and all those mentioned are assets in the rock garden.

Among the wild jumbled mountains of the northern Pindus are Tymphi and Smolikas: the latter is the second-highest mountain in Greece, and is composed of acid rocks and serpentine, at least in parts. It has a special flora which was much acclaimed by Giuseppi and others, but the military would not unfortunately allow us to visit it. Tymphi, at least in its lower parts, is more accessible, though in its remoter parts it is said to be still relatively unexplored, and wild goat, boar, cat and bear still dwell there.

Between the massifs of Smolikas and Tymphi a fine river runs under the high cliffs of the Vikos Gorge. In the rocks by the river we found *Pterocephalus perennis* subsp. *bellidifolius*, a dwarf mat-forming scabious well known in a closely allied form in our gardens. With it grew abundant rosettes of *Ramonda serbica*, distinguished from *nathaliae* and the Pyrenean *myconi* by the blue-black "beak" formed by the anthers. It is perhaps a little more scarce and difficult in the garden than the other two. Aubrieta too grows in the Vikos Gorge—I think *A. intermedia*, though there are several species in northern Greece. They are the parents of our garden hybrids, and well deserve a place in their own right.

On the foothills of Tymphi we found *Lilium candidum*, the Màdonna Lily. There has I believe been some argument as to whether it is truly a wild plant of Greece—like so many of the plants we have seen in Macedonia this is found also in S.W. Asia—but it certainly seems to be truly wild on Tymphi, growing amongst scrub and rocks on the open hillside. *Digitalis lanata*, a biennial foxglove with attractively marked flowers, grows in the same area; and a beautiful form of *Colchicum bivonae*, which I think is probably the one formerly called *C. bowlesianum*.

And now we come to what is I suppose the most renowned locality for Macedonian flowers—though it is indeed on the very border with Thessaly. Mt. Olympus lies close to the Aegean Sea, and plants from its lower levels are certainly under Mediterranean influence. The usual approach is from the sea-board and up through the village of Litochoron, though it can also be approached by a steeper ascent from the west. A new road from Litochoron into the heart of the mountain has made it much more accessible. On the lower slopes are Mediterranean type plants such as *Cistus incanus* subsp. *creticus*—very lovely but like a good many of the cistuses liable to be killed in English gardens by frost or desiccating winds in the spring. There are at least two fritillaries on Olympus—*F. messanensis* and *F. graeca*. I think most of us would acclaim *Jankaea heldreichii* as the doyen of Olympian endemics: it grows from quite low levels in the Enipeus Gorge right up to "Refuge A", above

2000 m. Such plants as I saw grew in the shade, either on north-facing rocks or under trees. The Jankaea is by no means an easy plant to grow in an alpine house; and still less so in the open garden. So far as my own limited observation goes, in the wild, even when it is in rock-crevices, it grows in rich humus. Now that Mt. Olympus has been made so much more accessible the Jankaea might have become in danger of unscrupulous collecting—but now the whole mountain is an area where plant-collecting is prohibited.

A good deal less charismatic, but attractive in its own quiet way, is little *Aquilegia amaliae*. Better known as a garden plant is *Saxifraga juniperifolia* subsp. *sancta*, cheerful, enduring and very early-flowering—an Asian plant which turns up also on Mt. Athos, whence perhaps its "holiness". Other saxifrages around "Refuge A" are the variable and beautiful *S. marginata*, *S. scardica* with leaves as spiky as its name (and there is said to be a rose-pink form of it, offered by nurserymen as 'Erythrantha') and *S. spruneri*. *Viola gracilis* creeps prettily through the screes. *Campanula oreadum* is an Olympic endemic with large long bells over small tufts of tiny leaves. *Omphalodes luciliae* grows high on Olympus and is not very common. Another rare and beautiful endemic of Olympus is *Viola delphinantha*, which I did not see—probably it was still under the snow in June. But in the eyes of the Warden at the Refuge (who was an enthusiast for his plants) the accolade went not to any of the plants I have mentioned, but to the spring gentian, *Gentiana verna* subsp. *pontica,* whose deep blue brilliance adorned the rocks around the Refuge. It is a scarce plant in Greece, and I would not quarrel with his judgement.

In conclusion I should say that there is far more to Macedonia than its flowers. The people are helpful and friendly and there are few significant problems for the traveller there now. The scenery is in many places lovely, there are beautiful birds and butterflies, and any time that one could spare from plant-seeking would be well spent in visiting the architecturally and historically fascinating buildings from the days of classical Greece to the present time.

Ericaceae
(Rhododendron Classification)

JAMES CULLEN

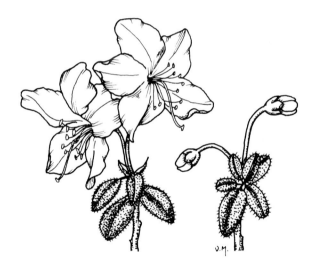

Rhododendron calostrotum

Though my given title is 'Ericaceae', I want to deal entirely with rhododendrons, as I have spent several years working on this genus. In particular I shall discuss the scaly or lepidote species; these form a substantial part of the genus, which is, in fact, known as subgenus Rhododendron; and this includes most of the dwarf species which form a suitable group to consider in the context of Alpines '81.

Now, I am a plant taxonomist, not a grower. I deal with the definition of species and how to tell them apart, rather than with how they are, or should be, grown. Of course, these two aspects are inter-related, particularly in a place like the Royal Botanic Garden, Edinburgh, but my concern is almost entirely with the first of them. I want to take this opportunity of explaining to you some of the problems we encounter in carrying out the business of plant classification; and this explanation will, I hope, give you some insight into the reasons why names change—apparently arbitrarily, you may think, though I hope to convince you that this is not so—using the dwarf, scaly rhododendrons as examples.

One point I must make clear to start with. Most taxonomic work is done using herbarium specimens: dried and preserved plants or plant parts, annotated with details of where and when they were collected, what the habitat was like and who made the collection. Some people are very disparaging about such specimens, referring to them as "heaps of hay". However they form the solid basis of our work. Living plants in gardens are useful, but can be only a secondary source of information. They are most useful if they relate to collections whose origin is known—that is, if we have for them the same sort of data as we have for herbarium specimens: in fact, the ideal situation is the one in which there are available both herbarium and living representatives of the same collection. Living plants for which we have such information will be referred to as "material of known wild origin", and it is this in which botanic gardens are particularly interested, as it forms a genuine scientific resource. Other plants of miscellaneous origin, whether bought from a nurseryman or exchanged among friends, are of lesser value as all sorts of things might have happened to them during their time in cultivation.

Even material of known wild origin has to be viewed with a certain amount of suspicion. Not even the best-run gardens would dare to claim that labels are never switched, or that material which should be propagated by cuttings or layers is never propagated by seed and grown on under the same collecting information. So, one has to be a little careful in accepting some claims of wild origin at their face value. Herbarium specimens, on the other hand, do not suffer from these problems, and do represent a small sample of what was growing where the collector says it grew, in such and such conditions, on a particular day. Living plants, particularly those introduced as seed, are not such a direct sample. Those that survive in cultivation are selected, mainly accidentally, by the procedures used in cultivation. A packet of seed introduced from the wild will contain large numbers of seeds that would never have developed to maturity; some of this fatality would have been accidental in that those seeds might have ended up in places totally unsuitable for germination; but some of them would have been eliminated in the seedling stage because of their poor genetical adaptation to the situation in which they found themselves. And so on. However, in the garden, if we are careful, a high percentage of the seeds may well develop and be brought through to maturity. Of these, some will propagate vegetatively more easily than others and, over the years, these are the ones which will survive in collections. Also, the gardener, looking over his batch of plants, may well weed out those that appeal to him least from various points of view: the poorer growers, the least shapely, those with the smallest flowers, etc. All these activities tend to make the living plant we see in a garden a less direct representation of what was actually growing in the wild, than the equivalent herbarium specimen.

One final advantage of herbarium specimens is that one can accumulate large numbers of them in one place, and they are always available there for study. This is simply not the case with living plants, and the larger they are, the greater is the problem. As an example, in the herbarium at Edinburgh there are 250 annotated specimens of *Rhododendron rubiginosum*. In the garden at Edinburgh (including, for this purpose, the gardens at Benmore and Logan) there are 25 accessions of the species, of which 15 are of known wild origin. I hope this will explain, at least in brief outline, why herbarium specimens form the basis of taxonomic work. The living plant has its place, certainly, but this must of necessity be a subsidiary one.

Bearing all this background in mind, we can now turn to Rhododendron. All the groups of the genus that I am going to mention come from the Himalaya and China, with the exception of the three species of Subsection Rhododendron, which come from Europe. The map on plate 19 which was very kindly prepared by Dr R. B. Burbidge, shows the distribution of all the scaly rhododendrons in the Sino-Himalayan area, extending from east Afghanistan to Szechuan in China, and showing the number of species that occur in each 1° latitude/longitude square. This indicates very clearly the concentration of species in western China, in particular in western Yunnan, the numbers of species falling off gradually as one moves east or west from there.

From scaly rhododendrons in general, we can now turn to the dwarf species. As the main example, I intend to use the group that used to be called the Saluenense Series, but which now bears the formidable name of Subgenus Rhododendron Section Rhododendron Subsection Saluenensia, or just Subsection Saluenensia for short. This contains plants which are quite widely grown as ornamentals for their convenient size, their large magenta flowers which are usually produced in abundance, and their pleasant aromatic smell.

If we turn to *The Species of Rhododendron,* that standard work on Rhododendron identification prepared during the twenties and published in 1930, we find that the group was thought to contain 11 species. Later on, the group was revised again, by H. H. Davidian, who published his results in *The Rhododendron and Camellia Yearbook* for 1954: he reduced the group to 8 species, one subdivided into varieties. The latest revision, which I published in 1980, reduces the group to 2 species, one with four, the other with two, subspecies. One of the species included in the group in both *The Species of Rhododendron* and in Davidian's revision is removed entirely. The table opposite shows what has happened.

As you can see, the overall structure of the group is broadly similar in each case; all that has changed is that several formerly

Names used in Subsections Fragariflora and Saluenensia.

1980 Revision	Davidian, 1954	The Species of Rhododendron, 1930
Subsect. Fragariflora	Saluenense series	Saluenense series
R. *fragariflorum*	R. *fragariflorum*	R. *fragariflorum*
Subsect. Saluenensia		
R. *calostrotum*		
subsp. *calostrotum*	R. *calostrotum*	R. *calostrotum*
subsp. *riparium*	R. *nitens*	
	R. *calostrotum* var.	R. *riparium*
	calciphilum	R. *calciphilum*
subsp. *riparioides*	—	—
subsp. *keleticum*	R. *keleticum*	R. *keleticum*
	R. *radicans*	R. *radicans*
R. *saluenense*		
subsp. *saluenense*	R. *saluenense*	R. *saluenense*
subsp. *chameunum*	R. *chameunum*	R. *chameunum*
	R. *prostratum*	R. *prostratum*
		R. *cosmetum*
		R. *charidotes*

recognised species have been sunk into the synonymy of others, and that the main taxa are now regarded as subspecies rather than species; and, of course, one species has been removed altogether.

I want to try to explain to you the reasons for these changes (which may seem inconvenient from the nomenclatural point of view), and what they imply. It is simplest to begin with *R. fragariflorum,* the species which I have removed to a new subsection of its own. There is no doubt that *R. fragariflorum* is broadly similar in general appearance to the plants left in Subsect. Saluenensia. It is a dwarf with small leaves and few-flowered inflorescences of rather large, reddish-purple open flowers with large sepals. In all of these features it resembles *R. calostrotum* and *R. saluenense*. But it differs in certain other features which I consider to be very important in the classification of the genus as a whole. Firstly, the structure of its scales is quite dissimilar. In *R. fragariflorum* the scales are very distant from each other, and are rounded, looking superficially like blobs of resin dropped on the leaf surface; they are almost stalkless, and lie directly on the leaf surface. In *R. calostrotum* and *R. saluenense* the scales are quite different. They are very crowded together, and have stalks of various lengths so that they form a "tiered" covering to the leaf, and their heads are flattened or slightly funnel-shaped with their margins finely scalloped (or crenulate as the taxonomic jargon has it). These two types of scale are totally unlike each other and cannot be confused; I have found the structure of the scales to be an important characteristic in Rhododendron classification generally, and there is no doubt that the differences here are very marked. Incidentally, the scales of *R. fragariflorum* are very like those of *R. campylogynum*—another dwarf, while those of *R. calostrotum* and *R. saluenense* are like those of such species as *R. anthopogon* and *R. primuliflorum* of section Pogonanthum with regard to their elongate stalks and "tiered" arrangement, and like those of *R. baileyi*, the sole species of subsection Baileya, in respect of their crenulate heads.

This difference in scale type is, in my view, significant and substantial. It is backed up by other characteristics which, in themselves are not so important, but, considered together as supporting the scale character, form an overwhelming constellation or syndrome of characters. The leaves of *R. fragariflorum* have finely scalloped margins, whereas those of *R. calostrotum* and *R. saluenense* are completely entire; the corolla of *R. fragariflorum* is hairless outside, whereas those of *R. calostrotum* and *R. saluenense* are finely and silkily hairy. Furthermore, in terms of distribution, *R. fragariflorum* occurs to the west of all the species of Subsect. Saluenensia.

On all these counts, then, there is reason to think that *R. fragariflorum* is more different from the species of Subsect. Saluenensia than they are among themselves. And this is the justification for segregating it into a distinct, monotypic subsection, Subsect. Fragariflora.

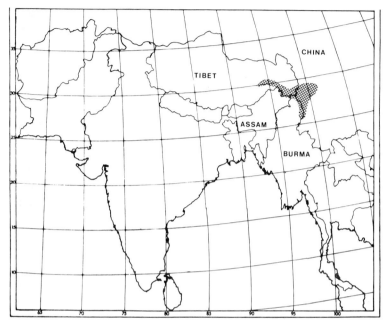

Distribution of Rhododendron Subsections Fragariflora and Saluenensia

When we turn to the species of this reduced subsection Saluenensia, we find a different set of problems. Members of the group are distributed quite widely in western China, from south east Tibet, through western Yunnan and extending into western Szechuan. They are represented in herbaria by numerous collections, which provide an adequate base for study. *The Species of Rhododendron* treated the group as 10 species, Davidian treated it as 7, whereas I treat it as 2 species divided into 6 subspecies. The basis for this sharp reduction in the number of species comes from a very detailed study of the specimens themselves. They vary greatly, as do individual characteristics such as overall size and habit, hairiness, size and shape of leaves, density of scales, size and colour of the flowers, etc. If we look at these specimens geographically, we find that they fall into a western group (mainly west of 98°E) and an eastern group (mainly east of 99°E), with, in the middle, mainly between 98 and 99°E and 28 and 29°N, a confusing set of plants which blur out the distinctions between the two wings. The plants from the western side of the divide are generally without bristles (when bristles occur they are found on the leaf margins and pedicels only), and are without tiny hairs at the apex of the ovary where the style fits into a small depression. This western group can be rather imprecisely divided into a northern group which consists of rather tall plants (up to 1·2 m) and a southern group of more compact plants. This north/south subdivision is certainly not clear-cut but represents an irregular gradient or cline, as taxonomists call it. It is as though one could walk from the southern part of the range to the northern, observing the plants as one went: it would be noticed that most of the plants at the beginning of the journey would be small (though there might be a few larger ones), but, as one went on, they would become, on average, larger and larger.

The plants on the eastern wing are different: they are very bristly, with bristles on the one- and two-year-old shoots, on the petioles and on the lower surface of the leaf midrib as well as on the leaf margins and pedicels, and the ovary is hairy in the depression into which the style fits. This group is reasonably homogeneous, unlike the western group.

Now, these three groups (the northern and southern ends of the western wing, and the eastern wing) correspond with names that are already in use: the eastern group corresponds with *chameunum*, described as a species by Balfour and Forrest in 1920. The northern part of the western group corresponds with *riparium*, described as a species first of all as *R. rivulare* by Kingdon Ward in 1929: this name, however, was not usable, as there was already an *R. rivulare*, described by Handel-Mazzetti in 1921 (this is a quite separate, elepidote species), so, in 1931, Kingdon Ward re-named the plant *R. riparium*. The southern part of the western group corresponds with *calostrotum*, also described as a species by Balfour and Kingdon Ward in 1920.

In the middle of the area, between 98 and 99° the features of these three groups mingle and merge in a way that plays havoc with their distinctiveness. Plants from this area mix up the various characteristics in some very confusing ways, so that it is not possible to identify most of the specimens from this area as *calostrotum, riparium* or *chameunum*. This picture can be explained in two ways—as a group diversifying and spreading out from a common centre, crystallising out distinct eastern and western wings; or as two or three originally separated groups which have come together and hybridised, forming the confusing central mass.

Within this conglomeration, however, certain plant types seem to have stabilised, and appear to form populations, and these can often be recognised as being intermediate between pairs of our original three types from outside the confusion. Thus there are many tall, upright, bristly plants which are intermediate between *riparium* and *chameunum*; smaller, bristleless plants intermediate between *calostrotum* and *chameunum*, some of these, in particular those from very high altitudes, very small; and so on. There are three of these intermediate types that are unified enough, and occur in sufficient abundance to be recognised formally:

(1) Tall bristly plants intermediate between *riparium* and *chameunum*;
(2) Moderately-sized, non-bristly plants intermediate between *calostrotum* and *chameunum*;
(3) Very small, high altitude types intermediate between *calostrotum* and *chameunum*.

The taxonomist's problem in dealing with a situation of this sort is to try to present a classification which reflects the situation. Here we have two important elements: a basic division into eastern and western groups; and a mixed mass of intermediates, some of which are recognisable. I have chosen, therefore, to recognise two species, as representing broadly the eastern and western wings; and within these to recognise subspecies to cover what can be done with the intermediate mass, the intermediates recognised as subspecies being considered under the species that they most resemble. The concept of subspecies is valuable here, as the use of this rank warns the reader that here are several groups which are not completely distinguishable using any of the morphological characters available. The implications of this will be touched on later.

In recognising the two species, it is necessary to separate them on the basis of the characters mentioned before: so all the very bristly plants with hairy ovaries will belong to the eastern species; and all the more or less bristle-less plants with glabrous ovaries belong to the western one; and this provides the basis for the assignment of the recognised subspecies to the species.

When we come to apply names to these groups we find a further problem. The first name applied to any of these plants was *R. saluenense,* which was described by the French botanist Adrian Franchet in 1898. This is a suitable point to pay tribute to Franchet, who was a very astute taxonomist, and whose contribution to Rhododendron taxonomy is largely unsung, but who was certainly as significant as Balfour, Wright Smith, Hutchinson and the rest. The plants described as *R. saluenense* by Franchet, which are the syntypes of the name, were collected by J. A. Soulié, a French missionary, in northern Yunnan, near the Tibetan border, right in the middle of what I have called the confusing mass. These plants are tall, bristly intermediates between *riparium* and *chameunum*; because of their bristliness and hairy ovary, they must belong to the eastern wing, and therefore the eastern species must be called *R. saluenense,* because of the rule of priority which is basic to all nomenclature. This is a pity, because *chameunum,* which is a name that applies unequivocally to the eastern species, would have been a biologically more appropriate name. This problem does not arise with the western species, as *calostrotum* is the earliest name to have been applied to it, and this can be used for the species.

I divide these two species, *calostrotum* and *saluenense,* into sub-species, of which four belong to *calostrotum,* two to *saluenense,* and I will now briefly describe them, indicating their salient features. Their distributions are indicated on page 47.

1. *R. calostrotum* subsp. *calostrotum.* This is found in eastern Burma and adjacent Yunnan and is the small, southern end of the western wing. It often has leaves with a greyish matt upper surface (matt because of persistent, dried out scales) and it generally has 1-2-flowered inflorescences with the flowers on rather long pedicels.

2. *R. calostrotum* subsp. *riparium.* This is the larger, northern end of the western wing. It is not sharply distinguished from subsp. *calostrotum,* but is generally larger, with longer leaves, and inflorescences with 2-5 flowers on shorter pedicels.

3. *R. calostrotum* subsp. *riparioides.* This is a plant very similar to subsp. *riparium,* as the name suggests, but larger leaved and with

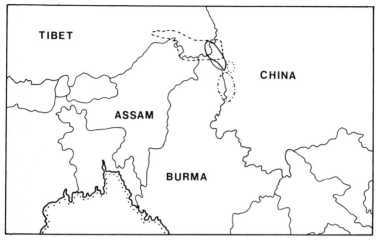

Distribution of R calostrotum subsp. *calostrotum*, dots and dashes; subsp. *keleticum*, continuous line; subsp. riparioides, dots; subsp. riparium, dashes.

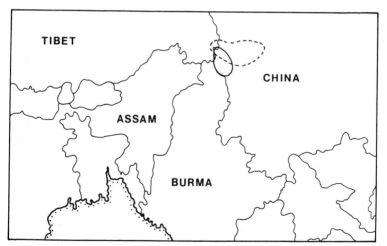

Distribution of R. *saluenense* subsp. *chameunum*, dashes; subsp. *saluenense*, continuous line.

the scales on the leaf under-surface much flatter than is usual, producing a felted appearance. It occurs in one small area of Yunnan, in the mountains to the west of the town of Wei hsi.

4. *R. calostrotum* subsp. *keleticum.* This is intermediate between *calostrotum* and the high-altitude, low-growing forms of *chameunum* which used to be called *R. prostratum.* It is a small clump-forming or creeping plant with small leaves which are usually shiny above. It occurs only in the central part of the total distribution and varies somewhat with altitude, those from the highest altitudes, around 4550 m (15,000 ft.) being very prostrate and having very small leaves.

5. *R. saluenense* subsp. *saluenense.* This, as I have already mentioned, is a tall, bristly plant, intermediate between *riparium* and *chameunum,* and found only in the central mass.

6. *R. saluenense* subsp. *chameunum* is a low-growing, extremely bristly plant with a distribution in Yunnan and just extending into Szechuan, which forms the eastern wing of the total distribution.

Now, before I go on to discuss these plants in cultivation, I should like to summarise the position in the wild. There are two species which are quite distinct on the eastern and western wings of the total distribution, but which merge in the middle. In this middle area are certain groups which can be identified in a reasonable manner; but there are also many individual specimens which do not fit particularly neatly into the groups defined: they combine the characteristics in various ways, and are very difficult to name accurately.

In the great age of horticultural/botanical exploration in western China, which began in the 1880s and lasted more or less to the beginning of the Second World War, many plant collectors were involved. The most important from the point of view of plants introduced to horticulture were George Forrest, Frank Kingdon Ward and Joseph Rock. All these collectors, but in particular the first two, were interested in novelties. The Rhododendron mania of the first 30 years of the century produced a tremendous demand for new rhododendrons, and so the collectors were on the look out for anything that diverged from what was already known. As far as the Saluenensia rhododendrons were concerned, they had a field day

Primula cuneifolia   (*Plate 9*)

Diapensia lapponica (Pink Form)   (*Plate 10*)

Orchis rotundifolia   (*Plate 11*)

Helleborus purpurascens   (*Plate 12*)

Helleborus orientalis   (*Plate 13*)

Corydalis caucasica   (*Plate 14*)

Corydalis transsilvanica   (*Plate 15*)

Gentiana cruttwellii   (*Plate 16*)

Phlox adsurgens 'Wagon Wheel'   (*Plate 17*)

Primula barnardoana   (*Plate 18*)

in the area I've described as the central mass. Here were lots of odd plants which diverged from the normal in various ways. These were eagerly gathered, sent back to Britain, grown on (some of them, at any rate) and given names: this accounts for the plethora of names in *The Species of Rhododendron*.

At Edinburgh we have material of all six of the taxa growing, mostly from material of known wild origin, much of it backed up with herbarium material. This gives us the chance to check up on the living material, making sure it has the same characteristics as the herbarium material from the same population. Of course, other material of these groups is quite widely distributed in gardens. Its origin is generally unknown and it is, as might be expected, pretty variable. Some of it probably originated in the central mass in China, and some of it possibly includes the results of accidental hybridisation in gardens. Some of the plants are clearly identifiable with the two species and six subspecies which I have discussed, whereas others will not fit exactly. Some clones have, of course, been selected and given cultivar names, e.g. *R. calostrotum* 'Exbury' and *R. calostrotum* 'Gigha'. These are mostly just selections from *R. calostrotum* subsp. *calostrotum,* made on the basis of variation in flower colour, which has no significance in terms of the botanical classification.

I hope I have given you here an explanation of the kinds of changes which have taken place recently in Rhododendron classification, and the reasons for them, together with some of the effects on the naming of plants in cultivation. Within the scaly rhododendrons as a whole, many such changes have taken place. The principles I have outlined in connection with subsect. Saluenensia apply throughout, and it is not my intention to deal with other groups in the same sort of detail. But I should like to conclude with a brief review of some of the other dwarf groups, indicating the more outstanding changes and some of the reasons for them.

The largest group of dwarf rhododendrons is subsect. Lapponica—the group formerly known as the Lapponicum Series. This was revised in 1975 by Professor and Dr Philipson, who recognised 26 species, as opposed to the 51 species treated in *The Species of Rhododendron.* I have accepted their classification, merely adding to it *R. setosum*—a species from the Himalaya of rather obscure relationships which is more at home in this group than anywhere else. The species of the subsection are all rather similar in general appearance and their identification is not easy, being based on rather trivial-seeming characters such as scale colour and size, size of calyx lobes and the number of stamens. Many of the species are widely grown, and can be exemplified by *R. hippophaeoides* and *R. intricatum*. Several familiar names have disappeared into synonymy in the Philipsons' re-classification, notably *R. scintillans*, which they have shown very convincingly must be called *R. polycladum*.

Subsection Rhododendron, formerly known as the Ferrugineum Series, consists of the same three European species recognised in *The Species of Rhododendron*. The only change is that the name *R. kotschyi* has had to be replaced by the earlier *R. myrtifolium* for the east European species—a change which was made in Flora Europaea vol. 3, published in 1972. The type species of the genus is *R. ferrugineum*, which is why the Subgenus and Section to which it belongs have to be called 'Rhododendron'.

Subsection Uniflora, which broadly corresponds with what used to be known as the Uniflorum Series, is related to Subsect. Saluenensia. Since its first recognition it has had a rather chequered history, containing various species. In my revision it contains four species, of which one, *R. ludlowii*, is quite distinct in possessing yellow flowers; this creates no problem. Of the other three, one, *R. pumilum* is widespread in the Himalaya, whereas the other two, *R. pemakoense* (which includes *R. patulum*) and *R. uniflorum*, which is divided into two varieties, var. *uniflorum* and var. *imperator*, are extremely restricted in distribution. In fact, these two species, which were formerly considered to be four species, are known from only seven collections in the wild. They are quite widespread in gardens, however, and this is one of those rare cases in which there is more living than herbarium material. Unfortunately, much of the garden material is of uncertain wild origin, and it is very variable, some of it being surprisingly different from the herbarium specimens. Whether this is due to accidental hybrid-isation in cultivation, or not, is not known. Very little can be done in a case like this until more material is available from north-east India and Tibet.

In Subsect. Boothia, which is much the same as what used to be known as Series Boothii Subseries Boothii, there are three species of dwarfs which present few taxonomic problems—*R. megeratum*, *R. leucaspis* and *R. sulfureum*. Of these, the last is doubtfully hardy in most parts of Britain, and so it is rarely seen.

Closely related to Subsect. Boothia is Subsect. Glauca, which is more or less equivalent to what was once called the Glaucophyllum Series. This group, which is easily recognised by its bi-coloured scales borne on a white-papillose leaf undersurface, can be exemplified by *R. glaucophyllum* itself, and *R. brachyanthum*. The main problem in this group is material in cultivation under the name *R. shweliense*. This is a rare species, collected only twice (by George Forrest); plants that I have seen under this name in gardens have all turned out to be a hybrid of *R. glaucophyllum* and not the genuine article at all. The only exception I have found is a plant growing at Rowallane, which looks as though it might be the real *R. shweliense*. Unfortunately, the specimen I saw was very poor, having languished in the post over a holiday weekend, and therefore I am not certain. I should be interested to hear from anyone who thinks that they might have the genuine *R. shweliense* growing.

Subsection Campylogyna consists of the one species *R. campylogynum*. This is variable, and was formerly divided up into several varieties on the basis of plants in cultivation. These varieties, however, seem to be little more than segments of the variation widely distributed in gardens, having no botanical significance.

Subsection Lepidota contains the very widespread *R. lepidotum*, which extends from Nepal to Yunnan, and two other species of restricted distribution, both of them from east Nepal—*R. lowndesii* and *R. cowanianum*. This last was formerly placed in the Trichocladum series, because of its deciduous leaves, but its relationships are very clearly with *R. lepidotum*.

Subsection Afghanica consists of one species, *R. afghanicum* which is one of two species found in eastern Afghanistan and adjacent Pakistan. It was formerly placed in the Triflorum series, but it is so distinct that it requires a subsection of its own. It is somewhat uncommon in cultivation, and doubtfully hardy at Edinburgh.

The last group I want to mention is Section Pogonanthum, which corresponds with what used to be called the Anthopogon Series. Note that this is a distinct section, not a subsection: this is because it is so different from all the other lepidote rhododendrons. Its scales are star-shaped—this is very difficult to see, as the scales overlap each other so much—the plants have a very characteristic pineapple-like smell, their corollas are tubular with a flat limb and the stamens and style are hidden away in the corolla tube. The group consists of thirteen species of which several are quite widely grown. Examples are *R. collettianum,* the other species which occurs in Afghanistan and adjacent Pakistan, *R. anthopogon, R. cephalanthum* and *R. primuliflorum.*

I hope that I have been able to give you something of an insight into the way taxonomic activity goes on, and the reasons for the changes in name in the genus Rhododendron which have occurred recently. All these taxonomic changes that I have been talking about, as well as those in the larger scaly rhododendrons are published as volume 39 part 1 of the *Notes from the Royal Botanic Garden, Edinburgh.* This appeared in December 1980, and is available from HMSO bookshops, at £7.50.

Conservation of Plants in the Wild

ALFRED EVANS (Ed)

Saxifraga florulenta

According to a little book I have, CONSERVATION has preservation, maintenance, perpetuation, protection and keeping listed as synonyms. It also gives as antonyms abolition, eradication, destruction and suppression. One could join in the game and add annihilation, cessation, extermination and EXTINCTION.

On the shelves in our library there are many volumes on all manner of botanical and horticultural subjects, but in the section reserved for books dealing with rare, threatened and endangered species one title which I think very apt and which spells out the message of plant conservation more than any other is "Extinction is Forever". It is a report of the "Status of Threatened and Endangered Plants of the Americas" and is published by the New York Botanic Garden.

Just think of it, through our thoughtlessness certain plants can disappear from the surface of the earth. We would then join trips to the mountains to see bare rocks, the soil already having been washed out to sea because of erosion. No *Gentiana acaulis*, no *Dryas octopetala*, no dodecatheons, primulas, Meconopsis, erythroniums or aubrietas. "What nonsense," I can just hear you saying! "How could all these millions of plants that we enjoy in the wild each year simply disappear like that? Goodness gracious, *Dryas octopetala* can stabilise shifting sands, dwarf Salix virtually act like gloves and envelope completely some of Europe's highest mountains, holding the soil in place, the numberless flowers of lupins are responsible for the blue haze which sometimes hangs over the meadows of some of North America's high peaks. There is no danger." I wonder, is that true? Aren't we really being too trusting?

Thankfully, Conservation is the "in" thing just now and as nearly everyone would agree, it is the accepted thing to be biased in support of any discussion preserving wild life. At last it is our turn, I hope.

Buildings, furniture, paintings and even man's creations in the way of garden design all receive support from government bodies, interested societies and even wealthy individuals. Enormous financial aid has been poured out over the years towards helping to preserve or conserve these man-made objects—man's achievements—but what of nature's efforts, this wonderful phenomenon of which we are so very much a part? Man has made use of nature quite liberally and often selfishly for his own ends, and now when he sees that he can control his own environment, informed minds realise that, without nature's co-operation and involvement, this power is a hollow achievement. The world got on well before we arrived on the scene, it gave us birth, and now, like unruly children we seem to find pleasure in tearing the place apart. Will we finally grow up to appreciate what mother nature has provided by herself over millions of years, and which we now use for our bodies' needs and pleasure, and treat what is hers with the respect we would give to our parents' possessions? I hope so, otherwise the world once more may have to manage without us.

As gardeners—and alpine plant enthusiasts at that—how then can we aid conservation? How can we in our small way help to arrest the destruction of species in the wild? I think first of all we must become aware that there is a problem; aware of the need to look after what we have and not unthinkingly uproot plants in the wild for our selfish pleasure. However, not for a moment do I suggest that we should say "stop" and that the world should remain un-altered as it is today. No—there would be little merit in that—there must be progress and change for even nature adapts and adjusts continuously, the plants advancing or retreating with changing conditions. Let us enjoy nature by all means, but at the same time let us protect it and teach others to appreciate it and not deliberately destroy and spoil what is so beautiful. It is part of our heritage and it is not ours to lay waste.

Surely by now we have reached the stage in alpine plant apprecia-tion where we recognise that plants growing in their natural habitats are somehow more in tune with each other than when they are "tarted up" in an alpine house or even lovingly tended in a rock garden. They may even have a longevity in the field which is denied them in cultivation. I do not say that we should not try to grow some of nature's distinctive, highly ornamental species, that would be completely negative, and some of my colleagues and friends are highly successful at that anyway, but let us try to procure our plants by non-destructive means. Let us leave the actual parent plant in its chosen environment and hopefully, from wild collected seeds, accept the even greater challenge of bringing into existence and nurturing a completely new plant, one raised by our own efforts from seed. Goodness knows there is every opportunity available for achieving that today. Quite apart from the accumulated knowledge and the numerous examples of the grower's skill, what other organised club has members so widely scattered across the globe as has rock gardeners? Moreover, how many societies have as many active, interested, generous members who, in time, can become close personal friends, and who will go to great lengths to procure for us seeds from natural sources and, lastly, what gives us the right to decimate plant communities? After all, the ease with which we can now participate in trips to areas where alpine flowers abound denies us very little. Tours are so well organised that we can be transported in comfort to some of nature's prettiest natural gardens where we may see alpine plant treasures on the grand scale all within a few hours. Capture the moment on film and if your holiday amongst the flowers has thrilled you, then the elation will return every time you project your transparencies.

Plant conservation is an extremely important part of today's living and, seriously, it involves our most basic requirement, the food chain. Our own facet is but a very small part of the whole picture and many books and academic papers on the topics have been published. Botanists in their high-powered ways try to open our eyes to the dangers of mass collecting, but at the end of the day the plain message is surely to plead that we respect and appreciate what is there, treat it sensibly and enjoy the experience. The picking or not picking of flowers I must leave to your conscience, but it would indeed be an unhappy moment if we ever reached the stage where a mother had to deny her little daughter the pleasure of weaving a daisy-chain.

I know that many members of alpine societies are well aware of the existence of the *Red Data Book*. This lists plants which are threatened with extinction worldwide and is a publication of the I.U.C.N. (the International Union for Conservation of Nature and Natural Resources Survival Service Commission). The list grows longer every year and, as an indication that we alpine gardeners operate within the pages of this volume and to what extent, I have added symbols to the plant index at the end of this article in order to indicate how many of the plants discussed in the papers given at the

5th International Rock Garden Plant Conference are listed in the *Red Data Book*. I said that the list of threatened species was compiled on an international level. It does not take account of the many attractive and interesting outliers from the main stream of the species—as *Diapensia lapponica, Phyllodoce caerulea* and *Saxifraga cernua* are in Scotland. There they are extremely rare. Their depletion in that country affects the overall population of plants hardly at all, but think of the tragic loss to Scotland. *Cypripedium calceolus* and *Pulsatilla vulgaris* are similarly placed in England and so on. One could find examples of this sort in every country. Their conservation is just as important to us nationally and locally.

So, statistically, if we were to assume that there are 250,000 flowering plants in the world—just another one of these arbitrary figures—but in this instance considered by some to be a very reasonable estimate, it is currently stated that 250 plants are threatened. That figure simply records the number we know of and at a conservative estimate one could be quite safe in assuming that there are at least as many again of which we are unaware. On running my eye down the printed list I have counted 29 which I think are of particular interest to the growers of alpine plants. In fact 5 have been discussed at this conference. Therefore, armed with this knowledge, we can firmly state that we have discussed 2% of the threatened plants of the world and, put another way, in the papers read 0·5% are listed as threatened.

The species listed in the *Red Data Book* which affect rock gardeners are:—

Androsace brevis	Italian Alps
Arctostaphylos densiflora	California
Artemisia granatensis	Spain
Celmisia morganii	New Zealand
*Celmisia philocremna	New Zealand
Cypripedium candidum	North America
*Daphne arbuscula	Hungary
Daphne rodriguezii	Minorca
Dianthus callizonus	Central Europe
Dianthus urumoffii	Bulgaria
Dionysia mira	Oman

Draba ladina	Switzerland
*Fritillaria liliacea	California
Gunnera hamiltonii	New Zealand
Hudsonia montana	North America
Iris lortetii	Syria
*Iris winogradowii	West Caucasus
Lilium rhodopaeum	Bulgaria
Myosotidium hortensia	Chatham Islands
Onosma tornensis	Europe
Paeonia cambessedesii	Balearic Islands
Primula palinuri	South Italy
*Ranunculus crithmifolius ssp. paucifolius	New Zealand
Saxifraga biternata	Mediterranean Region
Saxifraga florulenta	Maritime Alps
Silene diclinis	Spain
Silene holzmannii	Greece
Silene viscariopsis	Macedonia
Viola hispida	N.E. France.

Conservation of Plants in Gardens

CHRIS BRICKELL

Jankaea heldreichii

The urgent need to agree on and implement conservation policies for wild plants has been graphically and vividly illustrated on many occasions. But what of our garden plants—can it be said that they are in equal danger? Does it matter very much if there is a gradual loss of horticultural plants or is it important that they should be conserved? And if conservation is required how can this be achieved?

It is arguable that we have managed to get along perfectly well by using the wild plants nature has so abundantly provided and selecting or breeding from them to obtain the food, clothing and medicines required by man as well as satisfying his aesthetic needs. Why should this not continue?

We are all very much aware of one reason and that is the appalling loss of wild plants which occurs each year. This means that the basic reservoir on which we have drawn in the past is rapidly disappearing and lost species cannot be replaced. Many of the plants evolved by man, often from species no longer known in the wild, contain the potential through their genes to pass on characters of immense importance to our economic future, and directly or indirectly man's future depends on these plants. Yet our knowledge of cultivated plants is, in most instances, very scanty, so it is foolish to discard many of them as we have and are still doing without first evaluating their worth. The consequences of losing the genetic potential of these plants are obvious and a very compelling reason, therefore, for instituting conservation policies for plants of economic importance.

Can a similar case be made for our garden plants? I believe very strongly that it can, but it is essential that we do *not* blithely adopt an all-embracing policy of conserving garden plants purely for the sake of preserving them. Such an approach would be self-defeating as, apart from stretching what few resources we have to the limit, it would be pointless to attempt to maintain complete collections of cultivars of cabbages, pinks, apples, daffodils, rhododendrons or any other plant merely because they have been given cultivar names. Most have only a passing value and many need not have been named at all. There is, of course, no reason why enthusiasts should not attempt to assemble complete or near-complete collections of the genus or group in which they are interested but the highest priority *must* be given to certain important categories which it is vital to maintain if the conservation of our garden plants is to be successful; and to be successful we may initially need to gather together many cultivars that, when evaluated by agreed criteria and found wanting are then discarded.

Let me briefly outline the categories concerned and the reasons why I consider them to be of importance.

1. *Historical Importance*

We accept, almost unquestioningly that it is important to preserve historical collections of a wide variety of objects—pottery, clothing, rocks, paintings—so that man's endeavours to create a civilised world are not forgotten. Records of these developments and achievements are neatly catalogued in museums—but where are the records of man's achievements in harnessing plants for use in gardens and commercial horticulture? Written records, often incomplete, exist—drawings, paintings, photographs and dried specimens may have been prepared but they do not tell the whole story. To do this, it is essential to gather together and keep living collections of our cultivated plants containing historically important cultivars, and to include those considered as being representative of particular periods of garden fashion.

2. *Genetic Importance*

Many hybrids and cultivars might well disappear from our gardens without any deleterious future effects. But among those that have already been lost and are now being discarded may well be cultivars or mutants of species containing gene complexes able to provide an irreplaceable combination of characters important for improving the genus concerned. At the moment we simply do not know—so we cannot afford to discard plants that might be of value in supplying the genetic potential for resistance to diseases and pests or to improve quality, vigour and yield, just because they do not match up to our current requirements in other respects. As an example *Aster novi-belgii* 'Climax' an old cultivar with small blue flowers shows marked resistance to mildew, the bane of many large-flowered modern cultivars. It would seem to have in its make-up the genetic potential required to combat mildew in Michaelmas daisies but it has almost disappeared from the nursery trade as modern larger-flowered cultivars are deemed to be "improvements". Luckily it has been nurtured by members of the Hardy Plant Society so will still be available for future breeding programmes.

Included in this category should be cultivars of ornamentals, fruits and vegetables that are of value because of unusual qualities such as late-flowering or early maturing, since these are often by-passed during the main stream of a particular breeding programme as they are not directly relevant to the time. Alternatively they may be considered a nuisance to maintain as they do not fit into the pattern laid down for profitable commercial development and so are discarded. But the potential value remains, even for ornamentals and directly or indirectly many disciplines—farming, forestry, medicine, commercial and amateur horticulture—are effected adversely if the genetic value of these plants is not assessed before they are discarded or lost.

3. *Aesthetics and Garden Value*

The most compelling reason for most of us is that we grow plants because we like them and feel that they contribute greatly to our lives, both as objects of beauty and as a balm to help cope with the stresses and strains of daily living. Whatever your interest—collecting snowdrop cultivars, flower arranging or growing only the most intractable of alpines, you still need to obtain the relevant plants. And if some of these plants are no longer available your chances of deriving pleasure and satisfaction from achieving your particular goal are diminished considerably. There is unfortunately an elitist school of thought among growers of some types of plant the aim of which appears to be to limit the cultivation of their "treasures" to the select few, a restrictive attitude which frequently ends in the loss of the entire stock of the plant. Luckily this possessive approach to uncommon plants is diminishing and the vast majority of gardeners show an extraordinary generosity, even to virtual strangers, in sharing their plants. Exchange of rarities is their life-blood and those who cling to their treasures can only be pitied for their Scrooge-like approach.

We should remember too the aesthetic importance of gardens, and individual plants whose appeal can be justly compared with that of great paintings, sculptures or buildings. A threat to an important building or an irreplaceable painting creates an immediate public outcry; the loss of a great landscape garden or a valuable garden plant scarcely ripples across the surface of public consciousness. Why should this be? The reason is not hard to find. It is our lack of knowledge of what valuable plants and important gardens exist in Britain although in recent years co-ordinated efforts have been made to increase our knowledge.

4. *Usefulness to Man*

Apart from the very compelling economic reasons for conserving cultivated plants previously mentioned under "Genetic Importance" they must also be considered essential in the light of scientific and educational research. The advantages from the gardener's viewpoint may not appear of great moment, but as adjuncts to research into both pure and applied aspects of botany and allied sciences many undoubtedly have value, their chemical and physical make-up (in addition to their genetic characteristics) providing information extremely useful to scientists in their work.

Similarly cultivated plants are of use in education both in the developed and under-developed countries of the world where the role of plants in relation to man is little understood. Many of the species and cultivars we unwittingly destroy or discard could be of immense value to man and a knowledge of cultivated plants and their importance can help in an effort to encourage people to understand the need for plants in our lives; and to do this we need first to preserve and then to conserve by propagation the cultivated plants we still possess.

5. *Conservation of Wild Plants in Gardens*

In some cases it is possible to use our gardens as reservoirs in which species and their variants known to be rare and endangered in the wild can be grown and increased. Until recent years any conservation of wild species in gardens has been a chance occurrence, but now successful efforts are being made to maintain and propagate endangered species so that should a catastrophe occur in the wild and the remaining population of a species be wiped out, cultivated plants of known wild origin will be available for replanting if desired. If *Franklinia altamaha,* a beautiful American relative of the Camellia, had not been grown in gardens, it would now be extinct as it can no longer be found in the wild. Similarly cultivation in gardens has almost certainly ensured that *Ginkgo biloba,* the maidenhair tree and the dawn redwood, *Metasequoia glyptostroboides* remain as part of the world's flora, both known only in the wild in restricted areas of China and in very small numbers. You can contribute to this vital project by growing, propagating and distributing the varieties—but please, do not go out into the wild to collect them to cultivate. If you possess such plants as *Cyclamen rohlfsianum* or *C. libanoticum* propagate and distribute them—further attacks on the wild populations can only push them further towards the brink of extinction in nature and by making them available the need to collect from the wild will be diminished considerably.

If we accept the justification for preservation and conservation what has to be done? The delegates to the RHS Conservation Conference in 1978 certainly thought the case had been made for the conservation of gardens and garden plants (RHS Journal, April 1979, pp 161–171) and as a result the National Council for the Conservation of Plants and Gardens (NCCPG) was formed the following year to implement the resolutions agreed by the Conference and to formulate a programme to be carried out as staffing and finance allowed.

The NCCPG felt it essential to establish the important basic requirements and to pose a number of questions:

(a) What cultivated plants are important and what cultivars are still available?
(b) Which should we maintain? And why?
(c) How can conserved stocks be maintained and used?
(d) Who is to be responsible?

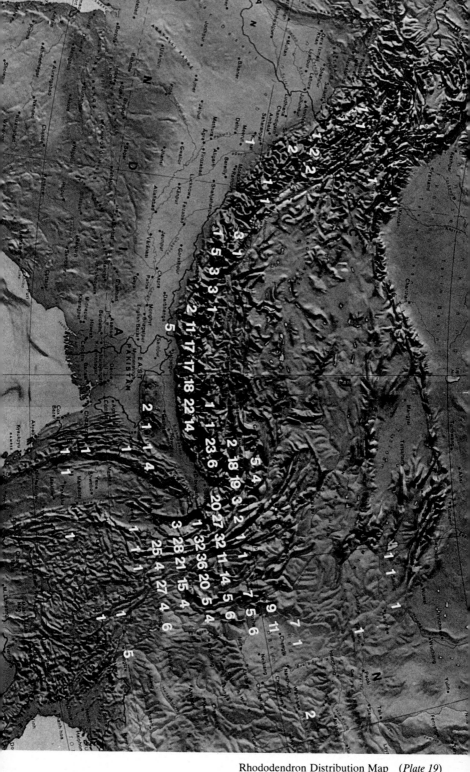

Rhododendron Distribution Map   (*Plate 19*)

⌕ Primula reidii   (*Plate 21*)

◊ Codonopsis convolvulacea 'Alba'   (*Plate 20*)

⌕ Celmisia sessiliflora   (*Plate 22*)

Anemone parviflora ⌒ (*Plate 24*)

◊ Pedicularis lanata (*Plate 23*)

Diapensia obovata ⌒ (*Plate 25*)

Saxifraga stolitzkae   (*Plate 26*)

Saxifraga hypostoma   (*Plate 27*)

Clintonia umbellata   (*Plate 28*)

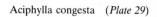

Aciphylla congesta   (*Plate 29*)

Ranunculus buchananii   (*Plate 30*)

Leucogenes grandiceps   (*Plate 31*)

None of these questions could be answered simply but, in order to establish objectives and a programme of work to carry out the resolutions of the RHS Conference, the NCCPG has set up a small co-ordinating staff based at Wisley. Initially its work is being concentrated on plants from temperate zones which can be grown in the open in Britain and among its main objectives are:

1. To monitor the position of gardens with important plant collections and, when necessary, advise on appropriate action to encourage their preservation through the NCCPG in co-operation with other bodies active in this field.

2. To encourage suitable bodies to undertake the listing of plants not covered by existing lists. Possibly under certain circumstances, to undertake pilot projects in listing. To assess on the basis of this work what plants are rare in cultivation or even extinct.

3. With the aid of knowledgeable individuals, specialist groups, registration authorities and interested nurserymen, to analyse these results and to indicate:

(a) criteria for choosing cultivars, hybrids and species whose continued preservation is important
(b) the desirable and important cultivars, hybrids and species that are no longer available via the trade, and
(c) which, among the rare but available cultivars, hybrids and species, it is important to preserve.

4. To act as a clearing house for those engaged in this field in any capacity, eg, nurserymen seeking propagating material of rare plants, and scientific and educational bodies in search of plant material.

5. To establish "National Collections" of different groups of plants to act as banks for the preservation of plants in cultivation and as sources of propagating material. These collections would form permanent exhibits for educational and research purposes.

6. To encourage introduction and propagation of threatened species and important cultivars and hybrids not represented in British gardens, maintaining contacts with appropriate bodies and people abroad where necessary with a view to encouraging as wide a dispersal as possible of such plants in British gardens.

The NCCPG believes that much of this work can be carried out most satisfactorily by independent but associated local groups; to date over 28 have been formed and it is hoped that eventually a nationwide network will be established comparable to the County Naturalists' Trusts.

6. *National Collections*

Apart from establishing very important links with other conservation organisations and the formation of local groups one of the main tasks of the NCCPG has been to foster the establishment of National Collections. These are reference collections, as complete as possible, of a group of plants, often comprising a genus such as *Cassiope* but quite frequently a section within a genus such as the Petiolarid primulas, or even the variants of a single species such as *Primula allionii.* They are run by organisations or individuals in collaboration with the NCCPG and in most cases a "reserve collection" will also be formed to make sure that if a disaster befalls the original National Collection or part of it, there is an alternative source of material from which further stock can be propagated. The types of organisations which have already agreed to hold National Collections are given in the accompanying chart.

The purposes of the National Collections are:

1. To act as "Gene Banks" so that the genetic variation of the collection will be available for future breeding work and research in horticulture.

2. To act as "Living Museums" so that they are valuable aids to taxonomic work and identification. By comparison with existing stocks it should be possible, eventually, to ensure that plant names in the nursery trade are stabilised.

In addition it will enable nurserymen wishing to name and introduce new cultivars to make certain by comparison that their proposed new introduction is both distinct from and an improvement upon already existing cultivars. This could in most cases ensure that the provision of "new names for old cultivars" does not occur and that the future introduction of very similar cultivars is avoided.

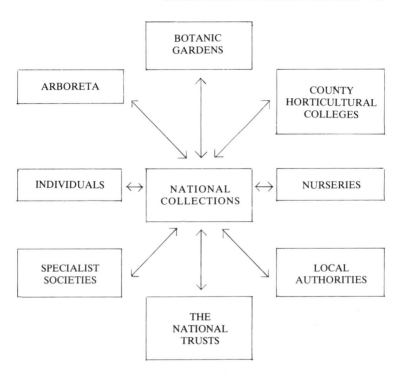

3. To act as sources of propagating material, particularly in the case of rare and unusual plants. Their purpose is not, however, to act as "stockgrounds" for nurserymen requiring propagating material each season, but to make available to the trade limited amounts of material so that plants in danger of being lost are propagated and distributed.

Although the organisation of National Collections differs to some extent, depending on the type of plant involved, they will normally include both cultivated plants—whether species, hybrids or cultivars—and plants of known wild origin particularly if they represent different areas of the plants' natural range so that a wide genetic base for the species concerned is maintained.

The main effort, at present, is directed towards conserving hardy plants but the aim eventually is to include tender and greenhouse plants in the scheme.

It is not an easy task to gather together, check the identity and establish groups of plants as National Collections. It is however, very heartening to find how many organisations wish to become involved in the scheme which applies not only to ornamentals but to fruit and vegetables. In the case of annuals the use of seed banks is being considered and a vegetable seed bank has already been established by the National Vegetable Research Station to conserve old cultivars.

With some plants such as roses, chrysanthemums, dahlias and daffodils the numbers of cultivars named is immense and it is clearly impossible, even were it desirable, to maintain all the cultivars still in existence. In such cases the criteria on which the case for conserving cultivated plants is based should be used to justify the inclusion of a particular plant in the National Collection. To be worthy of conserving it should be in one of the following categories:

1. Historically important in the development of the plant.
2. Genetically important, with characters which are likely to be of value in future breeding programmes.
3. Aesthetically of value or representative of an important period of garden fashion. Where applicable the RHS system of awards could be used to establish suitable criteria on which to base selection in this category.
4. Valuable for scientific research, medicinally, commercially or in other ways to man.
5. Known to be rare or endangered in the wild.

7. *What is Rare and Endangered and Why?*

One of the major problems is to locate the rare and endangered plants so that a possible source of material for future propagation and distribution is known. This can only be achieved through comprehensive listings and documentation in gardens and nurseries—a mammoth task which is now being tackled by the NCCPG. There is, however, a need to classify the reasons why garden plants have become rare or endangered so that we are aware of the types of plant that are still liable to be lost. These can roughly be divided into the following groups, some of which overlap to a certain extent.

DIFFICULT OR UNECONOMIC TO PROPAGATE COMMERCIALLY   Plants that are difficult to propagate or slow to reach saleable size are rapidly being dropped from the lists of many nurseries. If they do not come into the categories we consider merit conservation it is not of very great moment; but many are plants that gardeners would particularly like to grow and would often be willing to purchase at a high price. Where now for example can *Paeonia suffruticosa* (Rock's Variety) the Golden Oak, *Quercus robur* 'Concordia' or the bright yellow poppy relative *Dendromecon rigidum* be obtained commercially in Britain? Plants are still known in gardens but because specialist, and therefore expensive techniques of propagation are required they are likely to be propagated in small numbers only at present by the specialist nurserymen. Similarly the only way at present in which we can obtain the ladies slipper orchids such as *Cypripedium reginae* is from nurserymen importing plants from the wild as techniques to grow ground orchids of this type have yet to be developed satisfactorily. The stocks of Cypripedium species we purchase therefore, further deplete the species in the wild. A major effort is needed from research bodies to find means of propagating these horticulturally desirable ground orchids so that they do not one by one suffer the fate of our own native *Cypripedium calceolus* through over-collecting.

SIMPLE TO PROPAGATE BUT SLOW TO INCREASE   The supermarket approach in many nurseries and garden centres sadly but understandably means that plants of high quality easily propagated but of limited annual increase from individual plants are seldom grown or offered, although still sometimes stocked by the specialist nursery. Micropropagation may overcome this drawback when the techniques are more fully developed but by then it could be too late. If such plants as the deep metallic purple *Helleborus purpurascens,* the yellow flowered *Paeonia mlokosewitschii,* the superb hybrid *Meconopsis* × *sheldonii,* the wake robins like *Trillium sessile* and the double *T. grandiflorum* could be increased rapidly they would almost certainly be best-sellers. As it is they remain tenuously in the lists, occasionally being offered in very small quantities.

TENDER AND EASILY LOST UNLESS PROPAGATED REGULARLY   Understandably also the trade is not very anxious to cope with plants on the borderline of hardiness in Britain which are likely to be killed during the winter unless stock plants are maintained under glass. Many Salvia species and Osteospermum species and hybrids do not appear in the general nursery lists, good garden plants though they are, as regular annual propagation and over-wintering is required. *Cosmos atrosanguineus,* a relative of the Dahlia, with chocolate-scented, deep blackish-red flowers bloom-ing all summer lingers in a few sheltered gardens and is now available again though at one time it was almost lost. And what has happened to the old heliotrope cultivars, the scented "cherry pie" at one time obligatory ingredients of parks bedding schemes throughout the country. Seed raised imposters do duty for them but none match in quality the vegetatively propagated cultivars of old.

DIFFICULT TO GROW WITHOUT SPECIAL CARE   Alpine nurserymen still, praise be, retain the skill and expertise to grow and offer the stubborn Dionysia and Androsace species, *Calceolaria darwinii* and, less often, the rare and lovely *Iris nicolai* and the glorious Oncocyclus irises. These are not plants that we can or should expect the average nurseryman to stock but it is still important that they are maintained as even with the marvellous skills available in the AGS and SRGC many past introductions are no longer with us, as a glance at the indices of the AGS Bulletin and SRGC Journal will quickly show.

RARE OR UNCOMMON IN NATURE BUT NOT DIFFICULT TO INCREASE   A considerable number of plants, restricted in their distribution in nature, prove relatively easy to increase when brought into culti-vation. Once these plants are in the hands of nurserymen and individuals it should be easy enough for them to be propagated and distributed, which would have a marked effect on reducing further depredations in wild populations of the species concerned. Why for instance can one not obtain readily and at a reasonable price *Crocus gargaricus* and *C. tournefortii,* both easily increased but restricted in nature in their distribution? Similarly the beautiful *Daphne jasminea* known only from a few sites in Greece, roots without great difficulty from cuttings and yet is scarcely ever offered although happily one or two specialist growers have started to hold small stocks. Try also to obtain commercially *D. petraea* (even the clone 'Grandiflora') and *D. arbuscula* and you will search long and hard before you trace either for sale. And yet both root very readily from semi-ripe wood taken in summer and placed in a plastic-covered propagating tray with no bottom heat.

One of the problems is, of course, for the nursery trade to obtain stock plants and, perhaps more importantly, once they have the plants to build them up and retain them at a reasonable level. There is always the very understandable temptation to sell off most of your stock once you have it and then find that the propagating potential of your remaining stocks (if any!) is so limited that it is not worth offering for several years at least. Only a disciplined approach in adhering to a programme where sufficient stock plants are grown to provide an annual production of the required number of plants for sale, will give the steady flow of plants—and sales—which are essential if this type of plant is to be available on a regular basis.

OUT OF FASHION—EASILY PROPAGATED BUT GENERALLY NEGLECTED
Horticultural fashions like those of the couturiers change (although perhaps less rapidly!) and interests in particular groups of plants wax and wane often for no very apparent reasons. In recent years there has been a marked revival in growing "old roses" largely due to the work of Graham Thomas who has emphasised the value of many of them as garden plants whilst firmly making it clear that some are not of any great merit, or historical interest and could be discarded without any significant loss to horticulture. But there are still many plants, easily grown, readily increased and grown by a few gardeners which either do not appear to have been considered by the trade or for some reason are priced at an artificially high level. Why for instance is the delightful *Viola* 'Jackanapes' with its bi-colour bright yellow and dark purple-brown flowers not grown and sold in large quantities by every garden centre as a pot plant? Why is *Colchicum speciosum* var. *album,* in my view one of the most beautiful of autumn flowering bulbs, so over-priced? It increases rapidly, flowers regularly and should be no more costly than the ordinary Colchicum species and hybrids generally offered.

Examples in this category are not hard to find—many of them excellent garden plants that appear only to require a good horticultural PRO to make them more generally popular and available.

GOOD RECENT INTRODUCTIONS—WILL THEY BE PROPAGATED AND GROWN COMMERCIALLY?   Although there is a steady flow of new introductions of both species and cultivars into gardens it is not always easy for them to become established. Some like *Euonymus* 'Emerald 'n Gold' very quickly become standard garden centre lines whilst others, equally meritorious, languish and sometimes disappear altogether. *Fremontodendron* 'California Glory' a superb hybrid of *F. mexicana* and *F. californica,* was introduced from California by my predecessor at Wisley, Frank Knight, in 1962 and immediately propagating material was distributed to the trade. Sad to relate even with the accolade of an FCC in 1967 it was not until 1978 when it was propagated and marketed by RHS Enterprises that it "took on" in the trade and is happily now fairly readily available. Similarly *Rosa* 'Helen Knight', an excellent bright yellow, May-flowering hybrid of *R. ecae* raised at Wisley was offered to the trade in 1969 but not until 1980 was it propagated by the trade in sufficient quantities to make it available to the many people who wished to grow it. In a survey over a two week period at Wisley when it was in flower more than 500 people asked where they could purchase a plant and many others, no doubt, returned home to ask their local nurseryman to supply plants. These just happen to be examples where we know the full history but there are many other cases where fine new introductions fail to reach the public. Not all introductions, of course, are swans and a considerable number will not live up to their early promise so it is understandable that a conservative approach is adopted by the nursery trade. Let us hope that the establishment of National Collections and the possibility of direct comparison and assessment of cultivars in these collections will provide the stimulus needed to ensure the continuation of these neglected plants of high garden value.

LOST TO CULTIVATION AS FAR AS IS KNOWN   A cry that is often heard is that "so and so" which used to be a common plant in nurseries and gardens seems to have disappeared completely. In many cases, happily, the plant concerned is still growing tucked away in a garden, often unnamed, but potentially available if the owner will provide stock from which to propagate. Some will certainly have been lost to cultivation and it is probable that their loss will not really matter. But others which have been lost—as far as we know—are (or were) important for a particular reason. By diligent searching we may come across them and be able to cross them off the lost list and this is one of the projects we hope local groups will undertake in due course.

My own interest in the genus Daphne provides a number of examples of losses or near losses, the most valuable of which is *D. odora* 'Mazelii', a clone introduced from Japan in the late-19th century. As a garden plant it was apparently very fine and the characteristics of scented, winter-produced pink and white blooms in an inflorescence six inches or so in length, suggest that it could also be used viably as a pot plant in commercial horticulture. Regrettably we only know it now from a plate in *The Garden* for 1878. Commercially not of great importance but horticulturally desirable are the double white and double red forms of *D. mezereum,* both quite well-known during the last century, both now apparently lost. Similarly a most beautiful variegated (not virused!) form of this species that occurred as a seedling in Leeds in 1856 remains to us only as a plate in Lowe & Howard's *Beautiful Leaved Plants* (1861).

In recent years collectors have brought back seeds, bulbs and plants of numerous species of value and interest to gardeners from many parts of the world. How many of the plants brought back by E. K. Balls & Balfour Gourlay just prior to the 1939–45 War can we trace now? Even more recently the S.S. & W. collections in Nepal and those of Paul Furse in the Middle East—all widely distributed when they arrived—have dwindled so that only a few remain. These examples added to those one can trace fairly easily by looking back through the *Botanical Magazine,* the *RHS Journal* and other specialist journals, are significant reminders of the losses in garden plants that have occurred in recent years, partly due to the economic needs of the horticultural industry but also through a lack of any co-operative effort to maintain plants that the trade was not able to retain. The advent of National Collections and local groups will, we hope, change the pattern for the better.

In the end, however, success or failure in conserving plants will come down to the problem of supply and demand. We cannot expect the nursery trade to grow plants that the public is not going to buy. We may argue over what is a reasonable annual turnover of any one item—should it be dropped if sales/annum fall below 500 or should it be retained as a "lost leader" to entice people into the nursery?—but the retention or rejection of any particular plant will depend on pure survival economics. The nursery trade in my view, could boost its sales by increased publicity which at present is not its forte and might well adopt some of the marketing techniques used in other industries to good effect. But we who bemoan the lack of availability of the plants we want to grow must be prepared to buy the rare and uncommon plants, encourage others to do so and pay a reasonable premium for a plant which required more care, time and expense to grow than a mass-produced shrub or alpine which fits into the modern "factory" techniques essential to the industry if it is to survive.

8. *What can You Do to Help?*

If there is a local group in your area join it and become involved in its work. If not consider some of the following suggestions:

(i) Select a group of plants that interests you and
  (a) list those available in trade catalogues and those in your own garden
  (b) circulate other gardeners with similar interests to find out what they grow
  (c) visit shows, gardens and nurseries to note what they grow
  (d) pass on the information to the NCCPG to correlate with their records. Don't worry that you will be inundated with requests for plants—sources (unless commercial) will not be published.

(ii) If you grow plants that are uncommon, make sure you pass them on—your plant may one day die and you may then be looking for a source!

(iii) Make sure you have made satisfactory provision for the care of your plants so that they are passed on to capable growers in the event of serious illness or death.

(iv) If you are interested in gardens and landscapes locate and list those of importance in your area and pass on the information to the NCCPG

(v) Help to establish National Collections by providing propagating material of unusual plants.

(vi) Create a demand for the good plants that are so difficult to obtain by asking nurseries for uncommon plants in which you are interested and keep on asking!

9. *The Future*

Any policies of conservation *must* be looked at critically and practically. Blanket conservation based only on sentiment or the feeling that conservation with a capital C is a good idea is not enough.

If the NCCPG is to flourish and carry out its policies then a co-ordinated effort is essential from all those interested in growing and maintaining our garden plants. The NCCPG has only limited resources and so must rely on the goodwill and co-operation of individuals and specialist groups to provide information, expertise and inevitably a certain amount of funding in the future. It is up to you to decide—do you want to grow a wide range of interesting and beautiful plants in your garden or do you want only to have available the routine range to be found in many garden centres and the spasmodic supplies of uncommon and rare plants that will occasionally be available from the specialist nursery? Our heritage of plants and gardens is unique—should we not endeavour by every means at our disposal to ensure not only their survival but their revival?

THE CHOICE IS YOURS

Alaska

DICK REDFIELD

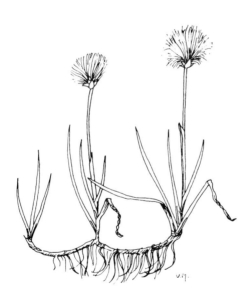

Eriophorum scheuchzeri

Initially, it would be helpful to the reader if he were to look at a map of the entire state of Alaska as I relate the travels of my party in search of plants. During the trips we paused briefly to look at just one or two plants in some areas and made more extended stops at other points to examine a wider range of species. This article covers three separate expeditions, the first in 1961, the second in 1965 and the last as recent as 1978. Although three weeks was the longest single stay, the combined dates cover the period from the second week in June through to the third week of July.

Transportation from home was accomplished by jet airliner from the east coast of the U.S.A. to Anchorage. This part of the journey took some nine hours and then, by means of a smaller plane, we travelled to Nome, which is situated on the south coast of the Seward Peninsula and almost as far west as one can go on the mainland of North America. There are no roads between Anchorage and Nome.

June is usually a wet month in this area and on our last visit, 1978, this was no exception. Rain fell on 27 days out of 30 and the three days at the end of the month when we were there were not the ones which were dry. Nevertheless we saw many interesting plants, amongst them *Androsace chamaejasme*, *Eritrichium aretioides*, *Oxytropis nigrescens*, *Primula tschuktschorum* and others. *Saxifraga oppositifolia* was plentiful but already past flowering. On the Nome Council road, just east of town, there were masses of *Primula borealis* interspersed with white-flowered forms here and there. Scattered among the primulas was an attractive lousewort, *Pedicularis sudetica*, some with reddish-purple and white flowers and others where the flowers were of one colour. The slopes of Anvil Mountain, near Nome, are said to be ablaze with colour when *Rhododendron camtschaticum* is in full flower. Unfortunately, at the time of our visit it was not yet in bloom, but we did see it flowering in a garden in Anchorage, along with a lovely, pure white form.

In 1965, we briefly visited the Katmai National Monument on the Alaska Peninsula. Very few plants were in flower at that early date in June but we did find the deepest colour form of *Loiseleuria procumbens* we have ever seen. It was almost red.

We picked up a car in Anchorage and this was our means of transportation for the balance of our travels. Proceeding north our first stop was at the Eklutna Flats. Here, in late June, we were greeted by the sight of thousands upon thousands of *Dodecatheon pulchellum,* stretching almost as far as the eye could see. Among them, but much fewer in number, were *Iris setosa* and that nearly black, but none the less beautiful, *Fritillaria camschatcensis.* Surely this is one of the most spectacular floral displays in Alaska. The entire area was swamped by high tides at the time of the 1964 earthquake and it was feared that the plants which had been submerged would be destroyed. However they bloomed as beautifully as ever the following year.

Our next stop was Hatcher Pass, a few miles farther north in the Talkeetna Mountains. Here we found a great variety of plants, among them the lovely *Anemone parviflora, Cassiope stelleriana, Diapensia lapponica,* including the rare, pink-flowered form, *Geum rossii* and *Primula cuneifolia.* Continuing northwards on the George Parks Highway, a relatively new road which provides a more direct route from Anchorage to Mount McKinley National Park and Fairbanks, we saw what appeared to be a small lake some distance from the highway. Closer examination revealed that it was a great mass of one of the many species of Eriophorum, perhaps *E. scheuchzeri,* that are found in Alaska, commonly called "Cotton Grass" or "Alaska Cotton". In many places we found shy little *Moneses uniflora* in considerable numbers, also the related *Pyrola asarifolia* and *P. grandiflora. Pulsatilla patens,* already gone to seed, was also plentiful.

From Fairbanks the Steese Highway meanders some 160 miles to Circle City on the Yukon River, "most northerly point on connected American Highway System". The areas close to Twelve Mile Summit and Eagle Summit, the highest point on the road at 3,880 feet, are some of the most accessible and best from which to view the native flora of Alaska. With no great physical effort we found *Rubus chamaemorus,* called "Baked Apple Berry" where it grows in eastern North America, *Gentiana glauca,* two attractive crucifers, *Parrya nudicaulis* and *Cardamine purpurea,* and *Dodecatheon frigidum,* a smaller species than *D. pulchellum.* Also seen were *Eritrichium aretioides,* varying from pale to deep blue,

Lagotis glauca, Rhododendron lapponicum, Cassiope tetragona, the very prostrate *Ledum decumbens* called by some botanists *L. palustre* ssp. *decumbens* or var. *decumbens,* and a most interesting and beautiful Pedicularis, *P. lanata,* resembling a ball of cotton in bud and then expanding into a very showy, purplish-pink when in full flower. Other species included *Oxytropis nigrescens,* a charming, prostrate legume, and *Arenaria arctica,* a relatively common and widespread species in Alaska. Here it was in beautiful display in a crevice in lichen-covered rocks.

From Circle we retraced our path to Fairbanks, then followed the Richardson Highway which leads eventually to Valdez on the coast. There are many points of interest along the way but we headed directly for Thompson Pass, about 25 miles inland from Valdez. Again we found a great mixture of plant species including *Caltha leptosepala, Claytonia sarmentosa, Phyllodoce glanduliflora, Ranunculus eschscholtzii* and *R. pygmaeus, Potentilla villosa, Salix reticulata* and *S. rotundifolia, Saxifraga bronchialis* and *Primula cuneifolia,* the last in greater numbers than we had ever seen previously, including the albino form.

The Glen Highway between Palmer and Glenallen affords excellent views of several of Alaska's major glaciers, including the Matanuska. An overnight stay at the Glacier Park Resort offers a closer look at this glacier and some of the interesting species found in these habitats, such as *Hedysarum mackenzii, Dryas drummondii,* whose yellow flowers never fully open, *Epilobium latifolium* and the "Fire Weed", *E. angustifolium,* in an unusual pale pink form. In suitable woodland areas along this stretch of highway we found *Orchis rotundifolia* in great numbers, including the rare albino, *Calypso bulbosa, Cypripedium passerinum* and *C. guttatum.*

The final area I want to consider borders the route of the Denali Highway, beginning at Paxson on the Richardson Highway and extending some 160 miles to McKinley Park Station, then for 90 additional miles to the end of the road at Kantishna. Unfortunately, this last section of road is no longer open to general traffic and on our last visit, in 1978, we were unable to drive through the park and stop for plant exploration wherever we wished. However, there is a cabin camp at the end of the road, Camp Denali, outside the park, where it is possible to stay and have meals provided. The hills surrounding the camp afford excellent plant-hunting territory. Just before leaving the Richardson Highway we were treated to a very colourful panorama from the gravel flats beside the Delta River, looking towards Rainbow Mountain across acres of *Hedysarum mackenzii*. Excellent views of the Alaska Range may be had from the Denali Highway and many interesting plants are to be found beside the road. In fairly recently disturbed sections, mats of *Silene acaulis*, in a brilliantly coloured form, were common. Scattered here and there amongst the tundra vegetation were patches of an interesting Saxifraga relative, *Boykinia richardsonii*, said to be one of the favourite summer foods of the caribou. *Polygonum bistorta* is one of the common plants in such areas. On a rocky hilltop not far from the road we found a thick patch of the lovely *Campanula lasiocarpa*, not an uncommon plant, but generally found in more scattered stands. Once within the park there are numerous sites which provide excellent displays of plants. Polychrome Pass, Highway Pass at 3950 feet, the highest point on the road, Stony Hill and Thorofare Pass are among the best. Included in the plants to be found are *Geranium erianthum* and *Mertensia paniculata*, both common roadside plants in many parts of the state, but here the Mertensia was greatly reduced in stature. Other species identified were the state flower of Alaska, *Myosotis alpestris*, *Aconitum delphinifolium*, *Anemone narcissiflora* and *A. parviflora*, the beautiful lemon-yellow *Papaver radicatum*, *Saxifraga flagellaris*, *Androsace chamaejasme*, *Pedicularis oederi*, *P. capitata* and *P. lanata*. At Stony Hill and Highway Pass we found some of the more uncommon plants, such as *Draba stenopetala* with another species, perhaps *D. densifolia*, an attractive white-flowered form of *Oxytropis nigrescens*, *Potentilla uniflora*, *Synthyris borealis*, *Claytonia scammaniana*, the most brightly coloured species in this genus, the rare and lovely *Douglasia gormanii*, *Saxifraga oppositifolia*, with a few plants still blooming in mid-July, *Eritrichium aretioides*, a more prostrate form than that found at Nome or Eagle Summit, and a very dwarf form of *Arnica frigida*. In the hills surrounding Camp Denali there are many interesting plants to be seen, including the usual, paler flowered form of *Loiseleuria procumbens*, *Silene acaulis*, *Claytonia sarmentosa* and *C. acutifolia, Gentiana prostrata,* a tiny annual, and *G. glauca, Primula cuneifolia, Arnica lessingii,* with solitary nodding flowers, *Campanula lasiocarpa, Arenaria arctica* and *Arctostaphylos alpina. Dryas octopetala* is everywhere. *Dryas integrifolia* with similar flowers but entire leaves is less common and generally found at lower elevations along with *Andromeda polifolia* and *Pinguicula vulgaris.*

No report on Alaska would be truly representative without at least a brief mention of some of the wildlife likely to be seen in McKinley National Park. Without any special effort we saw numerous Dall Sheep and Caribou as well as a number of Moose, Grizzly Bear and Red Foxes. Nesting birds included Ptarmigan, Golden Plover, Common Loon and Golden Eagle.

In June and July the lengthy hours of daylight provide wonderful opportunities for long days of plant hunting, and the views of Mount McKinley in the small hours of the morning and again in the evening can be spectacular if you are fortunate enough to have fair weather. Not until almost midnight does the mountain don that beautiful rosy glow from the setting sun.

Corydalis

BRIAN MATHEW

Corydalis bracteata

The large genus Corydalis belongs to the family Fumariaceae (which is sometimes included in Papaveraceae) and is comprised of some 300-odd species which occur in much of the northern temperate zone. There are quite a lot of annuals, some excellent herbaceous perennials, quite a number of caespitose rock plants and a sizeable group which possess fleshy tubers. It is this tuberous group with which I will be dealing here, known collectively as the Subgenus Capnites of De Candolle and which in turn can be divided into several distinct sections.

These tuberous species have evolved mostly in regions which have a dryish summer period during which time the plants exist as dormant tubers. They are all spring-flowering, making rapid growth as soon as winter is over and ripening their seeds in a very short space of time. The whole period of growth is as little as three months in some cases.

Before moving on to the sections and the species they contain it is worth describing the structure of the Corydalis flower for it appears at first to be rather complex. The small sepals fall off very early and are seldom seen. There are four petals, very unequal, giving an irregular flower shape. The upper one has a spur which is often the most prominent part of the flower, the lower petal projects into a lip and the two inner, much smaller ones are curved inwards to join at their tips. They enfold the stigma and stamens which stay enclosed unless a pollinating insect lands on the lip. If this happens the lip and the inner petals are depressed and the stigma and style are released in a trigger-like way so that pollen is sprayed on to the stigma.

The vegetative characters of the plant are very useful in defining the various sections and species. The leaves may be opposite, alternate or whorled and are compound with the leaflets dissected into lobes of varying shapes and sizes. On the stem above the tuber but below the leaves there may be one or more scales, but in some species there is no scale. Another useful feature is whether the bracts subtending each flower are smooth-edged (entire) or toothed. Some species have flower stems and leaves which rise more or less erect from the tuber while in others the stems creep horizontally before turning upwards to emerge from the soil.

For the purpose of this article it is necessary to consider only four sections, with a brief mention of a fifth since it contains one of the most famous "rock garden" Corydalis with a rootstock which is halfway between tuberous and non-tuberous. To dispense with this first, I am referring of course to *C. cashmiriana* and its allies, which belong to Section **Rapiferae**. Here, the rootstock consists of some thickened fleshy roots, as well as fibrous ones, and a cluster of tiny scales producing a small loose-scaled bulb. The species are mostly Himalayan and Chinese and would appear to prefer cool climates with humid summer growing conditions, although only *C. cashmiriana* has been tried in cultivation as far as I know. The species of the truly tuberous groups thrive best in well-drained conditions which are drier in summer during their dormant period. They occur mainly in the Mediterranean region and in the drier parts of western and central Asia, although a few extend through to eastern Asia and Japan, and into Alaska.

The sections which are to be considered here are (1) Sect. **Radix-cava**, (2) Sect. **Pes-gallinaceus**, (3) Sect. **Leonticoides** and (4) Sect. **Dactylotuber**.

1. *Section Radix-cava*

This group is characterised by having a perennial tuber, rather misshapen and often with a hollow on the underside. There is no scale leaf on the stem and there are two alternate stem leaves.

The best known species is *C. bulbosa* (syn. *C. cava*) which is a common plant in Europe. It grows about 15 cm in height and varies considerably in flower colour but is usually in the muddy-purplish or pinkish range, not a dramatic plant but useful for naturalising in the rock garden or beneath shrubs. A more attractive garden plant is its subspecies *marschalliana* which has a raceme of lovely creamy-white or yellow flowers. This occurs in the Balkans and east to the Caucasus and northern Iran. I find it a suitable plant for the peat garden.

The tubers of *C. bulbosa* get quite large but do not proliferate readily. Sometimes more than one growing point is formed and then the tuber can be broken up during its dormant period. *Corydalis bulbosa* and its variants should never be dried out too much in summer or the tubers will shrivel and die.

2. Section **Pes-gallinaceus**

This group contains those species with rounded tubers which are replaced annually, often dividing up into two or more at the time of replacement. There is one large, often recurved, scale leaf at or just above ground level and there are two alternate stem leaves.

This group contains some of the easiest of all the tuberous species, including the much-loved *C. solida* which is a common plant in Europe and western Asia, and is extremely variable in colour and inflorescence. It can be anything from white to pale pinkish-purple through to deep dull purple and the flowers may be packed together in a dense raceme or spaced out up the stem. The lower floral bracts are always lobed with four or more lobes, or toothed, but the upper ones are sometimes entire. *Corydalis densiflora,* occasionally seen listed as *C. solida* var. *densiflora,* is a worthwhile variant with many very narrow leaflets giving the foliage a graceful "ferny" effect. *Corydalis intermedia* (syn. *C. fabacea*) is very similar to *C. solida* but has all the bracts entire. Related to *C. solida* is *C. transsilvanica,* a gorgeous plant with deep salmon or pinkish flowers—it may be only a variant of *C. solida* but it is such an improvement that it is well worth obtaining.

From Russia comes *C. caucasica* which can be distinguished from *C. solida* in having a widely expanded lower lip to the flower. In the form cultivated in Britain the flowers are white, but in the wild they can decline to a dull purple so it appears that we are lucky in having a "good" form. *Corydalis bracteata* is very similar to *C. caucasica* but in the former the bracts are toothed while in the latter they are all entire. *Corydalis bracteata* is not widely grown at present but is worth seeking, especially in its yellow form which is most attractive. It also occurs wild in western Russia.

All of the species mentioned above are easy to grow outside either on the rock garden or in peat banks. They make a very useful early spring display in an alpine house.

The same applies to the striking eastern Asiatic *C. ambigua* (syn. *C. jezoensis*) which in good forms has beautiful clear blue flowers equalling in brilliance those of *C. cashmiriana.* It occurs wild in Japan, Sakhalin, the Kuriles, Kamchatka and northeast China and is hardy in Britain, although it may be frosted if its young growths appear during an early mild spell. I prefer to grow this in a cold frame for this reason. Unfortunately the tubers do not divide up quite so readily as in the other species of the group I have mentioned. Like most Corydalis, *C. ambigua* varies in flower colour and some forms in the wild may be a dingy purple. It differs also to a great degree in the amount of dissection of the leaves and in the size and shape of the lobes from rather rounded to very narrowly linear.

Other species in this section include:

pumila—C. Europe. Smaller flowers than *C. solida*, purple, carried on short pedicels.

paczoskii—USSR. Few flowers on the raceme, each with a straight spur; purple.

angustifolia—USSR. Yellow-flowered; bracts three-toothed; narrow leaflets.

integra—E. Aegean, S. Turkey, N. Iraq. Pink flowers; spur strongly curved; bracts entire.

remota—E. Asia, Japan. Related to *C. ambigua* but has toothed bracts (entire in *C. ambigua*).

repens—E. Asia, Japan. Related to *C. ambigua* but has smaller white to pale pink flowers.

3. Section **Leonticoides**

The species in this section have perennial tubers, often rather irregular in shape. There is no scale leaf on the stem and there are two opposite leaves, sometimes three in a whorl. The stems usually travel horizontally before emerging from the soil (so that in a pot they tend to come up all round the edge!). The stems often bear a mass of minute hair-roots on their underground sections.

This group contains some of the most attractive species, but since they occur mostly in the drier parts of west and central Asia they are not always the easiest to grow and propagate.

Corydalis rutifolia is one of the most widespread, from Crete and Cyprus to Lebanon and Turkey. It varies enormously in the shape of the leaves from being rather broad and rounded with few divisions to very much dissected into narrower leaflets. In the latter case it approaches *C. verticillaris* from Iraq and Iran and the two "species" may be forms of one widespread and variable plant. The flowers of *C. rutifolia* are usually pinkish or purplish with darker spots near the apex of the petals, and sometimes the upward curving spur is deeper purple-red giving a bicoloured effect. *Corydalis boissieri* from Iran is usually regarded as a subspecies of *C. verticillaris* and this is one of the most attractive forms with large flowers and long, gracefully curved spurs.

Corydalis aitchisonii is a superb plant with very grey rather broad leaflets and large yellow flowers up to 5·5 cm long which change to orange when past their peak. It is a native of eastern Iran and the adjacent part of Russia and northern Afghanistan where it grows on rocky hillsides. *Corydalis sewerzowii* is very similar but is distinguished by the amount of dissection of the leaves. They are both beautiful plants for a bulb frame where the foliage can spread out and show itself to advantage—in a pot it is often too cramped. Like most, if not all, members of this section the tubers do not divide naturally and propagation is a slow, but sure, business from seed. I find that hand pollination is necessary by depressing the lower lip of the flower until the stamens and style spring out from the two inner petals.

Corydalis popovii is becoming more well-known in cultivation and rightly so, for it too is an impressive plant although it needs to be grown in plenty of light if it is to stay neat and tidy. If slightly shaded its stems become very long and ungainly but grown well it makes compact clumps of grey-green leaves and produces purple flowers with deeper tips to the petals. The spur is long and down-turned at its apex. *Corydalis ledebouriana* (syn. *C. cyrtocentra*) has shorter purplish flowers with an up-turned paler spur and is of much less decorative value than the preceding species. It occurs in Afghanistan and Russian Central Asia.

Corydalis diphylla from the north west Himalaya, especially the Chitral and Kashmir regions, is well-known in cultivation and is a somewhat easier plant to grow. It has rather elegant blue-grey foliage with small somewhat pointed leaflets and racemes of flowers which have a white spur and deep purple petals. There seems to be little difficulty in increasing this by seed and it is usually obtainable from nurseries.

Corydalis afghanica is an exciting little plant but unfortunately it is probably not in cultivation at present. It is compact with distinctive pinnately-divided grey leaves with reddish margins. The flowers are 3·5–4 cm long—large for the size of the plant— and white or pale pink. It grows in the neighbourhood of Kabul.

Other species which belong to this group include: *Cc. firouzii, macrocentra, persica, darwasica, chionophila, nevskii, hyrcana* and *griffithii*. Some of these are in cultivation but are rather rare at present.

4. *Section **Dactylotuber***

This differs from other sections in that its tubers are divided into 2–5 lobes with roots emerging from the tip of each lobe. The stems carry 1–3 small scales which are appressed rather than held out horizontally or reflexed as in Section ***Pes-gallinaceus***. There are usually three or four stem leaves.

Although this section contains several species, few if any are in cultivation.

Corydalis pauciflora has a wide distribution from central Asiatic Russia in the Altai mountains, east to Kamchatka and Alaska. As its name implies it is few-flowered, usually only two or three, but these are of a reasonable size and are a good blue. *Corydalis alpestris* (syn. *C. nivalis*) from the Caucasus and northeast Turkey is very similar but slightly more robust with up to five flowers. These are pale blue to purplish blue, sometimes described as "Delphinium Blue" or "almost *C. cashmiriana* blue". It is very compact, growing in screes at up to 4000 metres altitude. In cultivation it will almost certainly require very good drainage and cool conditions with no drying out in summer. In the wild it flowers as late as June or July but is nevertheless spring-flowering, blooming next to the melting snow.

Corydalis conorhiza, which has a tuber divided into only 2–3 lobes, is a slightly taller plant with three to eight flowers. They are usually reddish-purple with paler inner petals and the rather tubby spur is hooked downwards at its tip. Like *C. alpestris* it grows at fairly high altitudes and flowers as soon as the snow retreats, which may be as late as July. It is a plant of mountain turf and rocky slopes in the Caucasus and northeast Turkey.

Other species in this section include: *Cc. pseudoalpestris, pallidiflora, arctica* and *emanuelii.*

PROPAGATION OF TUBEROUS CORYDALIS   Those species which naturally divide vegetatively are increased easily merely by separating the tubers from time to time. With the species which do not behave in this way it is occasionally possible to divide the tuber provided it has developed more than one growing point—*C. bulbosa* occasionally does this—and it may be a useful method if a particularly fine form has been selected.

Seed represents the only form of propagation for many of the species, and to be successful I find that it must be sown immediately it is ripe—this is usually while the capsule is still green. Even allowing the seeds to dry for a day or two before sowing is enough to delay germination for an extra season, or can prevent it altogether. My own method is to sow them immediately they ripen and keep them watered throughout the following summer. The pots are placed where they will receive frost during the first autumn–winter after sowing. Germination usually takes place about February or March and once this has happened the pots are moved to the protection of a frame or greenhouse. Corydalis are not rapid from seed, often taking three to five years to reach flowering size from sowing. The species of Section **Pes-gallinaceus** are the quickest in this respect, and Section **Leonticoides** the slowest.

Helleborus

BRIAN MATHEW

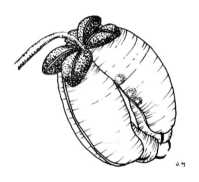

Helleborus vesicarius (fruit)

Hellebores form a small genus of about 16 species distributed widely in Europe, with a few outlying ones in Turkey, the Caucasus and China. They are a confusing group botanically and the delimitation of the species is not an easy task, especially in those with green flowers. Fortunately it is possible to divide the genus initially into three clear sections based on their habit of growth rather than flower characters, and only one of these sections causes trouble for the botanist! The three groups are (1) Caulescent (stemmed), (2) Acaulescent (stemless) and (3) *H. vesicarius* a species unrelated to any other.

1. *Caulescent Group*

This contains *H. foetidus, H. argutifolius* (syn. *H. corsicus*) and *H. lividus.* Here the leaves are produced on a semi-woody stem which carries the cluster of flowers at its apex.

Helleborus foetidus is a west European plant, as far north as Britain, usually growing in calcareous woodlands. Its finely divided dark green leaves are attractive in themselves, but when these are overtopped by the pale green bracts and numerous flowers in late winter it is really quite an impressive plant. The individual flowers are small and bell-shaped, often with brownish tips to the sepals. It is an easily grown species, seeding freely. There are variations and some of the forms are much more floriferous than others so it is worth selecting these for their increased garden value.

Helleborus argutifolius (syn. *H. corsicus*) is Corsican (it is recorded also in Sardinia) and is the best of the stemmed group for general garden use. It has striking leathery, bright green toothed leaves, each of which consists of only three leaflets. It is a robust plant, usually 50–100 cm in height with several stems in each clump and large inflorescences containing 15–30 pale green bowl-shaped flowers. The stamens arch over strongly in a very distinctive manner. Like *H. foetidus* it is a very hardy and easily grown species, although preferring sunnier situations where it is more compact and free-flowering. Self-sown seedlings frequently appear.

Helleborus lividus, though a close relative of *H. argutifolius,* and a Majorcan plant, is easily distinguished by its shorter stature (usually less than 45 cm tall), deep green leaves with creamy veins and few, if any, teeth on the margins of the leaflets. The flowers are fewer in number (less than ten) and are usually suffused with pinkish-brown, as are the undersurfaces of the leaves. In Britain it is undoubtedly slightly tender and may be killed in bad winters. However, if grown with the protection of a wall, or treated as an alpine house plant it is very satisfactory and will produce seeds quite readily. Unfortunately it frequently crosses with *H. argutifolius* to produce plants of an intermediate appearance (*H.* × *sternii*) so that if true *H. lividus* is required steps should be taken to prevent cross-pollination.

2. *Acaulescent Group*

In these species the leaves and flowers are produced separately, directly from the rhizome, and there are no true leaves on the flower stems although they may carry rather leafy bracts. This group contains *Hh. niger, orientalis, viridis, cyclophyllus, odorus, bocconei, multifidus, dumetorum, purpurascens, serbicus, atrorubens* and *thibetanus* (syn. *H. chinensis*).

Helleborus niger, the "Christmas Rose", needs little in the way of introduction since it is by far the most well-known of all the species, although not the easiest to grow. It is a mountain plant, mainly from the eastern European Alps, and is usually a plant of light woodland although I have also seen it on grassy hillsides. It is a variable plant and accordingly many names have been given to particular forms— the trouble with this is that to maintain a true stock it is necessary to divide the plants rather than raise new ones from seeds which may give rise to variable seedlings. Over the years there have been a number of named clones but it is doubtful if many of these survive, the large-flowered "Potter's Wheel" being one exception. In the Italian Alps and northern Yugoslavia there is a variant with markedly bluish-green foliage and large flowers with non-overlapping tepals. This has been described as subsp. *macranthus,* but even it appears to merge with subsp. *niger.* I once grew a semi-double form which was an interesting curiosity.

Helleborus orientalis (syn. *H. kochii, H. olympicus* and *H. antiquorum*) is a name covering a host of variants some of which have been accorded specific rank. The wild forms from northern Turkey, where it is very common, have creamy flowers suffused with green and occasionally there is a pinkish tinge. The shape and size of the tepals vary enormously, even within one population, so that there might be forms with broad overlapping tepals, narrow ones, pointed or rounded ones, and sometimes they are wavy at the margins. Farther east in the Caucasian region there is more colour variation through to pinkish-purple, spotted or unspotted. Forms with spotted flowers have acquired the name *H. guttatus,* those with purple flowers and fine speckling, *H. abschasicus.* In gardens these various forms have crossed together, and sometimes hybridised with other species, to give us the great range of fine plants we have today known as "*H. orientalis* hybrids".

In addition to these two well-known species, *H. niger* and *H. orientalis,* there is a group of closely related, mainly Balkan, species which bear green or purple-violet flowers. These are the most confusing botanically, and they almost certainly hybridise in the wild which causes further problems.

Helleborus viridis is the best-known green-flowered species and is very widespread in Europe. The western and northern variant, subsp. *occidentalis,* grows wild in Britain and is one of the least attractive of the group with smallish unscented flowers and rather coarsely-toothed leaves. The southern European subsp. *viridis* is a more garden-worthy plant with larger flattish flowers, often of a rather brighter, paler green. By far the best of the green ones is *H. cyclophyllus* which has large scented yellowy-green flowers 5 cm or more in diameter. The young leaves are silvery-downy on the underside, rather an attractive feature in the early stages before they unfold. It is an extremely common species in southern Yugoslavia, northern Greece, and Bulgaria but is rarely seen in cultivation, although not at all difficult to grow. It thrives best on lime-rich soils in a sheltered semi-shady situation, as do most of these Balkan species. This species produces yellower flowers than any of the others and is the obvious parent for breeding purposes if a yellow-flowered race of hybrids is sought. In Bulgaria I have seen forms which could be described as nearly yellow and crosses between these and the creamy *H. orientalis* are showing possibilities in this direction.

Helleborus odorus is very similar and is distinguished by the follicles (fruits) being joined at the base rather than completely separate from each other, as they are in *H. cyclophyllus*. This is scarcely of great importance to the horticulturist, and from a garden point of view there is little difference between the two species.

In central and southern Italy, *H. bocconei* and its subspecies *siculus* are the representatives of the green-flowered group, and they are not greatly different in overall appearance to *H. cyclophyllus,* with quite large, scented flowers. The leaves however are divided rather more and they often have very coarse teeth on their margins. Subspecies *siculus* differs from subsp. *bocconei* in having glabrous leaves. The division of the leaves into many leaflets is taken to extremes in the Dalmatian *H. multifidus* where each of the 9–15 leaflets is subdivided into up to 12 narrow lobes. The flowers are green and scented and rather small, but the plant is worth growing for its foliage effect. It occurs in rather dry scrub on limestone on the Adriatic coast of Yugoslavia, and correspondingly seems to prefer a warm sheltered position in cultivation.

The remaining green-flowered species, *H. dumetorum,* is a woodland plant growing in northern Yugoslavia, southern Austria, Hungary, Romania and Czechoslovakia. It is the smallest-flowered of all and unscented, but makes up for its lack of display by being very graceful, with foliage which has none of the gross leathery appearance of many hellebores. The pendulous cup-shaped flowers are overtopped by long leaf-like bracts, a feature characteristic of the species.

If the green-flowered species are somewhat puzzling in their distinguishing characteristics, then the purple-flowered ones must be classed as highly confusing! There are only two or three species depending on one's point of view, but each of these is highly variable and some botanists regard them as coloured variants of the green-flowered species. The best is undoubtedly *H. purpurascens,* if it can be obtained in a good form. It varies from a muddy brownish-purple to a lovely deep bluish colour, almost dove-coloured, with a grey grape-like "bloom" on the exterior. The latter form I find most attractive, and furthermore it is a dwarf plant, the flowers opening when the stems are only a few centimetres in height. *Helleborus purpurascens* usually has large flowers 5 cm or more in diameter with broad overlapping segments. The commercially available "*H. atrorubens* of gardens" is I think a form of *H. purpurascens*. Recently I have flowered some plants from wild-collected Czechoslovak seeds and they are very similar if not identical to those I obtained from nurseries in Britain. *Helleborus serbicus*, from southern Yugoslavia can have flowers similarly coloured to those of *H. purpurascens*, but they are smaller, usually 3–4 cm in diameter and on taller stems. The leaves too differ in being distinctly pedate in *H. serbicus* and more or less digitate in *H. purpurascens*, but in both species they are hairy on the underside. *Helleborus torquatus* is the name which was given to a particularly fine form of *H. serbicus* with blue-black ink-coloured flowers. This beautiful form can be found in south-eastern Yugoslavia, mixed with dirty brown and purplish forms which are barely worth cultivating. *Helleborus atrorubens* from northern Yugoslavia differs from both *H. purpurascens* and *H. serbicus* in having leaves which are glabrous. Its flowers are smaller than those of *H. purpurascens*, and often the tepals are narrower and non-overlapping. As with the other two species the flower colour varies and may be anything from dirty brownish-purple to a deep rich violet.

The last species to mention in the stemless group has not yet been seen in cultivation to my knowledge—it is *H. thibetanus* (syn. *H. chinensis*). I know it only from herbarium specimens and these show it to be a fairly slender species with small pinkish flowers about 3 cm in diameter. I have obtained seeds but these have not yet germinated and I await this event with much impatience!

3. *Helleborus vesicarius*

This is a curious species which has no near relatives in the genus and does not even look much like a hellebore, except perhaps in its individual flowers which resemble those of *H. foetidus*. It is a native of southern Turkey and adjacent northern Syria, and it overcomes the warm-dry summer period of this region by behaving like many of the bulbous plants which accompany it. In late spring, after fruiting, the plants go dormant until the following autumn when new leaves appear. Flowering is in early spring and although the flowers are small, green and unexciting, the capsules which follow

Meconopsis regia   *(Plate 32)*

Gentiana urnula   *(Plate 33)*

Stellera chamaejasme   (*Plate 34*)

Cremanthodium oblongatum   (*Plate 35*)

Saxifraga flagellaris ssp. sikkimensis   (*Plate 36*)

Androsace tapete   (*Plate 37*)

Caragana Steppe in Dolpo (*Plate 39*)

◊ Meconopsis horridula (*Plate 38*)

Leontopodium evax (*Plate 40*)

Primula uniflora (*Plate 41*)

Androsace delavayi   (*Plate 42*)

Gentiana depressa   (*Plate 43*)

Rhododendron saluenense   (*Plate 44*)

Narcissus rupicola   (*Plate 45*)

Gentiana oschtenica   (*Plate 46*)

Campanula lasiocarpa   (*Plate 47*)

Mitchella repens   (*Plate 48*)

are most distinctive. These are pale green and inflated and quite enormous, so that a whole clump covered with them is a most impressive sight. The leaves are soft and pale green, looking more like those of a peony than a hellebore. Unfortunately *H. vesicarius* has not responded very well to cultivation in the open in Britain, and seems best treated as a plant for the bulb frame where it can be dried off to some extent in summer.

The Introduction
and Maintenance of New Plants

JIM ARCHIBALD

Alstroemeria pygmaea

The precedent for the inclusion of this subject in the Conference Programme would appear to be an excellent article by W. R. Sykes, entitled "A Decade of Plant Introductions", which appeared in the report of the 1961 International Conference. This was not delivered as a talk at the Conference but it obviously appealed to the organisers of such events as it reappeared in 1971 as "A Decade of New Plants", which was dealt with in somewhat piecemeal fashion by three speakers. I was originally asked to deal with "Plants established from Recent Expeditions". You will note that I was spared the word "decade", as this is really too short a time to assess the status of a new plant in cultivation, and I was given a reasonable fluidity in my interpretation of the word "recent" but what problems are intrinsic in those two words "established" and "expeditions"! It would be much easier and possibly more instructive to consider the clear-cut case of plants *not* established, but this is too vast a subject. There is also an implied British insularity in both those words, which I feel is out of place at such an international gathering as Alpines '81.

I am, however, British and I have only experience of most new plants in British gardens, so that must be and was the basis for my talk. I propose to present you with a critical survey, which will by necessity be personally biased and insular, of some of the plants which have been introduced into cultivation in Britain between 1960 and 1980, with an emphasis on those which have been propagated and distributed fairly widely. I think there could be lessons for all of us interested in alpine plants throughout the world, in considering this period.

In 1961, Sykes could honestly deal with "expeditions". In the 1950s, the activities of such collectors as Ludlow and Sherriff, Kingdon Ward and Peter Davis were of great importance. In 1954, certain parts of Nepal were just beginning to become accessible and we had the significant Stainton, Sykes and Williams expedition. Today, any one of you can go on an organised, package expedition to Nepal, Sikkim, Ladakh, eastern Turkey, Ethiopia, Soviet Central Asia or even China and Peru. The world belongs to the amateur plant-hunter. The past twenty years have seen us enter the age of the amateur, a situation which is likely to be with us into the foreseeable future. Obviously, for the British amateur the mountain ranges of Europe provide the most accessible hunting-ground for new material. A considerable number of species has been established over the past twenty years but there still remain many plants deserving of cultivation but barely known to gardeners, particularly in the mountains of Spain, north-west Africa and the Balkans. What is disconcerting is that we seem no closer to evolving techniques to cultivate successfully many European alpines, in spite of repeated introductions of fresh material from the wild. One of the more successful of recent introductions is *Ranunculus abnormis,* a yellow-flowered, tuberous-rooted species brought back from central Spain by Joyce and Lionel Bacon. *R. acetosellifolius,* the distinguished, white-flowered Sierra Nevadan endemic, has, however, consistently proved less amenable and, although several collections have been made, has seldom been maintained for long by more than a few growers. The same can be said for its associates from the Sierra Nevada, the charming *Viola crassiuscula* and the prostrate, yellow daisy, *Leucanthemopsis radicans,* which has been in and out of cultivation for the past fifty years and which I doubt exists at present in the hands of more than one or two gardeners, if at all. Its slightly larger, silver-leaved relative, *L. pallida* subsp. *spathulifolia* has been introduced by a number of visitors to the Cazorla area but its hold on cultivation is equally tenuous. A somewhat easier Spanish composite and one of the best dwarf, silver-leaved plants for the alpine-house is *Artemisia assoana,* possibly a very compact race of *A. pedemontana,* collected by Ivor Barton and his companions. The Iberian thymes can provide several splendid plants and *Thymus longiflorus* has received an Award of Merit from material which Lyn Weeks and I collected on the south side of the Sierra Nevada in 1970. The award was given to a plant shown as *T. cephalotos,* another member of the Pseudothymbra Section with similar tubular, purplish flowers among showy coloured bracts. This latter species from southern Portugal is also established in cultivation, though it is not generally grown by amateur gardeners. Also in 1970, Lyn and I collected material of the genus Sarcocapnos, of which *S. crassifolia* has proved an extremely fine and long-lived plant, though much less willing to provide seeds than *S. baetica* or the better-known *S. enneaphylla.* It has nevertheless been possible to maintain all these over the past ten years without difficulty in the alpine-house. This genus is much more in evidence in north-west Africa where it becomes quite variable with a large number of local races, none of which is known in gardens. Surprisingly, there has been very little collecting in the Atlas ranges since I visited them in 1962 and no new alpine or saxatile species appears to have been established, apart from *Catananche caespitosa,* an excellent, little silvery-leaved, yellow-flowered composite grown from a Peter Davis collection but proving difficult to propagate. Three high-altitude plants from above 3000 m in the High Atlas are now well established from seed I collected in 1962 : the fascinating little cultivar of *Linaria tristis,* clonally propagated as 'Toubkal'; the stemless lavender-blue thistle, *Carduncellus pinnatus* var. *acaulis* and the white *Saxifraga pedemontana* subsp. *demnatensis,* an easy plant to keep alive but a challenge to grow to perfection. Most visitors are drawn to these ranges before the high-altitude plants are in flower far less seed but early collections such as Sheila Maule's reintroduction of *Narcissus watieri* have provided valuable and vigorous new material. My own 1966 collections of *N. bulbocodium* subsp. *albidus* from both Morocco and Algeria are also now well established and distributed but it is to Chris Stocken that the accolade must go for his collections of the genus Narcissus in Spain. *Narcissus cuatrecasasii* (originally grown as *N. rupicola* Grazalema form or *N. rupicola* subsp. *pedunculatus*) and the dwarf *N. papyraceus* subsp. *panizzianus* are two of his introductions.

As far as eastern Europe is concerned, there has been a significant and I hope expanding exchange of material with amateur gardeners in Czechoslovakia. This is, of course, based on personal correspondence and must be considered apart from the official seed-exchange system operated between botanic gardens. The most worthwhile species which has been widely established is certainly *Soldanella carpatica* and its white form, though sadly the latter now seems much less vigorous than when we first had it. This is an outstanding and floriferous species and I hope that we can look forward to seeing many more fine plants well established in the near future. There is still much we could look forward to from Bulgaria in particular. Collections from Yugoslavia and Greece, however, have mainly been made by British and German travellers. Too little attention is paid to these accessible areas as sources of new material. The past fifteen years have seen not only the successful establishment but the substantial increase of *Crocus scardicus* in the skilled hands of Harold Esslemont. Starting off with material I collected in the Šar Planina in 1964 he has built up and distributed a considerable number of this fine orange-yellow species by treating it like the alpine plant that it is—wet in spring, cool and moist in summer and dryish in winter. Similar treatment by the same grower is also paying dividends with a collection of *C. vallicola* var. *suworowianus* I made in the Turkish Pontus Mountains in 1966 and Brian Mathew's Yugoslavian collection of the predominantly Albanian, high-altitude, yellow *C. cvijicii* also now appears well-established and increasing. Many collections of Crocus by Brian Mathew, John Marr, Martyn Rix and others are carefully maintained by a small number of enthusiasts and these can be considered established to this extent.

Southern Greece has offered a pleasant and attractive hunting ground for the amateur over the past twenty years and the most outstanding result for the gardener has been the establishment of *Daphne jasminea* as an alpine-house shrub. This compact, saxatile species has been collected by a number of people but the majority of plants in cultivation would appear to stem from an introduction made and established by Ivor Barton in company with Ken Aslet in 1964. Another Greek endemic shrub, *Lithodora zahnii,* is also now well established from material brought back by Alexis Vlasto. It is less spectacular than its close relative, *L. rosmarinifolia* from southern Italy—at least in the forms we have in cultivation—but is a very worthwhile addition. Also closely allied is *L. hispidula,* grown from material collected in Crete by Lionel Bacon, and we can hope that this will also be propagated and distributed. It may come as a surprise to Cyclamen enthusiasts that twenty years ago few of us knew much about the extremely variable races of *C. repandum* from the Peloponnese nor of *C. repandum* var. *rhodense.* During these years, the habitats of both these races have become easily and cheaply accessible holiday-areas and there have been numerous introductions. The same cannot be said for *C. libanoticum* but we are fortunate to have this in cultivation from authentic wild material (surprisingly distinct from the long-cultivated race of unknown origin) collected by Eliot Hodgkin and Bertie Blount. The Caspian forests of northern Iran are also no longer accessible and it is to be hoped that we can maintain stock of one of the more distinct races covered by the blanket name *C. coum* subsp. *caucasicum*. Though it is no doubt difficult to justify *C. elegans* botanically, its pointed leaves and elongated petals make it a tempting plant for the gardener, as well a being a challenging one, for it is much more difficult to grow well in Britain than the high rainfall of its native beech-woods might lead us to suspect. The high altitude, Turkish race of *C. coum*, *C. parviflorum*, is also temperamental in cultivation but with a number of recent collections becoming quite widely distributed, I think we can assume that this will soon become well-established and much better known. A paradoxical situation surrounds another Turkish species, *C. mirabile*, a little-known plant twenty years ago. Peter Davis originally introduced this and further collections made by John Watson and others saw it more widely distributed in the 1960s. Recently, however, this species has been imported annually on a massive scale from Turkey and is currently resold throughout the world, by way of Dutch bulb merchants as both *"C. neapolitanum"* and *"C. europaeum"*, thus by-passing the pointless legislation regarding wild Cyclamen. From my own experience of Cyclamen in the wild, I feel that we have little cause for concern even over large-scale commercial collection; I could argue that they benefited from such disturbance. This is a genus adapted to maintaining a high local population level and to withstanding the depredations of animals which root about the forest floor, whether they be pigs or men.

However, I doubt if such remarks could apply to another recently introduced species, which it seems appropriate to mention here, although I have no personal experience of it. *Sternbergia candida*, the only white-flowered member of the genus, was discovered in Turkey in 1976, described in 1979 and suddenly became commercially available in 1980, in considerable numbers, both through the pages of our specialist publications and the lists of those who advertise in them. Even one such as myself, who is but a passive opponent to the politics and opportunism of "conservation" and a cynical bystander to the progress of this bandwagon along its primrose path, with our societies casting themselves upon it, could not but marvel at the blatant hypocrisy of it all.

Just as our attitude towards wild plants may be influenced by the fashions of our time, so too our enthusiasm for particular genera may be stimulated by current vogue. Fritillaria have survived the damning criticism of Reginald Farrer to become very fashionable plants indeed. Enthusiasts, such as Martyn Rix, Jack Elliott and the late Vic Horton, have brought together and maintained remarkable and comprehensive collections of this genus during the past twenty years. Many have only a tenuous hold on cultivation and few have become widely distributed but it is to be hoped that Paul Christian's efforts to propagate and offer a wide range commercially will mean that many more become firmly established. Perhaps the species which has most endeared itself to alpine gardeners is *Fritillaria michailovskyi,* especially in its best forms, introduced from eastern Turkey by Brian Mathew, John Watson and others. Closely related and with similar mahogany-purple, yellow-tipped flowers, *F. reuteri* from the central Zagros Mountains of Iran also appears to be settling down well. Although less striking, *F. crassifolia* subsp. *kurdica,* brought back by most of us who have visited eastern Turkey or western Iran, has proved an especially adaptable plant, flowering relatively quickly from seed. *Fritillaria carduchorum,* only recently discovered, sometimes grows along with it in a few localities in eastern Turkey. It too is now well established and increasing well vegetatively from both Rix and Watson collections. It has distinctive, narrow, brick-red flowers and glossy, green leaves. Coming from comparatively high altitudes, it should be of particular appeal to the alpine gardener. Sadly, the beautiful, pink *F. alburyana,* also a very recently discovered and locally restricted plant from eastern Turkey, is not proving so easy to maintain in Britain, in spite of numerous introductions by John Watson and others. However, it appears somewhat less troublesome with some gardeners in continental Europe, growing material collected by Erich Pasche. The similar but more eastern Rhinopetalum group confront the grower with similar problems. The pink *F. gibbosa* and others still linger but seldom increase vegetatively and, in my experience, even the most conscientious attempts at hand-pollination between a number of clones, when one was fortunate enough to have them, are quite fruitless. Seed is, however, distributed by several botanic gardens in Soviet Central Asia and from this source,

F. stenanthera, another Rhinopetalum new to cultivation, has been raised by several enthusiasts in Britain. In this context, I must mention the seed-exchange lists of the world's botanic gardens and institutes as a source of new material for the alpine gardener. The sad dichotomy between the professional botanical world and that of the amateur specialist is reflected in the fact that, when gardeners were eagerly welcoming new material of such species as *Crocus michelsonii* or several of the Juno irises, these and many other plants also native to Iran and Afghanistan were listed in seed-lists from Ashkhabad, Dushanbe, Tashkent and Alma-Ata. For instance, from such sources I once grew and propagated (but have now lost) *Eritrichium sericeum* from seed collected in the Tien-Shan and others have established that most compact and desirable of acantholimons, *A. diapensioides.* At present, Soviet Central Asia is becoming more accessible to visitors, who travel in organised groups, and we can hope for further interesting material from this source. In general, however, I feel that our failure to deal competently with this great volume of important monocotyledonous material over the past twenty years vastly outweighs the successes. The many collections of Juno and Reticulata irises are but memories to most of us. Recently, we have seen Syrian *Iris nusairiensis* discovered, described, introduced and successfully cultivated, a pattern we have seen with *I. hymenospatha, I. porphyrochrysa* and many others. Will its fate be the same? As I cannot recollect having seen even such a homely Juno as the Spanish *I. planifolia* truly established over the past twenty years, I feel pessimistic. I shall say nothing of Tulipa or Colchicum! Even with Fritillaria, whose successes I dwelt on, I can wonder from my own, limited personal experience, whatever happened to the thousands of *F. kotschyana* seedlings which should have been raised from a substantial seed collection I made fifteen years ago in the Elburz Mountains or how long the last irreplaceable bulbs of Iranian *F. chlorantha* or Lebanese *F. alfredae* will linger in cultivation.

We have not succeeded any better with the dwarf herbaceous and shrubby plants of south-west Asia. No-one has done more than John Watson to collect and distribute seeds of such material from Turkey but we have little to show for his efforts, spread over the past twenty years. While it may not excite the specialist, his

Origanum rotundifolium has proved a reliable and worthwhile garden plant—a rare acquisition nowadays. His more recent collection of *O. amanum* has produced some very robust and floriferous clones which look as though they may prove better garden plants than the original, dwarfer and more delicate, Peter Davis introduction, for which I still have a weakness. *Dianthus erinaceus* var. *alpinus* and *Asperula nitida* var. *puberula* are both now widely distributed from Watson collections. Both are excellent plants and sufficiently choice to give the grower considerable satisfaction when they flower really well. For many years I have known a tiny and delightful Asyneuma under an early Watson number. This appears to be *A. linifolium* var. *eximium* and I think very highly of its compact habit and tiny violet stars on thready stems. The fact that European asyneumas do not appear to stimulate most gardeners should not be allowed to detract from the merits of several small, Turkish saxatile species. I do not think we have established *A. compactum* but we do now have plants of *A. pulvinatum* from seed collected by John Watson and Jim McPhail. This is going to be a sought-after, tight cushion-plant and a challenge to flower well. Apart from yellow *Draba rosularis,* a Watson collection from eastern Turkey, and the interesting, white Iranian *Saxifraga wendelboi,* which Jack Drake was skilful enough to establish from living material I sent back from the Elburz Mountains, growers of cushion-forming cliff plants have had to be content with the genus Dionysia.

In 1959, the same year as he discovered the saxifrage, Per Wendelbo collected seed of *Dionysia aretioides.* This was germinated and grown at Kew and has proved to be the most outstanding rock-plant introduced during the period with which I am concerned. This original introduction did not, as far as I am aware, percolate through to the amateur specialist. Twenty years ago, we had the anomalous situation of the late Doris Saunders addressing the 1961 International Conference on "The Genus Dionysia", knowing only of one species, *D. curviflora,* in cultivation and quite unaware of Wendelbo's introduction or of his monograph on this genus, which was published the same year. Paul Furse was also unaware of this first introduction when he collected seed some years later. Although I and others subsequently collected seed, it was from this Furse introduction that the species became widely established and that the finest clones have been derived. It always saddens me that we cannot credit the first introduction of this superlative plant to this charming, generous and most remarkable man. Indeed, we may search in vain for some original introduction, which is both well established and of outstanding significance in our gardens; a plant we can present as a token memorial to Paul Furse. If this failure is a monument to our inadequacies as gardeners, we can console ourselves with the facts that Furse's wide collections of dried herbarium specimens from Iran and Afghanistan have already ensured him a respected position in the botanical history of this area and that his accounts of his journeys will always fascinate those who may delve into the gardening history of our time.

It was also from Furse collections that *Dionysia tapetodes* became widely distributed, though I believe it was first grown in Britain at Ingwersen's nursery from Afghan material collected by Mrs Priemer. This yellow-flowered species is the most variable and widespread of the tight-cushioned Bryomorphae dionysias, of which it is the easiest to grow and propagate. Of the Iranian members of this subsection, I think my collection of *D. janthina* can now be considered well established though little known as we seldom see its pink flowers. Plants from my re-introduction of *D. michauxii* and Tom Hewer's collection of the related *D. lamingtonii*, both yellow-flowered, still survive and are propagated by one or two enthusiasts though their position is more tenuous. I had considered that the long-term prospect of maintaining the violet-pink *D. bryoides* was even more uncertain until Eric Watson told me that he is now raising his second generation of cultivated seedlings. We may yet see this widely established. In the Caespitosae Subsection, we still have one or two surviving plants of *D. diapensiifolia* and *D. caespitosa* fifteen years after I collected seed of them but these are very difficult plants to propagate and without constant propagation their future with us is likely to be short.

Species in the Revolutae Subsection have generally proved somewhat easier to propagate and, apart from *D. aretioides*, we still have *D. revoluta*, both in the type race from my collection and in its grey-leaved subspecies, *D. revoluta* subsp. *canescens* from Tom Hewer's seed. The high-altitude, pale-violet flowered *D. archibaldii* too is now surprisingly widely grown though at times in its early history it survived only as a single plant in cultivation. I am, however, always apprehensive for the long-term future of any species which has been propagated from a single clone and offers little hope of providing us with seed. These more obviously shrubby dionysias bring us to the primitive Mirae and Scaposae Subsections, which would be of little interest to most gardeners if their name was not Dionysia. *Dionysia mira* from Oman, Turkish *D. teucrioides*, Afghan *D. paradoxa* and *D. lacei* from Pakistan are all in cultivation though the best-grown plants of these are more likely to be seen at Edinburgh or Kew, where there is more freedom from the prejudices of amateur gardeners, who are generally going to lavish most attention on plants which they or others consider "good" or "worth growing".

By present standards, all the pink- and violet-flowered species from Afghanistan are certainly "worth growing" and are no more difficult to grow than any others, if we could only propagate them successfully. Twenty years ago most of these were unknown to science as well as gardeners. The first we saw was *D. freitagii*, raised from seed collected by Hedge, Wendelbo and Ekberg in 1969. Two years later, in 1971, much valuable material was received from the journeys of both Grey-Wilson and Hewer and Bob Gibbons and his companions. The enthusiasm and expertise of Chris Grey-Wilson in particular greatly extended our knowledge of the Afghan species. Seed of *D. viscidula* and *D. microphylla* germinated particularly profusely and many plants were raised. I can remember the unique sight of a group of well-flowered young plants of the former, bedded out in the black peat of a nurseryman's exhibit at an R.H.S. show. Too many plants meant too little care. Over-confidence and complacency have resulted in these species becoming extremely rare in cultivation within a few years. The most recently introduced Dionysia, *D. involucrata*, the most northerly species from the Pamir-Alai, has reached Britain from Czechoslovakian sources and is so far proving remarkably accommodating. It is most striking planted out in the new alpine house at Kew, producing its candelabra of bright-pink flowers over a very long period, and in the skilled hands of Stan Taylor, a batch of seed from cultivated material is already being raised. I hope that we are learning from past experiences. Sadly, I fear that there will be no opportunity to obtain further wild seed of this genus from either Iran or Afghanistan over the next decade.

Although Dionysia may be considered the development of Primula in this area, true primulas do occur also and we have acquired an excellent garden plant in *P. warshenewskiana* var. *rhodantha.* Material of this little, sugar-pink species was collected by Mrs Priemer and reached Britain by way of Wilhelm Schacht at Munich. It is this Afghan form which we know in gardens but I have been given material of the type-race from the Pamirs by Hans Simon. I fear I found this less easy to grow and have now lost it.

The genus Primula can take us eastwards into the vast mountain ranges of Asia. As others, better qualified than I, will tell you of this area, as well as about North America, Australasia, and South America, I shall be yet more discriminating in my assessment of the new plants which have been established recently from the rest of the world. In fact, this is not too difficult a task for there has been comparatively little, considering the vastness of the areas and the increased number of travellers. Many people have visited Nepal in particular and there have been a number of re-introductions of significance but I cannot, for instance, find any new alpine plant widely established from the journeys of Roy Lancaster and Len Beer. Of course, many travellers had left before the seed had ripened at the highest altitudes and others, like Chris Grey-Wilson, have been concerned with collecting botanical material rather than seed for gardeners. This was not the case with John Jackson, however, who made some interesting collections around the Annapurna Himal in late October, 1978. It is yet premature to judge if anything will emerge as established from this collection but, as I have yet seen no result from his many collections of the desirable *Stellera chamaejasme,* I suspect that it is once again our competence as gardeners which is questionable rather than the competence of the collectors. One very interesting new Primula, which has been grown from seed collected by a group of students from the Royal Botanic Garden, Edinburgh, is *P. barnardoana,* a very distinct species with pale-yellow flowers which I hope will be maintained in cultivation. The related genus Androsace has provided more, mainly due to the satisfactory solution to this problem of establishing new plants, worked out by George Smith and Duncan Lowe. By retaining a relatively small amount of new material in the hands of one or two skilled growers, who are able and prepared to propagate it, we now have *A. delavayi, A. globifera* and *A. muscoidea* var. *longiscapa* well established and widely distributed from George Smith's Nepalese collections. Proving somewhat more difficult and not yet widely known are *A. zambalensis* and *A. tapete.* Similarly, *A. mucronifolia* from Dieter Schacht's Kashmir collection is none too easy to keep, far less keep in character. Among the Smith saxifrages, *S. stolitzkae* is now quite widely grown, though, like the androsaces, not at all easy to flower well. I think we can look forward to more plants entering general cultivation in the future from this successful teamwork.

I shall leave China to whoever may speak on this subject in ten years' time except to comment that, even with the increasing accessibility to this vast country, we should remember that life has changed since Forrest organised his armies of trained collectors and that it is unlikely that we shall be submerged in a deluge of new material. Yet further east, Taiwan has produced the prostrate *Rhododendron nakaharai,* dwarfest of the azaleas and extremely late flowering, though it needs its wood ripened by hotter summers than we have in Britain to give of its best. This will doubtless be of great importance in hybridisation, as will the dwarfer forms of *R. pseudochrysanthum* from the same island at similarly high altitudes. Very dwarf clones of the variable Japanese *R. keiskei,* originating from that extraordinary reservoir of pigmy plants, Yakushima Island, have also rapidly endeared themselves to alpine gardeners. I feel, however, it is invidious to talk of new introductions from Japan, when the Japanese have a far longer history of gardening than we have in Britain. There are, however, many Japanese plants still little-known in British gardens. *Corydalis ambigua,* which has become quite well known and sought after in recent years, is but one example.

Another Primula, *P. tschuktschorum,* can move us across the Bering Sea from Asia into North America. It also illustrates an insoluble problem of establishing some new plants. While I do not think it is with us any longer, I can remember seeing a very large number of plants, which that exceptional grower, Jack Crosland, had raised from his own seed. These were widely distributed but no-one else seemed to be able to grow it. There is maybe no point in introducing and propagating new plants if there are not enough skilled growers to give them to; on the other hand, we can often only learn how to grow a species by losing it. It is unreasonable, however, to expect that others should make more effort than us and to look for repeated fresh collections from the wild. Twenty years ago, Carl Worth was making annual journeys to collect seed from the Rocky Mountains. We may still have *Aquilegia scopulorum, Eriogonum ovalifolium* and *Polemonium confertum* from his collections but these are scarcer in cultivation today than they were a decade ago. Many more species which he collected, not once but many times, are no longer grown in Britain. Today, thanks to the regular efforts of Sally Walker, plants from her Arizona and New Mexico collections, such as *Primula ellisiae, P. rusbyi* and *Dodecatheon ellisiae,* are widely distributed among British gardeners. Several Mexican plants of her collecting, from which I might single out the dwarf species of Tigridia as especially fascinating, are also being grown here by a few specialists. We cannot anticipate such collections will be repeated indefinitely. In the exceptional case of the very dwarf Dodecatheon, which we grow here as *D. hendersonii* (Sooke form), we cannot anticipate any more material at all, as I am told that its only known habitat on Vancouver Island has been built over. I am glad to say that this has been propagated in Britain, though it is a slow-growing little plant and not too easy to flower well. Also on the credit side, I think such plants as the temperamental, wine-red *Douglasia dentata* and *D. laevigata* var. *ciliolata,* the fine Columbia River Gorge race, are becoming increasingly well known here. Ten years ago, shortly after the last Conference, I received seed of the needle-leaved, Montana-endemic *Phlox missoulensis* from Jim McPhail and Bob Woodward and an ice-blue clone of this is now quite widely grown. Much larger, though I fear challenging to propagate, are the stunning forms of *P. nana* collected by Paul Maslin. It is early yet to form an opinion on these in Britain but they are currently growing superbly at Kew, planted out both under glass and outside, in both yellow and orange-red forms. I suspect that these, like the pink-flowered plant we already grow as *P. nana* subsp. *ensifolia,* may expect a limited circulation among a few specialists, though it will be exciting if they can be more widely grown. *Phlox* 'Chatta-

Viola columnaris   (*Plate 49*)

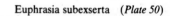

Euphrasia subexserta   (*Plate 50*)

Aquilegia flabellata 'Nana Alba'   (*Plate 51*)

Campanula pilosa 'Superba'   (*Plate 52*)

hoochee', a wild plant from Florida, in spite of the cultivar name, with its luminous lavender-blue flowers is now very well known indeed, whereas *P.* 'Fullers White', another form or hybrid of *P. divaricata*, rated more highly than it initially, is not at all well known. The selection, *P. adsurgens* 'Wagon Wheel' also does not seem to have lived up to early expectations of it in Britain and Kath Dryden predicts a more glowing future for another clone, 'Red Buttes'. Several variants of that other exclusively North American genus, Lewisia, have also come to the fore in recent years. We now have white forms of *L. tweedyi* and *L. cotyledon*, two of which have received awards as 'Alba' and 'Kathy Kline'. Particularly exciting, however, is the Jolon race of *L. rediviva*, which explodes into especially large, ivory-pink flowers and of which several generations have now been raised from English seed. Among monocotyledonous plants, very dwarf, pink forms of *Trillium ovatum* from the far west of Vancouver Island and grown as *T. hibbersonii* have become coveted plants. These have set seed and germinated well with several growers here. The name is difficult to justify botanically, as they appear to be the extreme end of a cline, but at their most compact they are distinct and desirable plants for the alpine gardener. Also now of somewhat doubtful status botanically, *Fritillaria roderickii* must be mentioned, not only as one of the best and easiest American species we can grow in Britain but also so that we can acknowledge the considerable amount of work Wayne Roderick has done in collecting material of the plants of western North America and his vast knowledge of these plants in their homes.

Turning our attention to the southern hemisphere, while others are dealing with the plants of Tasmania and New Zealand, no-one is talking about the few but interesting alpine plants from the mountains of south-east Australia. From this area, *Ranunculus muelleri* var. *brevicaulis*, with its varnished, bright-yellow buttercups, may well become established. I can remember being with John Kelly when he unpacked a small plant of this species sent by Otto Fauser. This plant survived and was subsequently rescued by Joe Elliott, with whom it has set seed on a number of occasions. The problem is growing on the seedlings but I think a solution will be reached. If so, we may yet grow the beautiful white *R. anemoneus*, which in spite of several fine seed collectings, does not appear to have been grown successfully in Britain. As both the starry, pinkish *Caltha introloba* and little *Aciphylla glacialis* from these same Australian Alps have grown well here in the open garden, I think we may feel some optimism.

So much material has reached British gardens from New Zealand over the past twenty years that it is difficult to nominate a few representatives or to determine which plants can be considered established and which are replenished periodically by fresh collectings of wild seed. In this particular case, we hardly need trouble ourselves over this, as many mountain areas in these islands are accessible to amateur enthusiasts without too much trouble and occasional seed collections from the wild are of trivial significance to natural populations. We do maintain many of these more recent additions, such as some of the celmisias, both from seed and cuttings in this country. I can remember when the first batch of cuttings from that choice little silver-plated shrub, *C. hectori,* was propagated at Jack Drake's nursery over twenty years ago and we still have this with us. This nursery has always been successful with New Zealand alpines, which enjoy its cooler, northern summer climate and Jack Drake has himself visited New Zealand, bringing back and continuing to maintain such interesting plants as the hybrid *Raoulia × loganii.* While this and the even more successful *R. hookeri* are propagated here, this is less frequently the case with the "vegetable sheep". Species like *R. mammillaris, R. rubra, R. eximia* and *R. buchananii,* which first made their debut here twenty years ago, are now comparatively well known, though their cultivation will, I suspect, always be limited to a few enthusiasts and we shall always be dependent on material from such sources as the members of the Canterbury Alpine Garden Society, whose excellent seed-list has contributed greatly to the distribution of such plants. There are, of course, many more-easily-grown New Zealand plants. We even have a British nursery, run by Graham Hutchins, specialising in these and, I am sure, listing much material which is new to cultivation here. One unexpectedly easy plant to grow and propagate, and with which I was involved initially, is *Cotula atrata* subsp. *luteola.* This fascinating little alpine with its ivory and maroon buttons over mats of grey and red-tinged foliage is restricted in nature to the

Kaikoura Ranges. Within a few months I was able to work up a good stock of this from material given to me by Anna Griffiths (I do not know who had sent the original stock to her from New Zealand)—not at all what anyone who has tried to grow the recalcitrant, black type-race, for which it often now masquerades in catalogues, might expect.

If we have benefited greatly by an influx of New Zealand plants over the last twenty years, we have seen virtually nothing new from the Drakensberg of southern Africa. *Helichrysum sessile* is being well grown by Stan Taylor, from material sent to Ralph Haywood by a relative in South Africa, but attempts to propagate this fascinating plant, with its extremely compact cushions of rosettes, have not yet been successful. It is over forty years since Helen Milford brought back material from that little, land-locked, mountainous country of Lesotho and how exceptionally adaptable and successful most of her introductions have been in British gardens. Everyone knows her *Euryops acraeus* but how many gardeners grow her hardy, high-altitude collection of the yellow *Cyrtanthus* (Anoiganthus) *luteus*. Every so often another Milford plant emerges from obscurity and what must have been many years of initial neglect. Where was *Diascia cordata* lurking for over twenty years until it appeared to establish itself in every alpine catalogue as a superlative, hardy, easy, long-flowering alpine? Several plants entirely new to science were collected and she is commemorated in such familiar alpines as *Helichrysum milfordiae* and *Crassula milfordiae*. How many gardeners, on seeing the yellow crocuses of *Romulea macowanii* var. *alticola* (this does at last have an authoritative name, after years as *Syringodea* sp. Basutoland, *S. luteonigra, R. longituba* and so on), appreciate that they are looking at a very-little-known plant indeed? There is not a single dried wild specimen of this from Lesotho in any of the world's herbaria but yet it sows itself in the scree of a Kentish rock garden. Considering the high incidence of growable, garden-worthy plants collected, the short time she spent in the field and the fact that she worked alone, Helen Milford's travels in Lesotho must surely be the most profitable journey for plants ever made. We must be able to expect some further good, growable plants from the highest Drakensberg and it is time someone went to bring them back to us.

The other part of the world which I should have considered would have had a great potential for British alpine gardeners is the temperate Andes of southern Chile and Argentina. We have made shockingly little progress with plants from this area over the past twenty years. In the 1950s we had much interesting material from lower altitudes in south-eastern Argentina brought back by Ruth Tweedie. *Oxalis laciniata* is now well known from her introduction and we still have a few plants like the little brick-coloured *Symphyostemon lyckholmii*, and the congested little shrub, *Nardophyllum bryoides*, which I do not think has ever flowered in captivity, more or less established. On the other hand, how many of us have seen *Cruckshanksia glacialis*, a superlative scree-plant with long-tubed, scented, yellow flowers, which was grown for some years from a Tweedie collection in a trough at Edrom Nurseries, by Alex Duguid, until some evil and covetous individual removed it. This and the more incredible but no more beautiful *C. hymenodon* with its spectacular rose-coloured calyces are but dreams to us, twenty years later. This will surely not always be so as we have had recent fine collections from these southern ranges by Lt. Col. Anderson and Dr Rolf Fiedler. It would be premature to attempt an assessment of our successes and failures with the seed distributed by either of these two collectors but we can certainly look back critically on our performance as gardeners with the material collected by John Watson and his companions in 1971. Once again, I feel we have given a very poor account of ourselves. The only introduction which has become quite well known was of a dusky buff-pink, as yet unnamed species of Mimulus, fancifully referred to by John as "Andean Nymph". While we have seen nothing of the sumptuous *Calandrinia affinis* or *C. sericea,* the little, garishly charming *C. rupestris*, with bi-coloured red and yellow flowers, might just become better distributed over the next few years. The most important plant for the alpine enthusiast, however, is surely *Ourisia microphylla*. Although a re-introduction, it is new to most of us and its profuse, pale-pink flowers over mounds of thready stems, clothed tightly in Cassiope-like leaves, ensure its appeal to the enthusiast. It is by no means easy to grow well or to propagate and the large number of plants which were raised initially has been dwindling steadily until recently. It has, however, been very successfully maintained at Kew and I think that they and the few enthusiasts, who have started to make a special effort with this, will make certain that this is not lost again. A larger spectacular scarlet Ourisia, possibly *O. alpina,* has been introduced and grown by Lt. Col. Anderson. One might hope that his proximity to those very skilled and experienced Scottish growers, Henry and Margaret Taylor, might lead to the establishment of some Chilean and Argentinian material, as the result of the same sort of fruitful liaison that was developed between George Smith and Duncan Lowe.

Several collections made by John Watson have become scarce through a neglect which I suspect stems from the fact that the genera are not at present fashionable with alpine gardeners. The genus Alstroemeria is the most striking case, as the collected seed of these germinated particularly well. We already had the tiny, orange-yellow species distributed by E. B. Anderson from material sent to him by Dr Wygnanki in Chile, as *A. pygmaea,* but several Watson collections, such as the beautifully marked, pale-pink *A. pulchra,* sumptuous violet *A. sierrae* and speckled *A. xanthina,* were still comparatively dwarf plants. They were not, however, satisfactory plants in the open garden, they dislike the confinement of pot cultivation and worst of all, I fear, were not sufficiently "alpine-looking" to become cult-plants like Dionysia.

The Chilean and Argentinian plants most likely to become the next cult-plants are, of course, some of the violas, whether they are of the habit of the rosulate *V. congesta,* the columnar *V. fluhmannii* or the cushion-forming *V. chamaedrys.* If Rolf Fiedler and others continue to send back seed, I might predict that we shall know rather more about growing these in ten years' time. I might also predict that we shall not be able to grow them in character without adapting existing concepts regarding pot-culture, composts and the treatment of the more difficult alpine plants.

In the case of that other genus of potential cult-plants, Nototriche, which can take us north into Bolivia and Peru, I should be even more dogmatic in asserting that we shall have to change our whole concept of cultivation to grow these. Fortunately, we have not yet had the opportunity to waste a collector's time and effort by losing these, for we are not yet ready for them. It is time for that clumsy and outdated makeshift attempt to adapt our climate, the alpine-house, to be replaced by something more effective. Even today, it would cost less than the price of ten metres of custom-built, conventional alpine-house for us to purchase the dehumidifier, refrigeration or air-conditioning equipment, appropriate lighting and circulatory fans to convert a spare room into a growing-room. What we cannot yet obtain is a ready-made programme to feed into the small home-computer which could control all these and enable us to reproduce with sufficient accuracy the climate, daylight-length and spectrum of the Bolivian altiplano. Gardeners are conservative souls, in general, but we have all accepted such artificial concepts as the alpine-house or even the rock garden itself as means towards the more successful cultivation of alpine plants. Perhaps the refriger-ated bench with its attendant lighting in the new alpine-house at Kew might make such paraphernalia more acceptable. There is no denying the success, which comparatively simple and limited equipment has brought to the maintenance of Arctic species in cultivation.

We may not, in fact, need any highly sophisticated arrangement to grow some species. When I visited the northern Andes of Colom-bia, I was so pessimistic about gardeners' capabilities to grow the plants of such mountains that I did not even collect seed from the genus Espeletia. Since then, Kew has successfully raised and grown *E. schultesii* from seed collected in Venezuela, though the plants are showing no sign yet of developing the extraordinary, columnar habit which they acquire on their native paramo. A few plants of Gaultheria, Pernettya and Gentianella from the limited seed collec-tion I made in Columbia in 1978 are progressing slowly in the hands of a few enthusiasts but the real problem with these tropical alpines is that their summer and winter are compressed into each twenty-four hours and that we cannot expect them to do more than half-heartedly survive in the protracted warmth of a British summer or the long cold northern winter. A fairly satisfactory solution with alpines from among the chilling, drifting clouds of the moister tropical mountains is simply to keep them growing all the time in frost-free conditions. As they are, in any case, used to a low light intensity, winter can be less of a problem for them than long, hot summer days. It was in a hot summer that I lost the exquisite, little

Gentiana cruttwellii from Papua New Guinea but this species as well as several other New Guinea alpines has been maintained at the R.B.G. Edinburgh since Paddy Woods brought back material in 1962. If enthusiasts are unwilling to adapt their growing conditions to suit these alpine plants, I see no reason why they should expect to have material to kill by treating it like a plant from the European Alps. On the other hand, large collections of the Malesian Rhododendrons are growing in the San Francisco area and parts of Australia. Even among these there are a few exquisite high-altitude plants, like the mat-forming, red, New Guinea *R. saxifragoides,* which should be of great interest to alpine gardeners. It is to be hoped that, if any experienced alpine enthusiasts, from areas where these plants might be growable outside, do come forward, material will be made available to them. Certainly seed from the exquisite little Dendrobium species, around *D. cuthbertsonii,* which grow in the moss- and lichen-encrusted "elfin wood" high on the New Guinea mountains, has been quite widely distributed by Edinburgh. Few alpine gardeners have either the expertise to raise orchids from seed or even to grow these tiny, jewel-like plants, which could be considered more genuinely alpine than the species of Pleione so fashionable with alpine growers at present. Is it too much to hope that one day we shall have special classes in our show schedules for tropical alpines and that New Guinea dendrobiums will be as well known as pleiones are today?

The genus Pleione has not always been popular, however. They have always been, I am told, held in rather low regard by most tropical orchid growers, and alpine enthusiasts showed a marked disinterest in them until very recently. Farrer does not mention them at all and Clay dismisses them briefly. The newcomer to alpine gardening might be forgiven for thinking that *Pleione forrestii* is a recent introduction for it has only been esteemed by alpine growers within the last twenty years. Its importance and significance to enthusiasts today are well illustrated by the remarkable and beautiful exhibit of its hybrids, staged at the Conference by Dr Harberd. It has, in fact, survived for over seventy years at the R.B.G. Edinburgh from an original Forrest collection. It is hardly fair to criticise Edinburgh for its initial slowness in distributing this species when one sees them as suddenly confronted by a horde of clamouring amateurs from a gardening world, which had shown nothing but apathy about the plant for fifty years. Such a problem could have been resolved diplomatically and impartially if some accepted channel had been created for the interchange of material between the professional, botanical world and the amateur gardener. It is surely up to our societies to create this. There must also be an acceptance by the botanical establishment of the fact that the amateur specialist-growers constitute a vast reservoir of expertise and plant material, which could easily be made available to them.

At present, however, it is becoming increasingly difficult to distribute and keep track of particular plants in the amateur world alone. The days when the grower could afford to be irresponsible and careless because there were sufficient skilled and knowledgeable nurserymen around to replace lost plants are long past and the expanding plant-sales at A.G.S. shows are of more significance as fund raisers than as means of distributing scarce material to competent growers. It is impossible to ascertain who might be able and willing to handle new material or to find out the status of a particular species in cultivation except through personal conversation with one's own immediate acquaintances. If this survey appears biased or inaccurate, this is the obvious explanation.

I cannot, for instance, give you an accurate assessment of the position in cultivation of three plants which were introduced by Peter Davis and all, I suspect, subsequently lost before being re-introduced on a number of occasions by John Watson: that distinctive pink, scree-crucifer *Ricotia davisiana,* the brilliant orange *Hypericum capitatum* and the little, blue borage, *Alkanna aucheriana.* The last is, I should guess, lost once again but I do know of a few plants of the other two—perhaps there are still many more. Those who do have such plants must never imagine that someone else is more competent than they are and must always propagate and distribute them to others whom they think may be able to grow them. In the absence of any organisation which might have given one person responsibility for maintaining a particular introduction, we must each assume this responsibility, ourselves. I have, for example, made up my mind to try to trace and bring together as many surviving clones as I can from the Oncocyclus and Regelia Iris collections made over the last twenty years, in the hope that it might be possible to increase these by seed. In planning this, I may well be trying to assuage my guilt at abandoning the cultivation of these plants some years ago but I also feel that my previous experience of them may be of some advantage in maintaining them in cultivation. It may be too late to recover *Iris heweri* but we can still hope to raise successive batches of seedlings from the existing clones of the beautiful *Iris afghanica* and to ensure that this is more widely established in cultivation, as one of the finest and most appropriate tributes possible to Paul Furse, who discovered this plant.

Such a scheme may seem too grandiose or pretentious to many of you but far greater challenges lie within easy reach of any European alpine gardener. I mentioned at the beginning of this article that we have made little progress towards the successful cultivation of some of our European alpines. We certainly cannot claim that species like *Gentiana pyrenaica, Eritrichium nanum* or *Ranunculus glacialis* are "established" in cultivation. Why not? Must we continue the pathetically negative attitude towards these plants for another twenty years? Conventional methods have not brought success, so we must try the unconventional: take an autumn holiday to collect some seed; raise a good batch of seedlings; try them under an ultra-violet lamp; put them in the deep freeze—anything is better than the present pessimism. If you would like a single plant to devote the next decade to, I suggest *Jankaea heldreichii,* surely one of the world's most beautiful saxatile plants and one which is as scarce in cultivation today as it was twenty years ago. One seed capsule of such a gesneriad contains thousands of seeds; can no one try to propagate this from seed in quantity?

In spite of the impression I may be giving, there have been successes and steps forward in recent years. The most notable is surely that *Paraquilegia grandiflora,* that incomparable cliff plant from the Himalayas and eastern Asia, has suddenly become widely available. Joe Elliott alone tells me that he has over two hundred seedlings at present. This was for so long the exclusive speciality of Branklyn, where I think the stock had come from a 1949 Ludlow and Sherriff collection which even then was a reintroduction, that many of us had despaired about ever seeing it widely grown. Not only do we have the violet Branklyn form from Bhutan but the little, western race, *P. afghanica*, has been raised from a Bob Gibbons collection, and the white Kashmir and Ladakh races have come from seed collected by Barry Starling and his companions and by Oleg Polunin. I think we may hope to do these more recent collections justice. At long last, too, the recalcitrant but beautiful Spanish *Viola cazorlensis* appears to be becoming established and successfully propagated, after hovering in and out of cultivation for over forty years. We have learned a great deal about these plants, as well as about the genus Dionysia, over the past twenty years and I think that there has also been a healthier attitude developing among alpine gardeners and a greater realisation that our main enemies are ignorance, over-confidence and selfishness.

Although I have attempted to be reasonably objective and constructive in my assessment of our recent alpine-gardening history, I am sure that I have antagonised some of you, who must be thinking what an overcritical and arrogant individual I am. I can assure those who may be ignorant of my record that I speak from a position of considerable authority. It may well be that I was actually asked to deal with this subject because no-one could think of anyone else, who has killed as many new introductions as I have. I think it is fitting that I leave you with what may well be recorded as my greatest achievements in this field. The more historic of the two is my recent assassination of the last cultivated plant of *Dionysia lindbergii*, which my late friend Peter Edwards had failed to kill in the seven years he grew it. It was especially noteworthy as possibly being the most beautiful of the dionysias and it will be an especially long time before a collector can see its soft, grey-velvet cushions studded with violet flowers, growing upside down under the overhangs of its native Afghan Darreh Zang, far less bring seed of it into cultivation. I believe that this might earn for me a position of greater significance than that enjoyed by my chairman, Roy Elliott, who can merely claim to be the man who killed the last *Primula rufa*. I have also recently killed *Dionysia afghanica*, which is a very slow-growing, firm-cushioned species with pale-violet, dark-eyed flowers, discovered and introduced by Chris Grey-Wilson in 1971. In this case, however, I have confounded myself by giving a plant to Eric Watson, who has cunningly kept his alive, thereby ensuring that he has the last plant. However, an old horticultural hit-man like myself does become a little bit tired of it all at times and it is really with some relief, perhaps tinged with a glimmer of maliciousness, that I leave the last *D. afghanica* to Eric.

Himalayan Plants in the Wild

GEORGE SMITH

Gentiana depressa

What a floral paradise is presented by the Himalaya. This region forms an arc 1500 miles long and 50 to 100 miles wide, made up of a lush maze of ridges and valleys, and a succession of enormous mountain blocks standing like a chain of icy islands in a green sea. The whole of this area is isolated florally to the north by the montane desert of Tibet and to the south by the fiercely hot plains of India, so that the two main influences on its alpine flora flow in from the ends of the arc. The lesser influence comes from the west and north-west, from the Hindu-Kush and the Pamirs, and the greater influence from the east and north-east, from the vast treasures of the west Chinese region. It is not surprising therefore to find that there is a marked east/west differentiation in the flora. This is greatly accentuated by the effects of the monsoon summer rains, which are heaviest in the eastern half of the Himalaya, the half nearest to the Bay of Bengal. All this means that the flora of Kashmir is quite different to that of Bhutan, and that there is a gradual increase in the wealth of alpine species as one moves eastwards, reaching a climax in the Bhutan-Assam-Himalaya, a sector alas almost totally closed, for political reasons, to visitors.

It seems at first sight astounding that notwithstanding the thousands of botanical tomes in existence, and after 200 or more years of exploration, the "Flora of the Himalaya" has yet to be written. The nearest one can come to it is Hooker's "Flora of India", a truly great work published more than a hundred years ago. This still forms the basis of a search for information on our subject. So much however has been discovered since then, that to complete the picture, one has to thumb the floral lists made by various travellers in more recent years, but best of all, spend days poring over the collectors' sheets in the main herbaria. For our region, the richest collections are at the British Museum (Nat. Hist.), and at the Royal Botanic Gardens of Kew and Edinburgh. Anyone seriously interested is welcomed and generously helped by the staff of those institutions. Until one has tried, one can have no idea of how real information may be obtained by browsing (metaphorically) through herbarium collections.

Very recently, a comprehensive work on the flora of the Central Himalaya has been published by the British Museum. It is a bibliography of the Flora of Nepal, and collates all the information gathered so far on species found, giving the main localities. It differs from a flora mainly in not supplying a botanical description of each species and in not defining distribution. Very much more work has yet to be done in the field by professional botanists before a full flora can be compiled. This serious gap in the botanical literature exists by reason of the sheer vastness and remoteness of the Himalayan region: although some of it has been thoroughly explored, most of it has only been looked at superficially, and much of it not at all. This is not to say that there are still many new species to be found, the great majority have been found; what is still lacking is an adequate knowledge of the geographical distribution and habitats of the known species.

It is not easy in a single article to do justice to one, much less several contrasting Himalayan regions. In the main therefore this account will concentrate on the Upper Arun region of east Nepal, an area which takes in the eastern flank of the Everest Massif and the Lumbasamba Himal, a range of mountains half way between Everest and Kangchenjunga.

The Upper Arun

Agriculture below 8000 ft and grazing above the tree line have of course had a strong impact on the natural vegetation cover of this well-populated region. Rice and maize cultivation have left little intact forest below 8000 ft. Between this altitude and the tree line at around 12,500 ft, however, a high proportion of virgin forest has survived. It has done so probably largely because in the monsoon season the higher ridges and slopes are almost continuously engulfed in cloud and rain. It is the magnificence of these forests which give east Nepal much of its special character. The greenery is overwhelming. The extent of grazing in the alpine zone is also less than in the more westerly regions, which means that vast areas of mountainside are still covered with thick scrub. Much of the original wild Himalaya is still to be found here!

The bulk of the forest is made up of broad-leaved trees, such as maples, magnolias, hollies, rhododendrons, together with the conifers *Tsuga dumosa* (Himalayan Hemlock) and *Abies spectabilis,* a fir which can reach an enormous size. The upper forest also contains a birch, *Betula utilis,* which however is more abundant in central and west Nepal. Frequently the forest can be made up almost entirely of any of six or so tree rhododendrons: *Rr. arboreum, grande, falconeri* and *hodgsonii* form tall gloomy forests, which with altitude gradually become weird, tangled, and impenetrable shrubberies comprising at least a dozen species, 10 ft to 20 ft tall, such as *Rr. barbatum, campanulatum, dalhousiae, thomsonii* and *campylocarpum.* In such forests there is practically no undergrowth, but in the mixed forest the shrubby and herb flora is quite significant. In more open forest or in clearings there are lots of viburnums, cotoneasters, roses, daphnes, barberries and *Pieris formosa* to name but a few of the more familiar genera, and then, especially near the tree line, there occur herbs such as *Primula sikkimensis, P. glomerata, P. petiolaris, Androsace hookeriana,* the taller Meconopsis such as *Mm. regia, grandis, napaulensis,* and some larger species of Pedicularis. Lower down, around 9000 ft, one can find in the gloom of thick forest the petiolarid *Primula boothii.* Of course epiphytes abound, so one finds *Pleione humilis* growing in the moss on trees, as well as numerous other orchids. Some trees can be so overladen with epiphytes that it is occasionally difficult to decide what is the host.

The long festoons of "Tree Moss" are a special feature. This is a type of lichen, which sometimes hangs like a curtain from the higher branches.

As the trees thin out at around 12,500 ft, more often than not one enters rough pastures, but where no trail emerges from the forest, then the succession is usually into dense, waist-deep scrub composed mainly of dwarf rhododendrons. The main species are *Rhododendron setosum* and *R. anthopogon,* stunted *R. campanulatum,* and to a lesser extent *R. lepidotum.* Mixed in with the rhododendrons are other shrubs such as Berberis, *Potentilla fruticosa,* cotoneasters, and junipers. In the Barun Valley on its shoulders at 13,000 ft this scrub is criss-crossed with broad bands of the large primulas such as *Pp. stuartii, strumosa, sikkimensis* and *obliqua.* At flowering time, probably in late May or early June, the colour must be absolutely fantastic, with the bright pink of *Rhododendron setosum,* the cream or white of *R. anthopogon,* and myriad primulas. Very noteworthy is that in the scrub hardly a blade of grass is to be seen.

Where the stunted woody plants are thin, then smaller herbs throng. It is here that we begin to find the treasures. If one is lucky, a whole slope dotted about with *Primula uniflora* appears—this very dainty soldanelloid with a shallow bowl-shaped corolla, in contradiction to its name, frequently carries two flowers in an umbel. Its colour varies from pale to dark violet-purple. Where the ground is particularly wet, the remarkable *Primula dickieana* appears, with its flat corolla of cream petals and a central disc of deep golden velvet. Here this species is almost at the western limit of its distribution, its range extending to south-west China. Here and there one also sees *P. buryana,* a white soldanelloid, but not as abundant as in central Nepal. There are everywhere, of course, stands of the larger meadow primulas. Amusingly, *Primula strumosa* has a particular predilection for the heavily manured areas in the neighbourhood of the shepherds' huts. Other delicate alpines are the perfectly proportioned *Gentiana phyllocalyx,* which produces its large, stemless single flowers from beds of moss in open scrub. Another wonderful gentian, one which seems to be quite at home in meadow, is the mat-forming *Gentiana depressa.* This late flowerer is very variable in colour, its tubby corolla being sometimes a delicate blue with lavender plicae, and brownish greenish markings in the tube, sometimes deep blue with brilliantly white plicae; there is endless scope here for the collector who, however, has to be there in autumn.

The mixture at this altitude, 12,000 to 14,000 ft, continues with great patches of *Cassiope fastigiata,* delicate specimens of *Rhododendron pumilum,* dwarf sulphur-yellow *R. lepidotum,* and a wide selection of Meconopsis, mostly the tall ones. *Meconopsis napaulensis* is seen in a range of colours from maroon-red to blue. Here, there, and everywhere, in pasture or light scrub, are large mats of *Androsace lehmannii* and the white-flowered form of *Androsace globifera,* species which were much more abundant in the Lumbasamba Himal than in the Barun Valley. At Topke Gola there are great cushions of *A. globifera* on flat rocks in the stream which must be submerged when the stream is in spate; also, beautiful specimens in full flower were bathing in the perpetual spray of a large waterfall—makes you think.

A universal meadow carpeter is *Potentilla eriocarpa,* or something very close to it. Lush ungrazed pasture, as in the Alps, is a rich mixture of many buttercup types, geraniums, parnassias, forget-me-nots, and a host of other tall herbs including primulas. A particularly attractive species flowering in July is *Primula capitata* var. *crispata* with a loose drooping umbel of small deep purple, very sweetly scented flowers covered on the outside with white farina. Associated with wetter meadows and boggy parts is none other than our own "Marsh Marigold", *Caltha palustris.*

Wandering further up the valleys the ground gets more stony, the scrub and pastures are no longer continuous, and the composition of the flora gradually changes. An examination of the flora at 14,000 ft to 16,000 ft is most enlightening. Most of the plants found at lower altitudes continue to be seen, but as some disappear, new ones occur. Thus species of Cyananthus become very much more common, and often, with their small blue trumpets, they are the dominant flowers, especially in well-grazed meadows. Of particular interest is a sulphur-yellow form of *Cyananthus incanus,* which occasionally outnumbers the blues. *Primula primulina* (syn. *pusilla)* appears on earthy banks in great quantity and is a joy to see. In the grass there are three members of the section Farinosae, *P. concinna, P. glabra,* and a small brilliant white *P. involucrata. Primula concinna* is tiny and stemless and *P. glabra* has a tight umbel of mauvish flowers the upper petals of which lean slightly backwards while the lower ones come a little forwards on a three inch stem, a bit like a Viola. *Primula involucrata* is equally at home in grass or grit. On steep gritty soft slopes and in flat mossy ground where nothing much else will grow, especially on exposed cols, one finds two species of the Minutissimae section: one is the very widely distributed *P. tenuiloba,* whose bluish-lilac stemless corolla resembles that of our *P. minima;* the other is the more rare pink to white *P. muscoides,* whose small mats bear the tiniest bells in the whole genus, a really fascinating species. Also in exposed places is the less common fairy-like *P. soldanelloides,* which gives its name to the section. Its white shallow-conical, hanging corolla is on a two-inch stem, and the plant is most often seen growing in moss on a boulder. A much bigger soldanelloid, growing on cliffs and even in earthy banks in much more sheltered habitats is *P. wollastonii:* its very characteristic tight umbel of blue-violet thimbles, covered in white farina on the inside and carried on three- to five-inch stems gives this species a beauty all its own. One more Primula must be mentioned, the small and plain *P. walshii*: this is very common in grass, especially at higher altitudes. It has small stemless pink or white flowers surrounded by disproportionately large strap-shaped leaves. It belongs to the Minutissimae section. It's quite clear by now that the Upper Arun is the place for anyone who is keen on primulas, and there are still more to come.

Turning now to androsaces, the situation is very different: at higher altitudes there are only two. *Androsace nortonii* is somewhat like *A. villosa* in appearance, and is essentially a very much reduced *A. sarmentosa*. It grows among thin scrub on gritty slopes. The other species, *A. delavayi*, is far more interesting and beautiful and may be found everywhere between the province of Kumaon (west of Nepal) and south-west China, but always above 15,000 ft. It is mat or cushion forming, and in Nepal its stemless flowers are white. Another is reputed to be there, *A. selago*, but I do not know of anyone who has found it.

The saxifrages are abundant and varied. There must be at least twenty species in the Hirculus section. They are all yellow flowered, and vary in form from the exuberant *Saxifraga brunoniana* with its long numerous bright red stolons and loose spikes of golden star flowers, to the tight cushions of *S. diapensia* covered in large stemless flowers. Most of the species form tuffets of leaves, sometimes spiky and linear, sometimes oval and fluffy, above which are borne single yellow flowers on half- to four-inch stems. *Saxifraga lychnitis* is different in that it has a spike of drooping conical corollas. *Saxifraga flagellaris* subsp. *sikkimensis* I did not see in flower, but subsp. *hoffmeisteri* was showing its yellow flowers with an uneven red blotch on most petals. The oddest is *S. hemisphaerica* which forms a very tight round woolly cushion, but whose flowers are apetalous. In the Micranthes section, to which our *S. stellaris* belongs, there are several species in the Melanocentra group; *Saxifraga melanocentra* itself is really spectacular, with large sessile one-inch flowers with wasp-like petals and a huge silky, almost black ovary. The commonest of the Kabschia section are *S. andersonii* and *S. kumaonensis,* both quite common all along

the Himalayan chain. The latter is somewhat variable, sometimes
having stemless, sometimes stalked, white flowers. The more rare
S. georgei also has white stemless flowers but with pointed petals,
and is modestly attractive. A red-flowered species, *S. lowndesii,*
was collected in the Barun Valley by L. W. Swann in 1954, but I was
unlucky.

The not terribly exciting *Gentiana prolata* is around, but never in
great abundance. On the other hand *G. ornata* can be very plentiful. A vigorous form of this species occurs in vast numbers at the
16,000 ft level near the upper Barun Glacier, where for hundreds of
yards it can make up a quarter or more of the green carpet on which
one is walking. It must be a breathtaking sight at flowering time,
which will be mid to end of September. When I was there at the end
of August there were only about a dozen flowers but, literally,
millions of buds. The same species on the east side of the Arun, in
the upper Ombula Chu Valley, is more graceful and dainty. Much
less abundant, but dotted about everywhere in meadow or on ridge,
is the lovely, small, deep-blue trumpet of *G. tubiflora,* with its tiny
Sempervivum-like leaf rosette. Another and very different gentian
is *G. elwesii,* whose cleistogamous, blue and white bullet-shape
corolla never opens, even in cultivation. A very rare gentian grows
in earthy pockets on cliffs and is totally absent from scree or
meadow above or below. It is *Gentiana staintonii*: this relative of
G. ornata has a deep blue squat almost cylindrical corolla and a
red calyx. Also in Gentianaceae is *Swertia multicaulis,* which is
dotted about everywhere. It is a largish species, with a head of
dozens of purplish-blue, four-petalled flowers on a stalk which
grows from virtually nothing to about a foot as the flowers
open.

Meconopsis horridula is also at its best at this altitude. This
species, which is found along the entire length of the Himalaya, is
seen here in a beautiful form with wide overlapping silky petals of a
delicate sky-blue. In the wild it is very compact, so its three-inch
blooms clustered on a nine-inch plant are in perfect proportion.
Drifts of cremanthodiums are everywhere; these are medium to
large yellow daisies with stiffly nodding heads from the cabbagy *C.
plantagineum* to the small and delicate *C. decaisnei.* Likewise
everywhere are asters, mostly *A. stracheyi.* One of the jewels of the

higher slopes is the pale pink to very bright rose-pink *Arenaria glanduligera* which forms tuffets two to six inches across and are so densely covered with 6 mm flowers as to hide the leaves totally. This is a very common species. In complete contrast, dotted about, inconspicuous and never plentiful, is *Campanula modesta,* one of the very few alpine campanulas in Nepal. It is very close to our *C. rotundifolia* but has a much narrower corolla of a deep purply-blue. Then there are several species of Trigonotis of which the most frequently seen is *T. rotundifolia*: this deep blue stemless forget-me-not forms brittle mounds and is highly decorative. Finally, though of course I have far from exhausted the list of flowering alpines in this altitude range, I must mention the dwarf form of *Corydalis cashmiriana.* This delicate elfin-like plant is most often seen peeping just above the surface of moss. Its crystalline sky-blue flowers stand singly or in pairs one or two inches high. Where this form grows in grit, it trails and does not rise. At lower altitudes one can find the more normal vigorous kinds.

Shershon is a shepherds' summer encampment. It lies at the top end of the valley by the lower glacier at around 15,500 ft. The two-mile walk to the terminal moraines of the upper glacier at 16,000 ft is still grazing land with a closed vegetation cover, even if the sheep and dzos have to digest a lot of *Primula walshii* and *Gentiana ornata.* At this top end some new species begin to dominate, notably *Rhododendron nivale,* which forms mats two or three feet wide and six inches deep. On the rocks a lovely and strange composite appears, *Tanacetum gossypinum,* a white silvery blob with golden buttons dotted about on it—the buttons are the disc florets, and there are no ray florets. Then there is a pale yellow edelweiss, *Leontopodium evax,* very different from the more conventional *L. jacotianum* found lower down which I forgot to mention. Increasingly numerous cushions of that extraordinary plant *Thylacospermum rupifragum* are to be seen: this species in the Caryophyllaceae is found at high altitude everywhere from the Tien Shan to west China and is remarkable not for its white flowers but for the incredible hardness of its cushion. You can stand on a large one and it won't dent. We camped on flat ground on the east shoulder of the valley at 16,500 ft, looking across to the end of the upper glacier. The ground is about 50% bare open soil and 50% of a green mat made up mainly of Carex. Among the other components are a purple Astragalus, *Cyananthus incanus,* one of the yellow saxifrages, *Polygonum affine, Swertia multicaulis, Thylacospermum rupifragum, Primula concinna, P. walshii, Arenaria glanduligera, Rhododendron nivale,* extremely stunted *Potentilla fruticosa* which has been with us all the way from the tree-line, and a dwarf umbellifer *Cortia depressa.* In addition there are *Campanula modesta, Meconopsis horridula, Corydalis cashmiriana, Viola biflora* as usual under the boulders, a tiny silvery composite with white "everlasting" flowers, and two great new finds, *Primula caveana* and *Chionocharis hookeri.* The Primula which is in the Rotundifolia section, holds the altitude record for the genus, and yet looking at it one would think it was a woodlander. It has roundish leaves on brittle stalks, ordinary looking magenta-pink flowers with a smell of pear-drops, on peduncles that can reach six inches in length. A possible explanation may be that it grows only in the shelter of boulders where I invariably found it. The lovely silky pale emerald green cushions of *Chionocharis hookeri* however grow in the open among the other species in the turf. By the time that I got there the blooms had long since gone, alas: this is a gem of a forget-me-not. Formerly known as *Eritrichium hookeri,* it produces deep sky-blue single stemless flowers, one per rosette, and gives the effect of being a blue *Androsace helvetica.*

On top of this ridge, with the summit of Everest visible only 12 miles away, two more treasures are yet to be seen. One is the dainty *Saxifraga punctulata,* probably in the Micranthes section, with its small chunky dark leafy rosettes and single flowers on two-inch stems. The corolla is spectacular, for the cream petals carry a regular pattern of sharp black dots, and two yellow eyes outlined in black dots at the base of each petal. The other, although the last to be mentioned, is by far not least and is the gorgeous *Gentiana urnula.* This very special species inhabits high exposed ridges. It has a two-inch tubular corolla which is urn-shaped when the corolla mouth closes or just before the bud opens. It has irregular very remarkable blue-black, violet, and greenish vertical stripes on a white background. The flowers sit stemless on a nest of tight leafy rosettes which are absolutely at ground level, with the leaves folded neatly in a square pattern, each leaf folded at 90°, a poem in economy. It really is worth all the toil and effort of a long trip to see *G. urnula* in the wild.

I would like to round off this account with a list of highest occurrences as recorded by L. W. Swann, who was attached to the 1954 Barun Mountaineering Expedition.

Carex	19000	
Stellaria decumbens var. *pulvinata*	20130 ⎫	
Arenaria festucoides	19300 ⎭	– – – – –Caryophyllaceae
Meconopsis horridula	19000	– – – – –Papaveraceae
Parrya lanuginosa	20100 ⎫	
Pegaeophyton scapiflorum	18100 ⎭	– – – – –Cruciferae
Sedum sp.	18800	– – – – –Crassulaceae
Saxifraga engleriana	18700	– – – – –Saxifragaceae
Sibbaldia sp.	18800	– – – – –Rosaceae
Gentiana urnula	20100	– – – – –Gentianaceae
Lagotis sp.	19600 ⎫	
Oreosolen wattii	19550 ⎭	– – – – –Scrophulariaceae
Leontopodium monocephalum	19600 ⎫	
Tanacetum gossypinum	19600 ⎪	
Saussurea gossipiphora	19600 ⎬	– – – – –Compositae
Anaphalis xylorhyza	19000 ⎭	

References:

1. "An Enumeration of the Flowering Plants of Nepal"
   H. Hara, W. T. Stearn and L. H. J. Williams
   Publ. Trustees of the British Museum (Nat. Hist.) London
   Vol I (1978), Vol II (1979), Vol III (to be published shortly)
2. "Forests of Nepal"
   J. D. A. Stainton
   Publ. John Murray 1972

Himalayan Plants in Gardens

DUNCAN LOWE

Androsace foliosa

My opening remarks almost began with a caution because of the short time we have had to gain experience in the cultivation of plants recently introduced from the Himalaya. "Short", of course, is relative for I realise that ten years have passed since the first material collected came into our hands. Nevertheless, those under discussion are still looked upon as newcomers to be watched over and tried, with a little more of this and a little less of that, until their response shows a real inclination to stay with us. A few have had little bother in settling down, some even graduating from pot to open garden but, taken as a race, they are as yet more difficult to maintain than the Europeans.

The species concerned here are true mountain plants: collecting only started after the tree line had been left behind and continued upwards as far as plants were found. Three plant families, (four genera), predominate and as might be expected, they are: Saxifraga, Gentiana, Primula and Androsace. Because we knew no other approach the plants were given the treatment and conditions suiting their nearest European equivalents and losses were formidable. Autopsies told us little but being convinced then, as now, that subtle variations in potting mixture constituents have negligible effect we concentrated on the conditions to which the newcomers were subjected. Aided by one or two informative accidents this approach led to a better understanding of their needs which, when related to the climatic aspects of their home ground, began to make some sense. In the regions where most of the specimens were collected monsoon rains are a daily occurrence in the growing season, the mornings are regularly dry and sunny but, after lunch, the deluge; quite a contrast to the successions of sunny days that can favour the Alps or Pyrenees. The altitude zone in which the majority of the plants were found starts where similar ground in the Alps finishes (around 3000 m) so the air is "thinner" and the sunlight less filtered. The third difference is temperature; no frosts have been noted by plant hunters even when camping by the snow line.

The behaviour of the "Himalayans" in cultivation corresponds in some measure to these observations. No amount of spring and summer rain seems to bother them, provided that their root run is perfectly drained. They respond to direct sunshine by flowering better the more they get, but only if they never lack sufficient moisture at their roots. Frost in excess of −4°C will damage their blooms and if more severe can even kill their leaves, or the entire plant in one or two species. The last is puzzling because plants of different genera, found sharing the same habitat in the wild, often respond quite differently to a hard night frost in Britain, some greeting the morning with crippled flowers and limp foliage, whilst others are unblemished.

In the dormant state they again, in general, differ from the "Europeans" in their needs, particularly the cushion types, for, whilst rosettes will rot if too damp, the plant can suffer dehydration if the root ball is allowed to dry out to the just moist state that would be perfect for say, *Androsace vandellii*. It is difficult to be precise as to the amount needed but, from experience, the soil mixture below the top dressing should be clearly damp to both sight and touch but not wet. Perhaps it might help to caution that plants have been lost by relying on the method whereby only the plunge material is watered, a tried and trusted practice for winter watering but likely to be inadequate for the Himalayan cushion plants.

Their vulnerability to pests is no worse and no better than that of other alpines, the only reliable means of protection being frequent examination and, in the case of aphids (the worst enemy), periodic spraying regardless of whether attack is evident or not. Many of the cushion-forming species have extremely hairy rosettes in which a considerable colony of aphids can develop unseen, the first clue to their presence being a loss of vigour in the plant with discoloration and wilting of leaves. Such symptoms can often be the beginning of the end.

An affliction uncommon in European species, though something like it is known to Dionysia growers, is "self-strangulation" and it can be infuriatingly common amongst the newcomers. The first sign of its happening is the sudden wilting of one or a few rosettes on an otherwise healthy plant. Sometimes the ailment will stop at that, leaving the affected rosettes to die and dry up but, it can also spread with alarming speed, reducing a turgid plant from full health to a corpse in a few days. Virus does not seem to be the culprit, for often, if an affected rosette is noticed in the early stages of wilting, snipped off and treated as a cutting, it will not only revive but go on to root and produce a healthy plant. The behaviour suggests that the plant suddenly cuts off the flow of moisture and nutrient along the feeding stem or stems, and it may do this at any time of the year, in wet or dry periods.

We amateurs would be very grateful for a scientific investigation of this phenomenon which is frustrating and defies all the usual "gardener's" attempts either to understand or control it. There is, however, some progress being made empirically in that we have found one or two resistant or disinclined clones, where it has been possible to raise a number of seedlings and this, perhaps, may be our longer term solution.

In order of difficulty and losses the primulas must head the list. Next come the gentians with the saxifrages and androsaces rating about equal for third place.

The saxifrages have produced problems in identification and even now several of the cushion-forming species still bear their field labels, such as: "tubby flowered kabschia type" and "grassy leaved hirculus?". Much labour lies ahead in the taxonomy of Himalayan saxifrages.

An attractive feature peculiar to many of the saxifrage species is ovality in the form of the flower, very noticeable in the throat and emphasised by the brilliant orange stamens which lie hard against the petals in their young stage. This characteristic is displayed to perfection in *Saxifraga hypostoma,* which forms a hard, hemispherical cushion and spangles it with completely sessile white flowers, whose petals overlap generously at their edges. The heart of each flower is golden and glistens with liquid nectar. Happily this saxifrage is not only beautiful but also hardy, quick growing and easily propagated from rosette cuttings.

There are some fascinating miniatures, looking somewhat like dwarf forms of *S. hypostoma,* several of which have still to be identified. One which has achieved its christening as well as being one of the best in health and charm is *S. quadrifaria,* with its almost flat cushion of 3 mm diameter rosettes and tiny oval flowers. Another named dwarf is *S. georgei* which has distinctive pointed petals and dark green foliage. Unfortunately the midgets are not as free and easy as *S. hypostoma,* since they tend towards rosette rotting during dormancy, but it is well worth the extra trouble of keeping the rain off them in winter and never allowing them to parch.

In splendid contrast to the white-flowered cushions, *S. flagellaris* ssp. *sikkimensis* covers itself in golden-yellow flowers which last for weeks. It is easy to please, is quite hardy and propagates itself strawberry fashion. It has one quirk however; the flowering rosettes are monocarpic and in spring every rosette flowers; however each rosette radiates restrained stolons (or runners?) tipped with plant-lets that eagerly root when they touch the earth and so progeny are assured. But in our long growing season the infants often mature enough to flower, in the autumn! To ensure that the entire stock does not fall to this floral suicide a few should be held back by deliberately disturbing them through such means as pricking out and repotting in late summer, once or twice, then they will over-winter without fuss and start the cycle all over again in spring.

Editorial limits prohibit anything like coverage of the saxifrages and this section must now be concluded with some name dropping and a note or two.

In addition to those discussed already we still have in cultivation *Ss. andersonii, georgei, imbricata, melanocentra, stolitzkae* and four unidentified species.

Cultivation

Cushion types are treated, in general, like European kabschias but are not allowed to dry out to the same degree in droughts or during dormancy. Most have set viable seed. All those still with us can be increased by single rosette cuttings or offsets. They do not need, and even dislike, glass overhead in the growing season, but the miniature forms benefit from cover in winter.

We have still too much to learn about the few "non-cushion" types to risk offering any advice.

The saxifrage story is one of fair success and the same can be said for the androsaces. Their afflictions and foibles have already been discussed but it is encouraging to report that, despite these, more than seventy-five per cent of the species introduced have been maintained in cultivation. These survivors are: *Aa. delavayi, foliosa, globifera, hookeriana, lehmannii, muscoidea* (several forms), *strigillosa, tapete* and *zambalensis*.

The muscoidea types have a constitution and behaviour very similar to that of the better known and closely related *A. jacquemontii* and will repay cultivation methods satisfying that species. Much easier are the herbaceous—like *A. foliosa* and *A. strigillosa* which have succeeded as "border plants" in some gardens, however they tend to be short lived and should be maintained by sowing seed that is fairly reliably produced. *Androsace lehmannii* grows in the company of primulas and although a cushion type, appreciates much more leaf mould in the soil mix. The remainder, *Aa. delavayi, globifera, hookeriana, tapete* and *zambalensis,* are still being treated as individuals and although there has been an occasional surge of response in one or two of them we are still a long way from being confident in offering guidance on their treatment.

In the north of England and Scotland Asiatic gentians are firmly established as a few species and many hybrids, *Gentiana sino-ornata* and *G. × stevenagensis* are typical examples. Of the gentians recently brought back from Nepal almost all have been introduced previously and it has become apparent why these did not persist as the old favourites did. The "ornata types" collected have about the same staying power as *G. farreri* or *G. hexaphylla.* Particularly in Scottish gardens *G. tubiflora* and, to a lesser extent, *G. staintonii* have settled in. From personal experience the ornata types prefer a more open root run and are showing promise in sunny, rich screes, in contrast to the partially shaded loamy beds enjoyed by *G. sino-ornata* and the like. We fought to keep the aristocratic, high altitude *G. urnula* but it slowly slipped away, as did one or two miniature species never identified. In consolation however *G. depressa* is strengthening its hold in cultivation. This beautiful creeping gentian came to us from the Schacht collection where it has been established for some time. In our experience, it requires regular division to promote good health, and plenty of sunshine to bring about the bounty of autumn flowers which in sheer beauty and extent repays any amount of care required. To keep it the owner must protect it from severe frost.

Finally we come to the primulas, mainly of the petiolarid, soldanelloid and nivalid groups, and let it be admitted that these have never been easy to please. Some favoured locations in Scotland have acted as havens for the older introductions, where skilled growers have been able to hold and propagate sufficient to maintain a flow of replenishments for the losses further south. It should be remembered that these represent the survivors from a multitude of species collected and introduced earlier in the century. And so it has been with the newcomers. They all begin well, growing rapidly and in several cases producing good seed, but after a year or two a decline sets in, thinning the ranks until only those with enough resistance or those which propagate readily, remain. Virus disease is probably the cause and has carried away at least eighty per cent of the species introduced.

Although essentially an obituary it is worth a few words to recall some of the beautiful things that stayed with us for a short time.

The tiniest was *P. muscoides*, the smallest of the minutissimae section, which lived long enough to produce its crystalline flowers, only 3 mm across. *Primula spathulifolia*, a fascinating crevice-dweller, never did flower but gave us, for a year, its clusters of silver-grey leaves. The bird's eye Primula of the Himalaya, *P. concinna*, produced its yellow-eyed pink flowers for several years and was amenable to division, allowing it to be quite well distributed amongst skilled growers, yet, as though responding to some signal, all of them faded away in the space of twelve months. So it was with *P. walshii* another tiny species and *P. uniflora*, an exquisite soldanelloid. In similar manner *P. boothii* declined in spite of our raising many plants from the seed produced in the first fruitful years.

Two survivors are *P. dickieana* and *P. wollastonii* and they remain for two interestingly different reasons. *Primula dickieana* is self pollinating or, more correctly, one of the collected plants possessed this virtue, and gave viable seed from which several plants survive. In addition the subdued leaves constituting the resting bud can, in spring, be peeled off like scales and, if treated as cuttings, can root and form young plants in a matter of weeks. *Primula wollastonii* also chooses spring to offer progeny but does so by sending up tiny complete plants from those roots that are just below surface. As many as six of these plantlets can rise from a 3 or 4 cm length of root, and if each is snipped out with a few millimetres of parent root they can be grown on in a propagator for a week or two then potted up to become adults in a single season.

There is little that can be said regarding cultivation. Like other "Asiatics" the collected plants were given an open fibrous rooting mixture, protected from over exposure to direct sunshine and generally looked after. No departures from established cultivation techniques showed much merit, and the conclusion is that disease and not maltreatment is the cause of ills.

Dwarf shrubs are represented by two notable rhododendrons, *R. anthopogon* and *R. lowndesii,* both doing well now as mature plants. In addition there is a pygmy *Potentilla fruticosa,* from the Ladakh area of Kashmir, which has yet to flower but is obviously hardy.

The space allotted allows no more and at best this has been a racing commentary on ten years of fascinating cultivation. More information is on record in the recent A.G.S. Bulletins where portraits of the noteworthy introductions have been presented as a series.

Glaucidium palmatum 'Album'   (*Plate 53*)

Paris japonica   (*Plate 54*)

Patrinia triloba   (*Plate 55*)

Salix reticulata   (*Plate 56*)

Recent Narcissus Classification

JOHN BLANCHARD

Narcissus hedraeanthus

Gardeners who feel that botanists should not change long established plant names have awaited the publication of the various volumes of Flora Europaea with trepidation. For bulb enthusiasts Volume 5 is at last with us, and we can take a look at how it deals with the genus Narcissus. The changes proposed are not too sweeping, and on the whole favour "lumping" rather than "splitting". The result has not met with universal acclaim, but it is likely to be the best working guide available for a long time to come. Some may well wish to retain varietal or cultivar names to distinguish different forms or clones of the very variable species and subspecies. This is a decision for gardeners rather than botanists.

The increasing number of plant hunters visiting Spain and Portugal, home of the greatest number of species, often find identification within the genus to be difficult. The authors of Flora Europaea recognise the difficulties, but do not always offer final solutions. The account which follows is not intended as a botanical critique, but as a gardener's guide. It is not a key to identification. It is an attempt to list the currently accepted names (including those of some African species) and to indicate which should now be used for some plants well known in cultivation whose traditional names have been discarded. Where I have dared to be critical, it is as the result of limited study of plants observed in the wild and from cultivated collected plants.

Anyone wanting more detail must of course refer to Flora Europaea itself. For ease of reference I have closely followed the order adopted there, and the sections are printed in heavy type. The genus is divided into nine sections. These, at least, are readily distinguishable.

SECTION TAPEINANTHUS.   This is a new section created to accommodate within the genus Narcissus the plant previously known as *Tapeinanthus humilis*. It now becomes *Narcissus humilis*. Although lacking the corona which is characteristic of all other narcissi, it has long been known that Tapeinanthus has a close affinity with Narcissus. This is borne out by the fact that it has hybridised with *N. serotinus* to give × *Carregnoa dubia*. However, dubia means doubtful and the authenticity of this bi-generic cross is questioned. Carregnoa is placed in synonymy under Tapeinanthus in Flora Europaea and in Willis.

SECTION SEROTINI.   This section contains only one species, the autumn flowering *N. serotinus.*

SECTION AURELIA.   This consists of one species, the autumn flowering *N. broussonetii,* which is found only in Morocco and so does not appear in the European flora. I have not seen this plant in flower. The species differs from *N. tazetta* in having only a rudimentary corona.

SECTION TAZETTAE.   Here we have had some drastic pruning, leaving only four certain species in Europe. The most distinctive is the autumn flowering *N. elegans,* which has little more than a rudimentary corona of yellowish or brownish-green colour. It is said that the leaves appear before or with the flowers, but I have not successfully grown the plant. Not only is it difficult to flower, but in cultivation it tends to have seasons in which it makes no leaf growth at all and, at other times and for no apparent reason, to disappear permanently.

The major species *N. tazetta* covers most of the bi-coloured plants and is described with three subspecies. *Narcissus tazetta* subsp. *tazetta* has pure white petals and a bright to deep yellow corona. It comes from the western Mediterranean area, and now includes the dwarfer plant hitherto known as *N. patulus. Narcissus tazetta* subsp. *italicus* from northern and eastern parts of the Mediterranean region has cream coloured or very pale yellow perianth segments and a medium to bright yellow cup. It includes *N. ochroleucus. Narcissus tazetta* subsp. *aureus* has bright to golden yellow perianth segments and a deep yellow to orange corona. It comes from south east France, north west Italy and Sardinia. *Narcissus bertolonii* loses its identity within this subspecies.

Narcissus corcyrensis from north west Greece is listed, but as a doubtful species. It is similar to *N. tazetta* subsp. *italicus,* but has solitary flowers and narrow petals, and hybrid origin is suggested.

There are three subspecies of the pure white tazetta, *N. papyraceus.* Only the smaller size of the flower, diameter 20–25 mm, distinguishes *N. papyraceus* subsp. *panizzianus* from *N. papyraceus* subsp. *papyraceus.* Both are widespread. *Narcissus papyraceus* subsp. *papyraceus* has larger flowers, and these two subspecies have glaucous leaves and compressed scapes. By contrast *N. papyraceus* subsp. *polyanthos* has leaves which are not glaucous and scapes which are almost terete. The only locality given for this species is southern France, but it is naturalised elsewhere. *Narcissus pachybolbus,* which may also have green rather than glaucous leaves, is non-European from Algeria, Morocco and Cyprus.

Lastly there is the quite distinct *N. dubius.* This is a small plant, 20 cm high at most with up to six small white flowers to a scape. It is said to come from a comparatively large area of southern France and eastern Spain, but is scarce in cultivation. It is an interesting plant botanically. Although regarded as a true species of section Tazettae, examination of its chromosomes indicates possible hybrid origin between *N. tazetta* subsp. *papyraceus* and *N. requienii* (syn. *N. juncifolius*) of the section Jonquillae. Although it is an allopolyploid (2n=50 compared with the normal 2n=14) it will hybridise freely with species of other sections. The progeny are themselves infertile, but this is normal where hybrids occur between species of different sections. It is distinctive in being fertile.

SECTION NARCISSUS.   The single species, *N. poeticus,* is divided into two subspecies. *Narcissus poeticus* subsp. *poeticus* covers most plants in the range. *Narcissus poeticus* subsp. *radiiflorus,* from south central Europe and the western part of the Balkan peninsula, differs in having perianth segments with a more or less distinct claw, the corona tending to be shortly cylindrical rather than discoid. All the stamens are partly exserted, whereas in subsp. *poeticus* three are exserted and three included.

Plants from the borders of Switzerland and Italy which are intermediate between the two subspecies and were previously described as *N. verbanensis* are tentatively put into subsp. *poeticus,* as are those with smaller flowers and wider leaves described as *N. hellenicus* (or *N. poeticus* subsp. *hellenicus*) but with the comment that they "require further investigation".

SECTION JONQUILLAE.   The jonquils can be difficult to identify as the species tend to merge into one another. Flora Europaea concedes this but puts them all into the same section, so declining to follow Fernandes who separates some into a section Apodanthae. His Jonquillae have matt black, wedge shaped seeds with no strophiole (i.e. the swelling surrounding the hilum—the scar left on the seed where it was joined to the placenta) as in section Bulbocodii; Apodanthae on the other hand have spherical, shiny black seeds with a strophiole, as in the sections Pseudonarcissi and Narcissus. As this is such an unvarying character, I should have thought it a valid and reliable botanical distinction. Also, I think it likely that hybrids between Jonquillae and Apodanthae are normally sterile. This, too, would justify keeping them as separate sections. I will therefore depart slightly from Flora Europaea in order to keep them apart.

The true jonquils comprise five distinct species with no subspecies. The key in Flora Europaea distinguishes them only by measurements, which is surely unsatisfactory as they are so variable. *Narcissus jonquilla* is the largest, both in diameter of flower and length of hypanthial tube (this is that part of the corona tube set between the top of the ovary and where the six, petal-like perianth parts merge with the corona). It can have as many as five flowers to a scape. *Narcissus requienii* (the name by which, to the sorrow of many, we must now call the erstwhile *N. juncifolius*) is a smaller plant with rarely more than two flowers to a scape. In my experience it tends, more than most jonquils, to have the corona of darker colour than the perianth. *Narcissus willkommii* is a somewhat smaller and more slender plant, but I defy anyone to make a positive identification from the description in Flora Europaea. *Narcissus jonquilloides,* a plant for which it has always been difficult to find an accurate description (and the hunting for which I have looked upon as a botanical grail), now loses its identity within this species. *Narcissus gaditanus* is the most delicate of the jonquils and a challenge to those who try to cultivate it. Its leaves are almost filiform and usually longer (often much longer) than the scape. The flowers are tiny (as little as 10 mm in diameter) and the corona comparatively large in proportion. Perhaps some forms may be considerably larger. *Narcissus minutiflorus* is now included in this species. *Narcissus fernandesii* is mentioned as being in most characters intermediate between *N. willkommii* and *N. gaditanus* and "its taxonomic status is obscure". The plants which I grow are nearer to *N. jonquilla* than either. Lastly there is no mistaking the autumn flowering *N. viridiflorus* with its dull green, concolorous flowers.

All species of the discarded Apodanthae Section are neatly formed and horticulturally attractive. The yellow flowered species are, with one exception, from Spain and Portugal. *Narcissus rupicola* is single flowered with a wide, flat corona often but not always six-lobed. The Moroccan *N. rupicola* subsp. *marvieri* is similar but somewhat larger, and is said to have green leaves. All the other species in this section have glaucous leaves. The flowers of *N. calcicola* and *N. scaberulus* are similar. *Narcissus calcicola* is usually a little larger, but *N. scaberulus* seems to be quite a variable plant. Both have cup shaped coronas, not lobed but sometimes crenulate. The vital distinction is that the margin of the leaf of *N. calcicola* is smooth, whilst that of *N. scaberulus* is scabrid (i.e. rough). Perhaps the greatest surprise in the Flora Europaea revision is *N. cuatrecassasii*. This is the name now given to the plant introduced into cultivation by Christopher Stocken, who called it *N. scaberulus* (Grazalema form). It was later identified as *N. rupicola* subsp. *pedunculatus,* a name which I never found acceptable because its corona has the form of *N. calcicola* and *N. scaberulus* and is unlike that of *N. rupicola.* I have always thought that Stocken's name was quite appropriate, and I find it remarkable that the plant should now be given specific status rather than becoming, at most, a subspecies of *N. scaberulus.* The two white flowered species are both North African from the High Atlas. *Narcissus watieri* has sparkling white flowers, with a corona of the same form as *N. rupicola. Narcissus atlanticus,* known only from a collection of seed by E. K. Balls, is creamy white with a cup shaped corona.

SECTION GANYMEDES.   *Narcissus triandrus* is the only species in this section. Three subspecies are recognised, though admittedly "somewhat ill defined". *Narcissus triandrus* subsp. *pallidulus* is the name now given to the plants from Portugal and central, southern and eastern Spain, varying in colour from pale cream to bright yellow and usually with solitary flowers, less often with umbels of two or three. These were previously known as *N. concolor* and before that as *N. triandrus* var. *concolor.* The bright yellow form was at one time called *N. triandrus* var. *aurantiacus. Narcissus triandrus* subsp. *triandrus* covers most of the rest of the section, those from northern Portugal and northern Spain and white or very pale yellow flowers in umbels of two or three, sometimes more but less often solitary.

Finally there is *N. triandrus* subsp. *capax*, the name we are now to give the plant from the Îles de Glenans off Brittany, hitherto known as *N. triandrus* var. *loiseleurii* and before that as *N. triandrus* var. *calathinus*. The distinction between *N. triandrus* subsp. *triandrus* and *N. triandrus* subsp. *capax* rests entirely on the length of the corona, which seems very unsatisfactory, since specimens of the former from the Picos de Europa and the north west corner of Spain can measure up to the given dimensions of *N. triandrus* subsp. *capax*, yet these are not accepted as being the subspecies from Glenans. Frank Waley, that alpine plant enthusiast who travelled widely in Spain and Portugal looking at daffodils, believes that the ends of the leaves of *N. triandrus* subsp. *capax* always coil upon themselves, and this characteristic is pronounced in some plants found in northern Spain, but no mention of it is made in Flora Europaea.

SECTION BULBOCODII. Anyone trying to classify the hoop petticoats finds that they come in a bewildering range of shapes, sizes and colours. They vary not only from location to location, but also to a remarkable extent within a single population. So it is not surprising that very few species and subspecies are now recognised. Following Fernandes, who reduced many subspecies to the level of varieties, Flora Europaea now admits only three species in Europe, and only one of these is divided into two subspecies. This is *N. bulbocodium* itself, which covers all European yellow and citron-flowered forms except *N. hedraeanthus*. The main subspecies *N. bulbocodium* subsp. *bulbocodium* must now include those variations to which the following varietal names have been applied; *citrinus, conspicuus, filifolius, graelsii, nivalis, vulgaris* and maybe some others. The only other subspecies retained is *N. bulbocodium* subsp. *obesus*, which is said to differ in having leaves which tend to be narrow and procumbent rather than erect (or nearly so), corona narrowed at the margin and the perianth and tube less tinged with green. I suspect that it would not be difficult to find borderline examples between the two. The pale yellow *N. hedraeanthus* is quite distinct, with much broader perianth segments and no pedicel. *Narcissus cantabricus* is the only European white-flowered species. To what extent *mono-phyllus* and *tananicus* should still be regarded as subspecies is doubtful, as Fernandes includes *monophyllus* as a subspecies from both Spain and Morocco but it is not mentioned in Flora Europaea. *Narcissus cantabricus* subsp. *tananicus* is endemic to the High Atlas, but Maire's Key in "Flore de l'Afrique du Nord" is inconsistent with Flora Europaea. *Narcissus romieuxii*, which Fernandes (unlike Maire) regards as a species in its own right and not as a subspecies of *N. bulbocodium*, is entirely African. He considers those with pale yellow flowers are *N. romieuxii* subsp. *romieuxii* and those with white flowers *N. romieuxii* subsp. *albidus*.

SECTION PSEUDONARCISSI.   The trumpet daffodils are the main victims or beneficiaries (depending on whether you are a splitter or a lumper) of the revision. Pugsley's 27 species are now reduced to six or eight at the most, and only *N. pseudonarcissus* itself has subspecies. *Narcissus longispathus*, from a comparatively restricted area in the Sierra de Cazorla, is distinct with its long spathe and long leaves. *Narcissus pseudonarcissus* on the other hand, is very widely distributed indeed—as far north as England and as far east as Romania. Most widespread of all is *N. pseudonarcissus* subsp. *pseudonarcissus*, though absent from Portugal and southern Spain. *Narcissus pseudonarcissus* subsp. *pallidiflorus* from the Pyrenees and northern Spain has a more expanded and recurved corona and includes *N. pseudonarcissus* subsp. *macrolobus*. The white *N. pseudonarcissus* subsp. *moschatus* from the same area now includes the smaller plant previously known as *N. alpestris* and Pugsley's *N. albescens* and *N. tortuosus*. The strongly bi-coloured *N. pseudonarcissus* subsp. *nobilis*, largest of the trumpets, abounds in the Picos de Europa and also extends eastwards to the central Pyrenees and westwards into northern Portugal. *Narcissus pseudonarcissus* subsp. *major*, concolored and golden yellow, has swallowed up *N. hispanicus* and *N. confusus*, whilst *N. pseudonarcissus* subsp. *portensis*, similarly coloured but with shorter leaves and less expanded corona, remains distinct. The "Tenby Daffodil", *N. pseudonarcissus* subsp. *obvallaris*, is mentioned as a variant between *N. pseudonarcissus* subsp. *major* and *N. pseudonarcissus* subsp. *portensis*, closer to the former, which probably arose in cultivation and subsequently became naturalised. *Narcissus pseudonarcissus* subsp. *nevadensis,* endemic to the Sierra Nevada, is unique in this section for carrying up to four flowers on a stem. *Narcissus bicolor* presents problems because it was described from a cultivated plant. The differences between it and the wild plant described as *N. abscissus* are slight, and it seems that *N. bicolor* is the valid name although the final paragraph relating to *N. bicolor* casts doubt.

Turning now to that end of the scale which embraces the miniatures we are immediately confronted with *N. minor* and *N. asturiensis,* two species which are hard to differentiate precisely. We are told that *N. minor* has petals which are sometimes twisted, but those of *N. asturiensis* never are, and that only *N. asturiensis* has the corona constricted in the middle and expanded towards the apex. This would put into *N. minor* plants from Portugal which I have grown and which, from their size and other characters, I had always thought indicated they were a form of *N. asturiensis. Narcissus minor* now includes *N. nanus, N. provincialis* and *N. pumilus. Narcissus lagoi* is mentioned under *N. asturiensis.* It was described from a single collection made near Lugo, and has probably never been in cultivation. Frank Waley has searched for it there without success. Though it has larger leaves and a longer scape than *N. asturiensis,* it is regarded as probably a variant of it or even a hybrid. Finally there is the well known and quite distinct *N. cyclamineus,* which is shown as coming from north west Spain as well as from north west Portugal.

I am well aware that this article will not answer all the questions relating to the correct identification of Narcissus but, by airing the problems, I hope the gardener will understand better the taxonomic difficulties which face botanists.

New World Fritillarias

ROGER M. MACFARLANE

Fritillaria liliacea

Fritillaria is a genus of bulbs in the lily family that has enjoyed a great increase in popularity in recent years. Although many factors have contributed to this, the main one is probably the increase in our knowledge of the species in their native habitats. This has clarified the taxonomy, led to new introductions, and taught us a lot about the conditions under which they grow. In this respect we owe a great debt to the pioneering work of the late Admiral Paul Furse whose selfless energy and enthusiasm, and the knowledge contributed from his trips to Turkey, Iran and Greece in the 1960s, started the new wave of interest in Fritillaria which persists today.

There are about 110 species of Fritillaria distributed throughout the northern hemisphere; in Europe there are 25, in Asia and Asia Minor 65 and in North America 20. The N. American group, while rather small in number, is quite diverse and often local in distribution. In this article I will briefly describe the habitats of Fritillaria in N. America, and also what we might learn from these regarding their cultivation. The first part can be documented reasonably well—the second part is more speculative.

With few exceptions cultivation is a transient state which, without the infusion of new wild material lasts only for years, perhaps decades. In the wild, individual species have evolved over a long period by selection in the presence of particular kinds of pressures and competition. The result we see today is one set of optimized conditions—delicately balanced but stable over a long period (in the absence of human intervention). It is often remarkable to note what small changes in microclimate—a different exposure, soil type, plant competition etc.—can lead to the presence or absence of a given species. It should be stressed that long term survival demands preservation of natural habitats. For the N. American species of Fritillaria these habitats can be classified as Grassland, Woodland, and Alpine or Sub-alpine Scree. Ease of cultivation depends mainly on two factors: how far the basic garden environment (e.g. temperature, rainfall, soil) differs from that in the wild; how adaptable individual species are to other than optimal conditions. Even if the garden environment is suitable for some species it is not for others. Thus, the second factor is perhaps the more generally limiting one. Bear in mind always that there will be some species that are essentially impossible to grow well—my philosophy is to leave these alone. Here are some of the ingredients that make up a successful wild environment, and some suggestions for translating these into a cultural context.

Soils

These are always well drained, often stony or on sloping ground. An apparent exception is the "adobe" clay soil of the grassland species, which grow where the summers are the hottest. It does however have a large capacity to soak up water and to dry out gradually, thereby insulating the bulbs from rapid changes in temperature and moisture. This kind of soil is not readily adaptable to cultural conditions. A compost consisting of equal parts of loam, leaf-mould or peat, and coarse grit (not fine sand) with some bone-meal for long term nitrogen and phosphorus, has been found to be a good basic mix. Scree plants should have one part peat or leaf-mould and one of grit. Good drainage is of paramount importance. Slow release fertiliser pellets applied once a year seem to give good results.

Temperature, Moisture and Light

The basic requirement is for ample moisture in the growing season (in the wild this is provided by concentrated winter rains or spring snow melt), followed by dryness in summer to enforce dormancy and protect the bulbs from rotting. During dormancy the bulbs are usually encapsulated in hard soil, or covered by rocks or a leafy mulch. As a group I suspect they resent real desiccation more than most European or Asiatic species. The grassland and scree species need plenty of light or they become drawn, while those from woodland habitats prefer light shade. Species from higher elevations e.g. *F. pinetorum* and *F. glauca* are significantly more difficult in cultivation—perhaps because they need the cold, dry winter with ample spring moisture.

Raised beds are probably the best places in which to grow fritillarias. Here the drainage is well controlled and temperature and moisture are uniform. They should be in an open sunny situation away from very invasive tree roots or heavy shade. An alternative scheme which also works well is to use half barrels or similar large containers. These can be moved (with difficulty) to experiment with different garden situations. Pot culture can be successful but requires more attention to watering.

Competition with other plants

This is much more important in the wild where competition for resources can lead to adaptation to otherwise unfavourable conditions e.g. the retreat to hostile serpentine soils by some species such as *F. purdyi* and *F. liliacea.* Generally (unless weeds take over!) it is not a problem in cultivation. Compatible plants which are annual or withstand summer dryness can be usefully ornamental and keep surface soil temperatures down e.g. Nemophila, Eschscholtzia, Delphinium and some grasses. A less attractive alternative, but a more controlled one is to mulch with coarse (15 mm) stone chips.

What follows is a brief description of the N. American species of Fritillaria, grouped according to their habitat.

Grassland Species

Those found in this environment are Californian. They grow in the heavy clay soils of the coastal areas and the Central Valley. Most of the former habitats have been converted to farmland or built on, so that as a group this is under the most pressure for survival. The grassland species are the first to flower, starting into growth soon after the winter rains in October or November and flowering from February to April. Their soil dries out in the hot summer months, but the bulbs are protected from desiccation by their depth (often 20 cm or more) and the good insulation of the "adobe" soil. The bulbs consist of several large scales arranged loosely around the base of the stem; there are no rice-grain bulblets. Natural increase is therefore almost entirely by seeds which are produced by interclonal pollination. Most of their leaves are arranged in a basal rosette which helps them to compete for light with the native grasses. In cultivation a deep well-drained loamy soil suits them well. The easiest to grow are *Ff. agrestis, biflora, liliacea* and *grayana* from the mild coastal or near coastal regions of central California.

Fritillaria agrestis has unpleasant smelling greenish flowers flecked with brown inside. The nectary is linear and there are lamellar ridges on the inside of the tepals.

Fritillaria biflora is closely related to the above, and grows in more coastal areas. It has long deep-chocolate shining bells, and rather broad basal leaves.

Fritillaria grayana (syn. *F. roderickii*) has short campanulate flowers which are brown with white tips on the outside of the tepals and carried on 10–15 cm stems above a basal rosette of narrow leaves. It grows well from seed. The wild distribution is extremely restricted on the north Californian coast and there is an inland population with mainly cauline leaves.

Fritillaria liliacea has white open-campanulate flowers, a broader nectary and much reduced lamellar ridges inside the tepals. The leaves vary from quite narrow (ca 5 mm) to broad (ca 3 cm). It is an attractive species restricted to the vicinity of the San Francisco Bay and sadly much depleted by habitat destruction.

The next two species come from the hot Central Valley, again with quite restricted and depleted distributions. They are unusual in having pink or purplish-pink flowers.

Fritillaria pluriflora has forms with campanulate flowers and some with narrower tepals and more open flowers. As with *F. striata*, white forms are also known. The leaves are somewhat glaucous and with undulate margins. This is a very attractive species which has been in cultivation, though rarely, for a long time.

Fritillaria striata differs from *F. pluriflora* in having recurving tips to the tepals and fine purplish striations on the inside of the flower. In addition it has a very attractive scent.

Fritillaria purdyi is the last member of the grassland group, yet its habitat often is suggestive of a scree plant. It grows in stony soils— at low elevations these are infertile serpentines—and is found from about 100 m elevation to about 1500 m. It has glossy bells of green-ish white with fine purple veining.

Woodland and Chaparral Species

The rice-grain bulbs of this group are shallower than those of the grassland species (ca 10 cm) and grow in a more open soil so that their bulblets can be distributed by burrowing animals. Their habitats vary from semi-shade and clearings in oak, madrone, fir and pine woodland to more open locations among chaparral scrubland. Generally this group has smaller flowers, a racemose inflorescence and narrow to lanceolate leaves usually in whorls on the stem. Again the lowland species such as *F. lanceolata* and *F. micrantha* are the most tractable in cultivation.

Fritillaria atropurpurea is quite widespread at higher elevations of the plateau between the Sierra Nevada and the Rocky Mountains. It is characterized by linear, alternate to scattered foliage and flat to open-campanulate flowers of greenish brown. It is not widely grown and seems difficult to make happy. There are some good dwarf forms from S. Oregon.

Fritillaria pinetorum from S. California is closely related to the above but differs in its longer and broader canaliculate leaves and its bowl-shaped outward to upward facing flowers—a character it shares with *F. falcata*. It grows in well drained granitic soils and comes from high elevations where snow melt occurs in June. It appears to dislike warm wet winters.

Fritillaria lanceolata is a lowland species and the easiest to grow. It has broadly campanulate flowers with pronounced shoulders at the prominent nectaries. The flower colour varies from green through green/purple tessellated to almost uniform purple-brown. Triploid forms from the coastal regions of California have large flowers and are strong growers, but being sterile do not set seed.

Fritillaria micrantha, from the foothills of the Sierra Nevada, has a racemose inflorescence consisting of 5 to 20 green to purple flowers which usually do not show marked tessellation.

Fritillaria recurva is another Sierran foothill plant but with an extended distribution in the chaparral of S. Oregon and the inner coast ranges of N. California. The bright red and yellow chequered flowers are unmistakable and provide hummingbirds with copious nectar. The style is only divided about one-quarter of its length. This is the most showy of the N. American species, indeed of the whole genus.

Fritillaria eastwoodiae is intermediate between *F. micrantha* and *F. recurva*, and may have arisen as a hybrid between them. It has rather numerous, small flaring flowers of varying shades of red or with red margins to the tepals. It has a very restricted distribution in the Sierran foothills on serpentine soils.

Fritillaria brandegei is another very local species, this time from the southern Sierran foothills and Greenhorn Mountains. It is most distinct morphologically, having small green starry flowers and an entire style. There is very little experience with it in cultivation, but what there is suggests that it fails to persist for very long.

Fritillaria camschatcensis has very dark, almost black, flowers and glossy whorled leaves. It grows in damp northern coastal areas, often tidal estuaries, and dislikes hot dry summers.

Fritillaria viridea is the odd one of this group in not having a rice-grain bulb structure. In other respects it is intermediate between *F. lanceolata* and *F. micrantha*. It grows in serpentine chaparral in the San Carlos and Santa Lucia Mountains, and is quite rare in the wild.

Alpine and Sub-alpine Scree Species

This is a small group in which I include *Ff. falcata, glauca* and *pudica*. In the wild they have a winter snow cover to provide cold dry winters and wet springs. They are difficult in cultivation and rather shy to flower. Of the group *F. pudica* is the easiest to grow, and a very beautiful plant.

Fritillaria falcata grows on soft mobile serpentine scree slopes. It is probably the most difficult to grow and since it is scarce in the wild its bulbs should not be collected. Its glaucous sickle-shaped leaves resemble those of *F. glauca* and the upward facing bowl-shaped flowers are close to *F. pinetorum*.

Fritillaria glauca generally has yellow campanulate flowers, but a purple-brown form is known. Its name derives from its predominantly basal, glaucous leaves. Ample spring moisture is provided by the melting snow cover.

Fritillaria pudica is one of the most widespread species, and has a distribution and habitat similar to *F. atropurpurea*, but prefers more open places among sagebrush. It is sometimes found as a snow-patch plant flowering at the edge of melting snow. Under these conditions its narrow, clear yellow bells held in ones to threes above narrow basal leaves are a very attractive sight.

Propagation is basically by seed (e.g. AGS seed list), or by rice-grain bulblets which take about the same time (4–6 years) to reach maturity. Natural increase by bulb division in the non rice-grain species is slow. Seed-set requires cross pollination of different clones. Most of the rice-grain species have triploid forms which are sexually sterile but usually more robust and better "doers" in cultivation. In the early stages of establishing a species new to cultivation, wild material is needed. Although rather slow this is best done by seed for a number of reasons. Numerous plants will be obtained for experimentation, they will settle in better to local conditions and a variety of forms will be obtained. Most import-antly, many wild populations will not sustain repeated attacks by collectors. Because of the transience of many species in cultivation and our ultimate dependence on wild populations, we must act responsibly in this area. Support should be given to nurseries that propagate material locally, even if the cost is somewhat higher.

North American Woodland Plants

ALFRED EVANS (ED.)

Goodyera oblongifolia

How does one introduce the subject of dwarf plants of the North American woodlands? How can one even attempt to cover the vegetative conglomeration in the extensive forests of that vast country and say that they are to discuss the woodland-type flora? One's first reaction must be that the task is impossible. There are surely so many species and genera represented in this type of environment, there must be so many of them truly garden-worthy that at the outset even to make a selection must present problems. Fortunately this project can be brought within more manageable proportions when one indicates that the plants are to be segregated into those which are considered to be hardy and non-hardy— somewhat arbitrary divisions—and that it is only the hardy ones we are to be involved with here. Additionally we need only think of those which are recognised as being valuable and attractive to rock garden plant enthusiasts. After all we are not discussing plants with a view to growing them in our normal open situation-type rock gardens. No, our aim is to introduce some of them into those little copses or even partly shaded corners which are in every garden and sometimes cause problems, especially among amateurs who may be without knowledge of a plant's basic needs.

Fortuitously, as members of a world-wide club, and that is really the fraternity to which rock gardeners belong, we also embrace within our hobby that vast range of fascinating, ground covering plants which are true woodlanders. I have to admit that I am forever amazed at how certain plant species which favour, and by that I mean are comfortable, in an eastern state environment can also be found just as contented and established among the conifers on the western seaboard. Plants certainly are tolerant and adaptable. Aren't we lucky? While we may go to great lengths to encourage plants from specific environments to settle in our small gardens we must also be grateful and recognise that they, too, want to live. In fact it is astounding just how much they will tolerate and even flourish in a situation which is apparently quite alien to them.

I think that one of the first things of which one is aware when walking through woodland is that the soil on which we tread is quite different to what we term garden loam. In fact, in many instances, there appears to be little or no mineral content whatsoever, a neutral soil-less compost. The whole forest floor is made up of decaying vegetable matter to some depth, and our plants are either seeding themselves with abandon or are spreading through the top layers by means of runners or stolons. No spade or trowel seems necessary to free the plants, for by running one's fingers through the forest debris the plants may be lifted cleanly and without damage to their roots. This is purely an observation on how puffy and loose some forest bases are and in no way is it intended to be an inducement to go into these favoured places to collect wild species.

It could be an object lesson to us however when we are considering our own soil in relation to that in which woodland plants grow. It is quite apparent that a loam, high in decaying leaves, bark, peat, pine needles or well made compost must surely promise us our best chance of success.

I have seen a great many gardens. I have also observed a great many well-grown plants and in the case of certain alpines, I have noted outstanding specimens which can be termed better in health and floriferousness than their equivalents in nature. In the woodland though, I am not so sure that this is the case. So many woodland plants seem to grow luxuriantly in their own habitat, while in the garden, although they may be said to flourish, it is the backcloth, the grand setting, which invariably is lacking. Add to this the sheer volume of plant material in the wild, and compatibility, both of which are often very much a part of the complete picture. To see *Trillium ovatum*, *Linnaea borealis* var *americana*, *Clintonia uniflora*, *Goodyera oblongifolia*, *Corallorhiza mertensiana* and *Achlys triphylla* mustered round the base of a single "Douglas Fir", all competing successfully with each other and even appearing to benefit from each other's company, then we must be looking at nature in harmony.

The gardener must be satisfied with a much smaller canvas and yet I am sure we all know of some very clever and artistic cultivators who, together with a feeling for their subjects and also possessing a partly shaded site, make a very worthwhile attempt at portraying a woodland scene. And there are those who manage in some of the least encouraging of corners to assemble and cultivate interesting collections of these lovely garden gems.

It is really quite enlightening to see how many plants related and completely unrelated to each other by family form associations and certainly, while some plant groupings may not be possible in nature, because of distance or geographical barriers, they are often very effective in a garden. Members of the lily family for example are quite prominent all over the North American continent, similarly Ericaceae, and their continued, beneficial juxtapositioning brings forth many attractive pairings. In our gardens, where we are the artists, it is we who must be blamed if one species is allowed to dominate and in consequence suppress another.

In my mind's eye I can still see the yellow *Fritillaria pudica* in an open woodland, and encountered it again on another occasion when I was collecting seeds. The erythroniums, although plants of the open meadow, and here I refer to *E. grandiflorum* and *E. montanum*, both beautiful species, cannot be termed woodlanders and yet, in the centres of clumps of scrub and drifting quite happily through forest clearings, they looked happy and were flowering well. *Clintonia uniflora* spreading by runners will quickly colonise a small area and must be kept in check. It produces broad foliage at ground level and then decorates this with large white stars formed singly. It is quite different in habit to the much sought after *C. andrewsiana* which forms a tight clump from which the glossy green leaves appear. This is followed by a flowering scape carrying a number of bright pink flowers. Seeds are frequently formed and they are embedded in purplish fruits. Somewhere between these two species so far as habit of growth is concerned is *C. umbellata*. This plant is well named for the six inch high flower stem is topped by a dense umbel of creamy white flowers. It increases steadily, and, in spring, its pale brown developing buds can be seen erupting through the soil. Trilliums have been well publicised in recent years. This is as it should be for here is one of nature's quality genera. North America is the home of the bulk of the species, a few less decorative ones being Asiatic. If I mention only two here it is simply that to go further would merely be singing an old song and one often repeated. But surely every gardener would want to possess a specimen of *T. ovatum* and *T. grandiflorum*? The first is from the western side of the continent and the other from the east. *Trillium ovatum* is the first to flower in gardens in Scotland by a good three weeks and as it has an erect habit of growth one can look directly into the centre of the flowers. *Trillium grandiflorum* on the other hand is shy. It has a more graceful posture, hanging its head and forming a beautiful trumpet with its overlapping petals. Both are white flowered and are easily grown, and although the flowers are single there are forms which produce double blooms. *Trillium grandiflorum* 'Snow Bunting' has been awarded a First Class Certificate from the R.H.S. while *T. ovatum* 'Kenmore', also a double, is so rare that it has never been presented to the award-giving committee. One other form which must be mentioned is a very fine pink flowered selection of *T. grandiflorum*, it is listed as 'Roseum' and is not one which becomes tinged with pink as the flowers fade. It is a constant, delicately toned pink, even richer in bud. It may be worth adding that there are other species of high merit, such as *T. chloropetalum* with fascinating mottled foliage, which have their champions. The disporums, too, are useful plants and, especially in autumn when they are adorned with golden-yellow fruits, such as in the case of *D. smithii*, they are doubly welcome. Even in spring the long, narrow, creamy, bell-shaped flowers hang gracefully beneath the soft green young foliage. Other species are *D. hookeri* and *D. trachycarpum* which fit well into a garden scene. Of Streptopus there are at least two which are worth including, *S. amplexifolius* and *S. roseus*, the latter being a little difficult to establish. In passing I think I should just like to mention that the Chinese species, *S. simplex* with its white, dainty fairy bells is one of the most graceful plants I know. It would be a pity if no lily were mentioned and the one I favour here is *Lilium columbianum*. I have a lovely memory of it growing on the slopes of Mount Rainier. I never saw clumps such as we tend to plant in gardens but I think it looked better in smaller numbers where the stateliness of the individual flowering spikes could be seen to perfection.

Among the orchids there are some that gardeners like to try. A few of the cypripediums seem to be available from time to time and *C. pubescens*, *C. montanum*, *C. passerinum* and *C. acaule* come to mind. They have been tried by a number of enthusiasts but none is really easy. I know of no one, though, who has been successful with *Corallorhiza mertensiana*. Living as it does, saprophytically, and having no green coloured tissue, its needs are much more complex than mere gardeners can cater for. This, the "Coralroot", is most attractive when the slender stems are seen singly or in clusters, peppering a clearing. The intricately chequered foliage of *Good-yera oblongifolia*, the "Rattlesnake Plantain", is also a little tricky in gardens but it is not impossible. The tall slim spikes and small flowers seem to be in proportion.

Some of the wild gingers are worth including in a collection of unusual plants. They may take a little time to build up into colonies but their foliage is extremely decorative as in the case of *Asarum hartwegii* with its mottled leaved forms. In fact the foliage closely resembles that of some Cyclamen. *Asarum caudatum* is particularly intriguing, almost ominous, with its long tails spreading from the purplish-brown flowers. What a pity it is that the blooms tend to be hidden.

Aquilegias are suitable plants for partially shaded sites and *A. flavescens* with its pale yellow-spurred flowers brightens up a corner and blooms over a longish period. *Achlys triphylla*, "Vanilla Leaf", is really a foliage plant, at least to me, for it is the lovely broad, yet thinly textured, partly divided leaves which impress me most. Its spikes of small white flowers are quite attractive but they really comprise a very small part of the appeal of the species. On turning the leaves over the exposing of the lighter undersides adds yet another attractive feature. Does anyone successfully cultivate this plant in a garden? Another member of the Berberis family, to which Achlys belongs, is Vancouveria and although there are very few species the one I should give pride of place to in my garden would be *V. chrysantha*. I understand that it was the last of the species to be introduced into Europe. It has divided foliage, grows to almost a foot in height and bears a few bright yellow flowers on each stalk. It is completely reliable and can be depended upon to do well in a shaded spot. The Berberis, or really *Mahonia aquifolium,* "Holly Barberry", and the smaller *M. nervosa,* "Oregon Grape", are plants familiar to us, but to see them in their native habitats loaded with their glaucous blue fruits, makes us appreciate them very much more. Nevertheless, as garden plants they are invaluable, tolerating shade, and forming solid colonies of prickly, evergreen, well proportioned foliage.

A group of plants, perhaps not amongst the more showy of genera or species and belonging to the rockfoil family, Saxifragaceae, go under names which sound closely like anagrams. In fact the first two are! The genera to which I refer are Mitella, Tellima, Tiarella and Tolmeia. They are subdued and quiet plants fulfilling their rôle in nature and in gardens, often in dense shade, where brighter and more decorative genera would fail. They are herbaceous and in summer the soil is adequately covered by their rounded though sometimes irregularly edged leaves. Frequently they are hairy, and never could they be classed as firm favourites. However, *Mitella ovalis* carries small cream coloured flowers which on close examination reveal petals which are virtually cut to ribbons. It is worth looking at the flowers with a hand lens in order to appreciate their filigree pattern. Later, black seeds sit uncovered in shallow capsules. *Tellima grandiflora* on the other hand is taller, more robust, and carries a few hairy leaves on the flowering shoots. The petals in this case are red but also they are heavily fringed. *Tiarella wherryi* is very much in demand because of the manner in which it carries the multitude of tiny flowers in a column, giving a foam-like inflorescence. *Tolmeia menziesii* must not be ignored. After all it is named after Archibald Menzies, a Scot, and ship's surgeon who sailed with Captain Vancouver. It carries foliage on its flowering shoots but, instead of having normal buds nestling in the axils of the leaves, small plantlets develop and at a certain stage they become dislodged and then take root in the soil, so spreading the colony. This phenomenon has given rise to the common name "Youth on Age". Perhaps a little word of warning should be added here, which is that these plants can take over in a garden but with a vigilant gardener that need not cause a big problem.

No one could possibly tread woodland paths without encountering pyrolas and no one having seen them could possibly resist their attraction. Some have a world-wide distribution and yet only a few are ever seen spreading in a cultivated site. The round-leaved *Pyrola asarifolia* with its long slender spike of pink to red tinged flowers, never mass produced and so always admired, usually forms part of a complex vegetative ground cover. Its shoots travel underground, often appearing at some distance from where the centre appears to be. The aptly named *P. secunda*, so called because of the manner in which the nodding flowers all face the same way, carries its greenish flowers almost as tightly packed as pearls on a string. The annual, soft green leaves add brightness to a shady dell. I wonder just how often this same species has been admired during alpine flower trips to Europe? Perhaps even more so the single flowered Pyrola, or more correctly *Moneses uniflora*—how often has it caught the eye of the photographer? This dainty species with fully pendant open flowers nicely marked on the central parts of the petals, can be four inches high but usually it is less. The "Pipsissewa" on the other hand, Chimaphila, produces its blooms in clusters. The flowers are still wide open displaying the inner parts of the flowers prominently but in *C. umbellata* they are carried in a fairly regularly shaped head, the colour being pink, while in *C. menziesii* the inflorescence is less tidy but the more decorative blooms have white petals. These species are evergreen with toothed foliage which itself bears a purplish tinge. Very closely allied and, in a way, indicative of the difficulties that one meets in attempting to cultivate plants in this family, Pyrolaceae, is *Monotropa uniflora* or "Indian Pipe". Living as a saprophyte on decaying vegetable matter and without chlorophyll it would set the gardener a real problem if he were to try to include Monotropa in his collection. Lucky is he where this plant occurs naturally on his property and where little clumps of the white and pink stems and hanging bells erupt in the shelter of thinly canopied scrub.

The "Partridge Foot", *Luetkea pectinata*, is a plant of the mountains but on the fringe of some of the higher, thinner forests it is sometimes found. It grows well in a rock garden and can produce masses of creamy yellow flowers. These are tiny and are borne in short dense spikes, the whole flowering stem being no more than six inches high. The extremely fine foliage, almost fern-like, adorning the trailing, spreading, thread-like stems is pale green. It is a member of the rose family.

Trientalis latifolia is a very close relative of *T. europaea*, "Chickweed Wintergreen", but not everyone recognises that they are different enough to be made separate species. The delicate far-searching underground stems emerge from the soil at frequent intervals and it is then that the clear white stars adorn the carpet. One usually treads warily even although to miss crushing a few stems is almost impossible. *Linnaea borealis* var. *americana* travelling fast over the surface of a moist woodland floor, roots as it goes, the young rootlets quickly securing the long thin stems. From each of the opposite leaves further shoots develop and these in turn carry the delicately supported, twin, bright pink bells. It is not known as the "Twin Flower" for nothing. This slightly larger leaved variety is easier to cultivate than the originally described European species. It may interest readers to know that this plant shares the family Caprifoliaceae with "Honeysuckle".

One could question the advice of planting Phlox in subdued light and yet there is one species which responds well in a shady corner. Admittedly this must not be too dense, but where the soil and atmosphere are dry, a shaded site can be just the right place for *P. adsurgens*. The coral-pink flowers can completely smother the broadish, glossy, dark green leaves. There is a cultivar "Wagon Wheel" much in evidence just now but the narrow petals are not nearly so effective as a good, full-flowered selection from the species. Although tending to flower itself out of existence, it can be kept going in gardens by taking cuttings and rooting them in summer.

Vaccinium angustifolium var *alpinum* may not be a woodland species. It can most certainly exist very successfully on open hillsides in very exposed places and late in the season it can transform a whole area, setting it ablaze with its rich orange-red, autumn tinted foliage. I say "also woodland", for amongst the dwarf conifers as on high mountains such as Mount Washington, it forms much of the ground cover. I wonder, could it colour up as well in lowland gardens? *Gaultheria serpyllifolia* syn. *Chiogenes hispidula,* also belongs to the Erica family. It is well known by its common epithet, "Creeping Snowberry". Although the flowers on this minute, creeping sub-shrub may be relatively insignificant, the same cannot be said of the berries. When formed they are most conspicuous as round pearls punctuating the trailing wiry stems. *Epigaea repens*, the "May Flower" or "Creeping Arbutus", has a quality of flower and foliage which lifts a collection out of the commonplace. It is a woodlander all right yet on grassy banks, at least on banks of low mixed vegetation rising from roadsides, large colonies of this truly desirable plant can be found. The delicate pink tubular flowers are carried in clusters at ground level and can be so numerous that the bank becomes a haze of pink. Shelter from wind and direct sunlight is necessary in gardens in Britain lest the foliage turns brown and the plant suffers.

And to end, what better than to choose two highly ornamental species noted for their fruits. One, *Mitchella repens*, "Partridge Berry", forms mats in light woodland and, being completely prostrate, is useful as low cover in dappled shade. Although bearing attractive foliage, with the tiny, opposite leaves brightened by veins prominently etched in white, the impact of the plant is greater in autumn when the twin red fruits being fused together and still with the remnants of the flowers remaining give an impression of two dark eyes. It is not a plant which is known for its fruiting qualities in gardens, unfortunately, but in view of the fact that, like Primula, it suffers from heterostylism, i.e. bearing short and long styles on different plants, cross pollination with the other phase would appear to be beneficial. The "Bunchberry", however, *Cornus canadensis*, must be the bane of all gardeners. In some places it simply refuses to bloom, in others it flowers well enough, but I have yet to hear of anyone in Britain who can boast a crop of fruit on his *C. canadensis* as one sees in the wild. They can be bright scarlet and succulent and will light up most effectively when illuminated by a low sun. In addition the foliage, too, can be quite decorative and colourful as it takes on an autumnal hue.

As I said at the beginning of this article the North American continent is vast. It is also rich in the types of plant we like to cultivate and, bearing in mind the importance of plant conservation in the wild, there are quite legitimate ways of procuring stocks.

Plant Collectors Through the Ages

BRINSLEY BURBIDGE

The collecting of garden plants is one of the few human activities which have recently reversed the inexorable trend towards professionalism. With a few exceptions (the collection of dried herbarium specimens for scientific study is still in the hands of the full-time botanist) plant collecting has gone the way of carpentry, house decorating and plumbing: it is now very much a do-it-yourself activity. Consequently the age of the professional collector is, sadly, almost over: cheap, rapid travel has seen to that. The hills are alive with the sound of trowels hitting rock and the snap of camera shutters, or husband and wife teams preparing for next winter's round of "Plant Hunting in South Georgia" type talks to every horticultural society in the land.

This is by no means a frivolous view of plant collecting in the last fifty years. With very few exceptions all worthwhile garden plants now come into cultivation via the enthusiastic gardener/collector followed by a complex network of informal plant exchanges and the highly efficient seed exchange schemes organised by the ARGS, SRGC, AGS and other horticultural societies. Even sponsored collecting is now in amateur hands (probably where it is best served) with excellent expeditions such as those by Cheese and Watson to the Andes or Binns, Mason and Wright to Nepal, getting much of their finance from the sale of "seed-shares" to the garden enthusiast.

An unfortunate aspect of the swelling tide of plant diggers is that motives are sometimes less than pure and scruples something of a rarity. We can only guess at just how many rare plants (covered by current laws to protect endangered species) are smuggled through customs for financial gain or for the pride of possession. Poaching in national parks is not confined to rhinoceros horn for its aphrodisiac properties: I have watched a red-data-book lily being dug within the confines of a national nature reserve. I have also seen sack loads of wild-collected orchid pseudobulbs (in which international traffic is prohibited) being loaded on to a private aircraft for shipment to a less than scrupulous nursery. There are classic plant localities which have been stripped by successive visits from plant collectors: how many of these plants ever survived to flower in the collector's garden? Perhaps I am taking too serious a view of plant collecting in the last few years, but I don't think so. The summer holiday collector is never in the field at seed harvest time. Therefore he collects only living plants. This little-and-often predation on fragile plant populations is far more damaging than even the most business-like seed gathering from collectors of the past.

We will return to seed and plant collections later but now let us examine the work of just a few collectors in the light of the motives and pressures which put them in the field. We will restrict discussion as far as possible to collectors of alpine and herbaceous material.

It is easy to imagine that practical necessity (medicine and food) was the sole reason for plants being grown in early gardens and to expect that plants which we now grow only for their decorative qualities would be late introductions to horticulture. These ideas are rapidly dispelled if we go back to the writings of John Gerard (1545–1612), especially to his "Catalogue" of 1596. Incidentally, the reason for so many plant species having 1596 as their date of introduction to Britain is that their first mention was in Gerard's Catalogue. If we look almost at random through the pages we find *Daphne gnidium, Epimedium alpinum,* Phlomis, Clematis, Cistus, Philadelphus and Cornus species. We also find an extensive collection of European roses and a great many tulips which had arrived (deviously, via the pilfering habits of Busbecq, the Viennese Ambassador) from the garden of Suleiman the Magnificent of Turkey. Few of these plants were specifically sought: most were exchanges with other landowners and learned men although Gerard did employ a Mr William Marshall to collect for him in the Mediterranean region. Marshall has the doubtful honour of having sent the first prickly pear to Britain.

If we want more active plant collecting it is necessary to move forward into the seventeenth century and look at the work of the Tradescants, John and John, father and son, who viewed plants with love and with a trained mercenary eye. The market for their plants was the gardens of the wealthy and the royal. Between them they added an astonishing number of species to cultivation. John Parkinson's "Paradisi in Sole Paradisus Terrestris" of 1629 contains numerous references to plants introduced by the Tradescants including, of course, the "Spiderwort" in which their name is immortalised, Tradescantia. Parkinson also reveals a little of the possessive relationship between the seventeenth-century employer and his staff—"The spiderwort is of late knowledge and for it the Christian world is indebted into that painful and industrious searcher and lover of all natures varieties, John Tradescant (sometime belonging to the Right Honourable Lord Robert, Earle of Salisbury and then unto the Lord Wotton of Canterbury in Kent, and lastly on to the late Duke of Buckingham)".

The elder John made his initial collections mainly from European nurseries and then, in 1618 he went to Russia. Many trees resulted from this voyage including the first Larch to be seen in Britain. Rather disappointingly most of his smaller introductions could easily have been found had he journeyed north to Scotland. They include *Rubus chamaemorus* (the cloudberry), *Vaccinium myrtillus* and *Chamaepericlymenum suecicum* (syn. *Cornus suecica*). Two years later he went to the Mediterranean and brought back *Gladiolus byzantinus, Hypericum calycinum, Acanthus spinosus* and several sun-roses, *Cistus monspeliensis, C. psilosepalus* and *C. ladanifer*. John junior also visited the Mediterranean and gave us the ancestor of our stocks, *Matthiola sinuata* which he called "The Greatest Sea Stocke Gilloflower".

In 1626 the Tradescants set up home in Lambeth and established a "Closett of Rarities" (later to become the Ashmolean Museum) and an extensive nursery. John the elder was a shareholder in the Virginian company and owned land there. From Virginia we have him to thank for *Parthenocissus quinquefolia*, the Virginia creeper, as well as *Rudbeckia laciniata, Tiarella cordifolia, Asclepias purpurascens* and the first michaelmas daisy, *Aster tradescantii*. Later the Tradescants added *Dodecatheon media, Oenothera biennis* and *Lupinus perennis* to the list. These are just a few. The pages of Mea Allan's definitive "The Tradescants" provide excellent reading and a continual succession of surprises about just how many plants were already cultivated in Britain by the end of the seventeenth century.

The Tradescants illustrate the collecting methods of the initial phase of plant collecting which lasted until the middle of the eighteenth century. This phase was dominated by royalty and the landed gentry whose main aim was to improve the appearance of their gardens. This need was satisfied in two ways, firstly by gardeners in their employ who travelled by joining naval vessels and diplomatic missions, taking advantage of whatever opportunities

Cornus canadensis (*Plate 57*)

Corallorhiza mertensiana (*Plate 58*)

Cornus canadensis (fruit) (*Plate 59*)

Fritillaria camschatcensis 'Aurea'   (*Plate 61*)   Fritillaria recurva   (*Plate 62*)

) Cypripedium acaule   (*Plate 60*)

Fritillaria alburyana   (*Plate 63*)

Mount Cook   (*Plate 64*)

Notothlaspi rosulatum   (*Plate 65*)

presented themselves to collect plants. Sometimes even ships' captains were sufficiently enthused to collect plants. Secondly there was an ever-increasing number of nurseries both in Britain and on the continent (especially in France and Holland) which employed collectors, but mainly bought from one another and built up stocks of plants for sale.

The publication of Linnaeus' "Species Plantarum" in 1753 rationalised the naming of plants and gave a great boost to the second phase of plant collecting (which very much continues today): the gathering of plant material for scientific study. This frequently only involves the collection of dried herbarium material: few, if any, living plants or seeds being gathered. Into this category come the French missionaries. Perny, Farges, Soulié, David and Delavay. The last did recognise the garden value of some of his finds and sent some seeds to France, but for the most part these men only made Europe aware of the treasures of China and the Himalaya without satisfying the appetite they had whetted. We have to wait for Fortune, Wilson, Farrer, Rock, Forrest and Kingdon Ward before we see any significant introductions from this area which contains the greatest concentration of ornamental material in the world. With these collectors we see a change in the method of plant collecting, the gathering of seed rather than living plants.

It is very difficult to imagine why so little emphasis was placed on collecting seed before the middle of the nineteenth century. Were collectors never in the field long enough to note and mark a worthwhile plant and later to return for the harvest? Was the longevity of seed not known? I think not. Here we have something of a mystery which is not fully solved. E. H. M. Cox in his "Plant Hunting in China" advances one reason for the neglect of introduction by seed, the fact that a large proportion of plants sent home from China consisted of florists' flowers from Chinese nurseries which would not necessarily come true from seed. He adds " . . . that does not explain the neglect of seed collecting. Many species capable of being introduced in the form of seed were laboriously shipped home as plants." Plant losses on a six-month sea voyage were depressingly high, one survivor in a thousand being an early nineteenth century estimate by a Dr Livingstone, a surgeon in the East India Company.

The Treaty of Nanking in 1842 resulted directly in Robert Fortune heading for China the following year. His detailed instructions from the Horticultural Society included the collection of bamboos, tea, peaches, roses and many other woody plants but only chrysanthemums represented the herbaceous department. Fortune's collections include little to interest the rock gardener and it is only with the involvement in China of the nursery firm of James Veitch and Son that the humbler alpine and herbaceous plants began to reach Europe.

Veitch published "Hortus Veitchii" in 1906, a superbly printed and illustrated account of the history of their nursery. It includes excellent biographies of their principal collectors and an account of the plants they introduced. The second half of the book contains a list of all the species which first came into cultivation (largely from China but also from many other parts of the world) through their nursery. It makes fascinating reading with 34 pages of herbaceous and bulbous plants including *Codonopsis tangshen*, *Corydalis wilsonii*, *Delphinium cardinale*, *Meconopsis integrifolia*, *Ourisia racemosa* (syn. *O. coccinea*), *Platycodon grandiflorum*, *Primula denticulata*, *Tropaeolum speciosum*, *Lilium auratum*, *Thalictrum dipterocarpum* and *Cardiocrinum giganteum*. This is a tiny selection. E. H. Wilson and several other collectors are included under the Veitch umbrella, none of whom we have space to discuss in this short article.

The turn of the century saw a further change in the method of expedition finance. The garden syndicate came into being and the new generation of collectors divided their spoils between a number of subscribers. George Forrest was probably the most prolific and effective of this new generation. He collected seed on a scale never previously attempted with often more than a dozen native collectors working in the field at any one time. Forrest's period in China coincided with, and to some extent provoked, "Rhododendronmania." Consequently he was obliged to concentrate on the genus to which he was to contribute so much. From his letters home it is obvious that he rapidly developed a deep love of rhododendrons, although his collections show that he never developed a single-minded dedication to the group. His best introductions, plants such as *Gentiana sino-ornata* and *Paraquilegia grandiflora*, are too well known to need further discussion and in a way, they represent the survivors. Many of his fine introductions were passed over in the excitement given to the more glamorous rhododendrons. His seed collections came back to Britain in such quantity that much of it was never sown and if sown neglect often followed. *Gentiana georgei*, a superb plant similar to *G. sino-ornata* but with purple trumpets striped and spotted with green and with a green base, has never been properly established. The compact, fragrant, yellow-flowered *Daphne aurantiaca* hangs on in cultivation as a rather leggy shrub probably from Forrest's 1906 (F2115) collection. His field photographs show a beautiful compact bun covered with flowers. Has this form never been introduced or do the few people who possess it treasure it too much to pinch out buds at an early stage to produce a more compact habit?

Rock collected in the same area as Forrest, the two frequently working only a few miles from one another. They both employed the technique of bulk collecting. Reginald Farrer and Frank Kingdon Ward collected in a far more personal way, covering much of the ground and seeing most of the plants themselves.

In 1911 Kingdon Ward began his career as a collector in the pay of A. K. Bulley who was also largely responsible for putting Forrest in the field. Much the same area, S.E. Tibet, Yunnan and N. Burma were explored, to which Kingdon Ward added Assam and the Tsangpo Gorge in Tibet. Bulley was, by this time, getting more rhododendron material from Forrest than he could handle and issued instructions to concentrate on alpine and herbaceous plants. For Kingdon Ward, exploration always came first, with plants and plant collecting very much of secondary importance. Quality rather than quantity marks his collections which included *Lilium wardii, Primula florindae* and *Meconopsis betonicifolia.*

Kingdon Ward was a prolific writer and each journey was followed by a travel book aimed at an audience with a profound knowledge of the plant kingdom but among explorer/collector/writers of the period Reginald Farrer must surely take first prize. Farrer collected in Kansu, some five hundred miles north of Forrest and Kingdon Ward "territory" and explored, with E. H. M. Cox, the mountains of north Burma. Many of his collections were lost during the 1914–1918 war and he had scarcely begun to collect again when he died in Burma in 1920, while drying the year's seed harvest. Of all the collectors I have mentioned Farrer had the greatest influence on our gardens: not as a collector but as a writer. Almost single-handed he pulled British gardening out of the Victorian era and began the craze for rock gardens. He was also largely responsible for the feeling, reinforced by experience, that the best plants for rock-gardens come from the Chinese-Himalayan region. His books are almost too florid for present-day taste but his love of, and enthusiasm for, plants still show clearly through the verbiage.

Farrer died in 1920, Forrest in 1932 and Kingdon Ward more recently in 1958. Air travel began to have its effect on plant collections not because of the increasing ease of travel to far-off places but because of the speed at which it could be accomplished. Formerly at least a year had to be set aside for any major journey. Now a 3-month trip is very long indeed and a lot can be done in a fortnight, given proper advance planning. In a way the professional collector is now almost superfluous. The gardener is increasingly his own collector and his exchanges with friends allow the rapid penetration of new species and varieties into cultivation. Unfortunately, as was mentioned before, the trend is now towards the collection of plants rather than seed with a consequently greater effect on wild populations.

Plant collecting was a process requiring a large input of effort and frequently a considerable degree of discomfort and hardship. It still is. Probably only this will prevent even more people taking off on their summer holidays with a trowel. It is perhaps churlish to suggest that photography should completely replace collecting as it has done with animals in the game parks in Africa but, unless some voluntary reduction in plant collecting takes place, the plant lovers themselves will be to blame for the extinction of the species they love.

New Zealand Alpines

JIM LE COMTE

Treat as other coriacea

New Zealand, with a total area only a little greater than that of the British Isles, includes North and South Islands, the considerably smaller Stewart Island to the south and a number of minor islands. The two main islands, separated by the 22 mile wide Cook Strait, are mountainous with many wide fertile plains. The Southern Alps, as one would expect, are in the South Island and are well known for their wealth of alpine flowers and contain Mount Cook, 12,349 feet, the highest mountain in New Zealand.

My brief is to discuss some native alpines but it would require many hours of intensive reading to get an insight into the alpine flora of New Zealand. To condense this into an article of not more than 3,000 words is impossible but I have made a selection of some of my favourites in the hope I may mention some of universal interest.

Most visitors to New Zealand stop over at Mount Cook and stroll up the valleys, which are carpeted with *Ranunculus lyallii* in many places. It blooms from October to January depending on the type of season. Ranunculus is well represented in New Zealand and, apart from two species, all have yellow flowers. The only ones that are white are *R. buchananii* and *R. lyallii* and of these the latter is undoubtedly the better known. It has been adopted by Mount Cook Airlines as their emblem.

If I had to choose a single plant from the gems of this genus my choice would be *R. buchananii* with its glistening, pure white, often double-petalled blooms rising above crinkled, grey-green foliage. It is a high altitude species and does not survive long in cultivation. Although plants flowered for a time in my garden they rarely remained for more than three years. One of the easiest species to grow is *R. insignis* which can make quite a show with its bold, shiny, dark green leaves and brightly sparkling, yellow flowers that have the appearance of being coated with yellow enamel. Some species are masters of camouflage for, when out of flower, it would be difficult to locate *R. crithmifolius* var. *crithmifolius* because of the manner in which the colour and texture of the foliage blends in with its typical habitat. It is a plant of semi-stable screes and bare clay areas found locally in the drier, more easterly higher mountains of the alps. Apart from the rare *R. grahamii*, *R. sericophyllus* is the species found at the highest altitude and there it is located on ledges and in rock crevices. It forms low, neat mats of bright green foliage and bears firmly structured, almost sessile, golden blooms.

It is interesting to note that of approximately 50 species of Myosotis native to temperate countries, New Zealand can claim about 35 and most of them are endemic. Probably one of the best known is *M. macrantha*, a plant of moist, shady places and carrying blooms in a variety of colours from lemon, through shades of mustard, lovely shades of golden-brown, to chocolate and muddy purple. One of the most interesting facts about Myosotis in New Zealand is that there are at least two pulvinating (bun-forming) species and *M. uniflora* illustrates this well. It bears small, creamy-yellow flowers in early summer and is a plant of the wide shingle river beds of Canterbury and central Otago where it sparsely colonises the more stable areas. The other cushion-forming species, *M. pulvinaris*, is at home in the mountains of central Otago where it forms tight mounds of small rosettes. These are made up of numerous, soft, hairy leaves which in turn are often obscured by the mass of white flowers. It grows well in cultivation but fails to bloom as profusely.

Many New Zealand mountains, especially those in the vicinity of Canterbury, comprise large areas of scree and these unstable expanses carry a very sparse plant population of nine or ten different, yet highly specialised plants. Most of these are not found elsewhere. When not in bloom they are extremely difficult to find because the greyness of their foliage merges with the greywacke scree. For example, the slightly succulent, Elk-horn-like leaves of *Lobelia roughii* are small and barely rise above the stones. The small white, to partly reddish flowers are borne on short stems up to two inches long among the leaves.

One of the most unusual scree plants is *Lignocarpa carnosula*, (syn. *Anisotome carnosula*) with very finely divided, fleshy, grey-brown foliage among which the tiny white flowers are almost hidden in summer. Individual plants may have either all female flowers or both male and bisexual ones and by the time the seed is ripe the upper parts of the plant are dry and brittle and eventually break off at ground level. It is then left to the wind to blow this material about as a tumble weed, shedding seed around the screes. *Ranunculus haastii*, because of being frequently shorn off by the moving scree, usually only bears a single flower. Sometimes there may be two, very rarely three or four, so that when one sees a plant bearing seven blooms it is very unusual indeed. A plant with four fruiting heads is also a rare sight. I find this species almost impossible to grow in the garden. The scree dweller which is easiest, on the other hand, is *Cotula atrata*. The finely divided, pale glaucous-green to purplish foliage gives a feathery appearance and each stem bears a solitary button-like head of purple-black flowers. Against this the golden anthers stand out in a spectacular way. *Hebe haastii* is also found on the screes but is not rigidly confined to them. Despite this variation in habitat it has not proved to be easy in cultivation. Each stem seems to blacken off progressivly from the base until, finally, only a tuft of green remains at each tip. It is one of the more desirable hebes, being very attractive, neat and worth persevering with. *Notothlaspi rosulatum*, "Penwiper Plant", engenders a feeling of incredulity when seen for the first time. The rosette, itself, is striking for each successive layer of leaves is slightly smaller than the preceding one and the whole presents the effect of a low tight cone. The overlapping leaves are grey in colour. Notothlaspi is a biennial and the scented, creamy-white flowers are produced in the second year. Following on this the flat seed pods, packed tightly together and layer upon layer, scatter the seeds as the dried off plant remains tumble about on the scree.

The fellfields are the habitat of many unusual plants. A typical example is *Pimelea traversii* which in appearance closely resembles a dwarf Hebe. It usually occurs in more sheltered sites among shrubs and tussocks where it can grow into erect tidy bushes. The pimeleas are extremely floriferous and are commonly called New Zealand daphnes, a genus with which they have a close relationship. They both belong to the plant family Thymelaeaceae. The small endemic genus Pygmea (now more correctly Chionohebe) belonging to the family Scrophulariaceae, has six species. *Pygmea pulvinaris* is the best known of this small genus and forms grey velvety cushions but more often it is found in the shape of small buns. Professor Philipson, in "Rock Garden Plants of the Southern Alps", described it as "Soft as the back of a mouse, and often as small". It is virtually covered in bloom in early summer and during that time rivals the finest European androsaces. When not in flower, the cushion-forming species are sometimes confused with Myosotis species of similar habit.

Haastia sinclairii can often be traced growing in the fellfield debris. The sprawling branchlets have upward curving tips that protrude from among the stones and are clothed in long white hairs but underneath that soft silky furriness there is a normal green leaf. It is the most widespread of all the haastias but is almost impossible to cultivate under normal conditions. On the fellfields and more stable screes one may find *H. recurva*, a species with a much more restricted distribution. It is often seen as broad mats of vegetation, the branches radiating from a central rootstock. It is just as felty and no less intractable than *H. sinclairii* but here the silky hairs are buff. This makes the plants difficult to see until one is almost on top of them. If one were to examine closely the terminal points of the shoots the silky covering is then quite apparent.

A desirable species and certainly the most famous is *H. pulvinaris* and although attractive when merely twelve inches across, I have seen plants several feet in diameter on the Blackbirch Range, Marlborough. These ancient plants are composed of a multitude of branchlets, each terminating in a shoot as thick as a man's thumb. They pack tightly to form a mound. Buff coloured hairs completely obscure the leaves and when handled are soft and velvety to touch. It is a plant of high crags where it is best left alone, for collected plants will almost certainly die.

Also growing on several Marlborough mountains, as well as some Westland mountains, is *Raoulia bryoides*. This is the smallest of the "Vegetable Sheep" which may even after the passing of a great number of years seldom ever exceed 18 (eighteen) inches in diameter. To those unfamiliar with Raoulia, it is very difficult to determine the differences between the species. However, Mrs Margaret Bulfin of Botany Division, DSIR, Christchurch did some research on Raoulia* and published a paper that makes it easier to identify *R. eximia, R. mammillaris* and *R. bryoides*. The key character is the arrangement of the hairs on the leaves and for this one requires a hand lens.

Raoulia mammillaris is similar in size to *R. bryoides* and is abundant, locally, especially in areas of mid-Canterbury. I find these two species fairly easy to identify by colour and general

* "Cushion Raoulias of Canterbury", Canterbury Botanical Society Journal No. 6. 1977, Page 27.

superficial appearances. *Raoulia bryoides* has a distinct silvery-blue shade whereas *R. mammillaris* is silvery-green. In both species the terminal points of the leaves are visible, this character being reminiscent of the tiny rosettes seen on encrusted saxifrages. Apart from the difference in sheer size, *R. eximia* differs in that the terminal points of the leaves are not visible, being clothed in silky hairs. The rosettes are also larger. On Mount Hutt, and on a few other mountains in Canterbury, *R. mammillaris* is found with *R. eximia*, considered the largest species, and certainly one with the widest distribution. It forms dense colonies in some areas and from a distance one can be excused for thinking that one is seeing a flock of grazing sheep. The mounds of vegetation, often six feet or more in diameter, and certainly very old, are made up of myriad, tightly packed rosettes, each being the terminal point of a thin branchlet. Moreover, the surface of the hummocks is so firm and hard that if rapped with the knuckles it gives off a sound similar to that of wood. I remember helping to measure a particularly fine specimen and it was 14 feet long. When growing in the vicinity of and over rock, *R. eximia* hugs the stone so tightly that both appear to be welded together. It is extremely difficult to introduce the blade of a knife between them. *Raoulia youngii* is found on rocky peaks and forms small loose cushions. It has relatively broad leaves covered in silver-grey wool, with flowers similar to the daisy-like blooms of *R. grandiflora*. *Raoulia buchananii* is a plant of the southern mountains of the South Island and is quite distinct. Being green in colour the effect is not so striking and although sometimes forming tight hummocks it usually spreads like mats, taking on the undulating shapes and contours of the rocks on which it encroaches. Occasionally one comes across bi-generic hybrids between Raoulia and Leucogenes where the two overlap. Hybrids between Raoulia and Helichrysum are also known.

Leucogenes, known universally as the "New Zealand Edelweiss" is claimed, especially by New Zealanders, to be superior to its European namesake. I have seen some very fine specimens of *Leucogenes grandiceps* on many mountains and they are worthy of a place in any alpine garden. Not being parochial, I must here say that I consider the North Island "Edelweiss", *Leucogenes leon-*

topodium, to be an even lovelier foliage plant and more floriferous in cultivation.

Hectorella caespitosa is a true plant of the high mountains and is quite common in the tundra tops of central Otago mountains. It is very compact, appearing smooth even although composed of numerous individual rosettes. The sessile, often unisexual blooms are cream coloured and are produced in masses. It can be grown in gardens but judging from my own experience, it loses its closely shorn appearance when removed from the high hills.

Another rock garden plant which is much sought after is *Pentachondra pumila*. This is a beautiful, tiny shrub with small, darkish-purple leaves and white flowers, and in late summer it is usual to see a profusion of bright red berries. It is interesting to note that because the berries take a year to develop, both flowers and fruit are most often seen together. This species rarely exceeds two or three inches in height and slowly spreads to form a cushion or mat. Although not quick to establish, it usually settles well in gardens and gradually develops into a mound of narrow-needled vegetation.

Phyllachne colensoi is a high alpine which can be abundant in damp places and moist hollows. Its domes of vegetation are prominent because they are a bright shade of green. *Phyllachne rubra* is from the southern mountains of South Island and has a more restricted distribution. It is easily distinguished from *P. colensoi* by the club-like swelling on the end of each tiny leaf. Both species have white flowers and these are in such profusion that the leaves are frequently hidden.

Over the last ten years my chief interest has been Aciphylla but straight away I have to acknowledge the fact that they may not be everybody's favourite plants. Because of this I shall mention only a few although the number of species known from the as yet unpublished revision of the genus* is about 45. One of the most spectacular of those which are dwarf is *A. dobsonii*. It grows at about 6000 feet in the mountains of the southern part of South Island. Its bronze coloured compound leaves form rosettes which in time

---

* Ed. note. Allan lists close on 40 species of Aciphylla and it will be interesting to see how this number increases following the new revision by DAWSON & LE COMTE.

become tightly packed into perfect, rounded domes. The creamy-white, snowball-like flowers stand out dramatically against the rich colouring of the rigid foliage. Of almost identical habit, but in this instance with simple leaves and of even smaller stature, is *A. simplex*. I have seen particularly fine, well flowered specimens on the Old Man Range. Both these species are hard, prickly and stiff to the touch. *Aciphylla crosby-smithii* is a similar type of plant, although the leaves are not so bronze, and to me it is also very attractive. Although plentiful in west Otago, its distribution is quite limited. The rosettes of *A. congesta* are very symmetrically arranged and although each rosette is only three to four inches across, the overall plant size is much greater when they merge together. The stiff, dark green leaves are perfect foils for the typical umbellate head of creamy flowers. The sheath and midrib of the leaves are purple while the tip of each segment is reddish. When surrounded by large mats of the silvery *Celmisia hectori*, the effect can be dramatic. Albeit similar to a degree, *A. spedenii* is a trifle smaller in stature than *A. congesta*. The foliage is glaucous-green and the new growth has a grape-like bloom but to add to its effectiveness as a foliage plant the tip of each segment is pink. This genus is dioecious, which means that male and female plants occur and in most cases the male inflorescence is by far the showier. *Aciphylla hectori* is quite a different plant being much smaller than those already mentioned. It has stiff, dark green, strap-shaped leaves of barely two or three inches and these form a loose basal rosette. The six to ten inch long inflorescences are golden yellow on male plants but are much darker in the case of the female. *Aciphylla lecomtei*, discovered in the southern mountains, has only recently been named. It, too, forms mounds of symmetrical, dark green rosettes and the showy creamy-white inflorescence is eight to ten inches high. It is proving a good garden plant and is easily cultivated. Up until recently it was erroneously called *A. similis*, a species which is not known to occur south of Arthur's Pass. While an official description for this new Aciphylla was pending it was tentatively called *A.* 'Otago', and under this name seed was distributed to rock garden plant societies. It has also been dispatched as *A. similis* by some donors from the southern part of South Island. The two species are easily separated;

the leaves of *A. lecomtei* have four pairs of leaflets while in typical *A. similis* there are five to ten pairs.

Anisotome is a genus of many species closely allied to Aciphylla but not all are attractive. *Anisotome haastii*, with its delicate, fern-like foliage and large heads of creamy-white flowers, is at its best only in damp positions. *Anisotome pilifera*, on the other hand, inhabits rock crevices and cliffs. It is larger than the previously mentioned plant, with coarser, much less divided foliage which has a glaucous tinge, and is spectacular when seen in bloom.

No programme on New Zealand alpines could be termed comprehensive without the inclusion of Celmisia. According to Allan almost sixty species are endemic to New Zealand and although some may be difficult in cultivation others, many of which are truly garden-worthy, are easy to grow. Some are rare while others are little known, and *C. macmahonii* var. *hadfieldii*, a cushion-forming species restricted to the Richmond Range in Marlborough, can be placed in both categories. It seems to prefer the shelter afforded by over-hanging rock ledges where its attractive silvery coloured silky rosettes are protected from the wet. *Celmisia cordatifolia*, a rare alpine species restricted to the same range, is in danger of extinction through the ravages of wild goats. It is known to grow only in rock chimneys or on shady ledges in deposits of peaty humus. The shape of the leaf is so pronounced that it occurs to me that it would have been more appropriate to have given it the specific name of *sagittifolia*. The true beauty of this plant is revealed when the leaf is turned over and the thick velvety layer of reddish-brown fur is displayed. Its particular requirements in the wild do not appear to be too difficult to provide in cultivation but even with much care, it has not yet been possible to keep this species for more than four years, whereas its even rarer variety, *similis*, which I believe to be a standardised hybrid between *C. cordatifolia* and *C. spectabilis*, is not quite so difficult. *Celmisia philocremna* was discovered only a few years ago in the Eyre Mountains and up until now has not been recorded from anywhere else. As the name suggests it is a crag dweller and its habitat can be reached only after a long and arduous climb. Quite unlike any other species, it has small rosettes of stubby and stiff, dark green, leathery leaves. The leaf margins are rolled and older plants may form into cushions.

The white daisy-like flowers are held on short sturdy stems and these in turn are covered in a woolly substance. This is most effective. Most alpine gardeners, be they beginners or experts, are familiar with the ubiquitous *C. coriacea*. Unfortunately I must now record some unpopular news, which is that one must now recognise it by another name. The International Code of Botanical Nomenclature states that the first name used when describing a species is the authentic one and during research, Dr David Given of the Botany Division, DSIR, discovered that the specific epithet, *coriacea* was applied to another taxon long before our popular plant received recognition. And so our much admired member of the genus Celmisia, and actually the one adopted by the Canterbury Alpine Garden Society as its emblem, has been renamed *C. semicordata*. The previously unnamed bronze-leaved form from the central Otago mountains now becomes *C. semicordata* subsp. *aurigans* while the extremely silvery-leaved variant until recently referred to as *C. coriacea* var. *stricta* becomes *C. semicordata* subsp. *stricta*. The specific name, *coriacea*, was first used by J. G. A. Forster in 1786 for the plant we know as *C. lanceolata*. This attractive foliage plant must revert to its original name, i.e. *C. coriacea*. The leaves are broad and bronzy-green in colour but are further embellished with a conspicuous orange stripe along each midrib. *Celmisia coriacea*, (syn. *C. lanceolata*), grows in the Fiordland area in the south west corner of South Island but it also extends into the west Otago mountains.

Finally and with a view to whetting the appetites of plant enthusiasts I shall end those notes by introducing a new plant. It is *Clematis marmoraria* and it is known only from Mount Hoary Head and Mount Crusader in Nelson. Above the treeline, the Clematis grows in crevices and among the semi-stable rocks and stones of these marble mountains. It was described by Dr Barry Sneddon of Victoria University, Wellington. *Clematis marmoraria* forms a compact mound, two inches high. The small leaves are much divided and unlike many of its sister species it neither climbs nor clambers over shrubs but slowly increases in width by means of underground stolons. Flowering in the wild occurs in early December but during October in cultivation. The creamy flowers are prolific and completely obscure the plant. I predict a big future for this plant once seed becomes available and if ever a pan of *C. marmoraria* in full bloom is displayed on a show bench I feel certain it will be awarded first prize.

There are many more beautiful and unusual alpine plants of New Zealand and although they lack the colour of their European counterparts they more than make up for it in foliage and form. Because of lack of time and space available, I am unable to share them with you but I hope my selection will encourage those who have still to discover the delight in cultivating plants from my country. I predict that many more will come to have a place among the choice plants cultivated in rock gardens. Many are already known to New Zealand botanists but not to gardeners and surely *Clematis marmoraria* is not the last treasure awaiting discovery.

Tasmanian Plants

KEN GILLANDERS

Wittsteinia vacciniacea

The impression many people have of Australia is of vast open spaces, sheep stations, surf beaches and plenty of sunshine. This concept is true but down in the southern part of the continent, several small areas are truly alpine. The Great Dividing Range, which starts in north-eastern Victoria and extends up through New South Wales into Queensland rises to an altitude of over 2100 m in New South Wales and Victoria and has about 984 sq km which may be termed alpine. These areas occur on mountains of 1530 m or more, beneath which are rather dry Eucalypt-clad slopes. The alpine regions consist mainly of extensive herb fields often intersected by small streams and sphagnum bogs. The general appearance of these mountains is not rugged but is one of weathered rounded tops, sweeping valleys and plains. The other alpine territories occur in Tasmania, an island of 68,000 sq km, due south of the mainland. Its latitude is 40′–43′ south and it is in the path of strong prevailing westerly winds, known as the "Roaring Forties". It is very mountainous and 6400 sq km is classed as snow country. However, a much smaller proportion of this could be termed alpine. Tasmania's highest mountain is only 1600 m high but there are many exceeding 1400 m. Here the alpine areas are more rugged with large rock formations and precipitous drops from many peaks. Glacial action is very apparent and a great many lakes and tarns are found throughout the island. Rainfall is very varied, being 350 cm per annum on the west coast and below 38 cm on the east. Most mountain regions receive no less than 152 cm. Soil in all the alpine slopes is acid, and this is particularly so in Tasmania where a pH of 4–5 would be average and often is below this. Most soils are formed from sandstone or quartzite but some are of volcanic origin such as on Mount Field and in the Hartz Mountains which are dolerite. Soils in Victoria and New South Wales are generally derived from granite or dolerite and are not peaty like those in Tasmania. The climatic conditions on the higher mountains of Tasmania are very harsh and the strong cold winds have caused many plants to adopt a compact cushion-like habit to survive. They give the appearance of being mounds of moss but in reality are dwarfed shrubs. I should like to devote the rest of this article to describing some of the more interesting species.

Abrotanella, Compositae, is of sub-antarctic distribution, the two species found in Tasmania, *A. forsterioides* and *A. scapigera*, being endemic. *Abrotanella forsterioides* is the most common cushion plant found on our mountains and the easiest to cultivate. It forms large dense cushions, sometimes up to 200 cm across and 30 cm deep. These are so hard that they can be walked on without leaving an impression. It occurs on mountain summits and moors in open moist positions, around small tarns and in bogs. Soil is practically non-existent in many of these areas, the growing medium being a very acid black peat. The flowers are extremely small and insignificant, the beauty of the plant being in its form and deep green rosetted foliage. It is commonly called "Cushion Bush". In cultivation, it grows very easily in an acid soil mixture to which has been added a good proportion of peat. In cool climates, it can be grown in full sun if kept well watered. It propagates very freely by dividing the rosettes, each of which should have several long thong-like roots. There are several bun-forming plants widespread in our mountains. Several genera tend to coalesce such as Nertera, Pernettya and Coprosma.

Donatia novae-zelandiae, Donatiaceae, is superficially very similar to *Abrotanella forsterioides* when not in flower. It forms cushions up to 90 cm in diameter which are very hard and dense. However, I have noticed that if by any chance the cushions of either species are damaged, they are at the mercy of the elements. Frost, water and wind fret them away and gradually destroy them. The flower of Donatia is a five sepalled cup of pure white set tightly amongst the foliage. This species is also found in New Zealand. The only other known species, *D. fascicularis*, occurs in South America. Cultivation is as for Abrotanella but it appears to be a more difficult plant in cultivation and is much slower to grow. It may be divided but not too severely, and does seem to sulk before growing away.

Phyllachne colensoi, Stylideaceae, is also found in New Zealand but in Tasmania is far more restricted than the other cushion-forming plants. It prefers exposed feldmark and open moors at about 1200 m, growing in peaty ground between rocks. Its very bright, yellow-green foliage distinguishes it from its neighbours and it seldom exceeds 50 cm in diameter. The creamy yellow 5–6 petalled flowers nestle in the foliage and are so abundant that they almost obscure the plant. It responds to cultivation quite well and will divide easily as plenty of roots develop from each rosette.

Pterygopappus lawrencei, Compositae, is a Tasmanian endemic and is almost always found in association with one of the species already mentioned. The light glaucous green rosettes are densely covered in fine matted hairs. Although the foliage is softer than Donatia and Phyllachne it still forms a very dense hard surface. The flowers are rather insignificant. Although it will grow quite well in cultivation, the plant tends to lose its firm compact form. However, I feel that this could be overcome by careful watering and by selecting the correct position. It divides easily and grows away quite well.

The genus Dracophyllum, Epacridaceae, is confined to Australia, New Zealand, New Caledonia and the Antarctic Islands. There are two species endemic to Tasmania.

Dracophyllum minimum is very similar to Donatia and Abrotanella when not in bloom. The white flowers are quite sessile and the corollas comprised of narrow tubes with five spreading lobes. While the others tend to send many roots down through the moist decaying matter in the centres of the cushions, the rooting system of this plant develops one central root. This makes it a much harder plant to propagate, as it cannot be divided. I have not tried cuttings but if it is anything like the other dracophyllums it will be most difficult. Its cultivation is similar to that of the other cushion plants.

Dracophyllum milliganii is quite variable, ranging in height from 15 to 90 cm. However, the average height is generally 30 to 45 cm. It forms a deep rooting central root system and although forming offsets, these never develop roots. The inflorescence has persistent bracts from which the clusters of white flowers appear. The reddish bracts and stems enhance the flowers. Its habitat varies greatly from exposed feldmark to sheltered valleys in the south-west of the state. Seed is the only method of propagation and this must be sown very fresh. It requires a deep peaty moist medium in which to grow, and regular watering.

Also in the plant family Epacridaceae is Trochocarpa. It is confined wholly to Australia. There are four species endemic to Tasmania—one quite suitable for the rock garden. This is

T. thymifolia, a rather dense shrub with small dark green foliage, as its name implies. In summer the small clusters of crimson bell-shaped flowers appear on the terminal shoots. The bluish-purple fruits are very persistent and are frequently displayed on the plant at the same time as it is in flower. The shrub will grow up to 90 cm in its natural habitat but generally it does not reach this height in cultivation. It grows amongst boulders on exposed positions on mountain summits and also in lightly timbered sub-alpine forest. It is very slow growing in cultivation but it may be sited in either sun or semi-shade. Cuttings, although difficult, will give a fair percentage strike. Seed is slow to germinate and possibly a treatment of the seed coat may help.

From a very restricted locality in southern Victoria "Lilacberry", *Trochocarpa clarkei* is known. It is a low creeping shrub up to 20 cm. The lilac fruits can be 1 to 2 cm in diameter and appear in clusters. It prefers an open position in stony well drained soil. I have not tried to propagate this species from cuttings but rooted pieces can be detached. Cultivation is as for *T. thymifolia*.

Widespread in alpine areas in Victoria, New South Wales and Tasmania and also occurring in New Zealand, *Pentachondra pumila* or "Carpet Heath" forms dense mats up to 120 cm across. It is found only in open exposed positions on the higher mountains in peaty acid soils. The white flowers which appear in summer are greatly enhanced by the large red fruits persisting from the previous season. Some of these flowers are extremely long lasting as they remain on top of the fruits till they are ripe. Pentachondra is best grown in a sunny open position and is rather slow growing. Pieces can be divided and will slowly grow away. I have not tried cuttings or seed of this species.

The last member of Epacridaceae that I will mention is *Wittsteinia vacciniacea*, "Baw Baw Berry", which is endemic to the Baw Baw Range and two other mountains in southern Victoria. There is still speculation as to whether this plant should be included in Ericaceae or Epacridaceae. This suckering shrub grows around boulders and *Eucalyptus niphophylla* in peaty debris. The leaves and stems are quite fleshy. The flowers are a greenish yellow and are followed by round, pale green fruits flushed red in the autumn. This plant is quite easy to cultivate in varying degrees of shade in a peaty soil. Cuttings strike very readily.

From Epacridaceae I should like to move to Ericaceae. There are very few members of the genus in Australia and, of the four that are found in Tasmania, three are endemic. The fourth—*Gaultheria depressa*—also occurs in New Zealand. *Gaultheria hispida* is very widespread in Tasmania, growing in rain forest, on rocky mountain sides and right down to sea level in the far north and on the west coast. It is a great coloniser of steep road cuttings on the west side of the Island, and during April and May presents a beautiful display, with bunches of large glistening white fruits. On these perpetually damp and often permanently shaded sites, it grows in clay and alluvial gravel with great vigour. Plants within the dense rain forests are rather straggly and will reach 180 cm but in the open they are more compact and 60 cm is an average height. The white flowers are borne in terminal racemes and appear in late spring. Seed germinates quickly and easily and provides the best method of increase. Cuttings will also strike.

Possibly better known in cultivation in the United Kingdom than in Australia is *Pernettya tasmanica*, a delightful prostrate shrub which has its main stronghold on the central plateau at an elevation of 1000–1350 m. It is said to occur also on the west coast down to sea level. The central plateau is very open and windswept and one of the coldest places on the Island. Here *Pernettya tasmanica* grows abundantly, creeping amongst boulders and through cushion plants such as Abrotanella. The small white, bell-shaped flowers can be easily missed, but the fruits that follow are most spectacular and vary in colour from rich red through pink, creamy yellow to white. They do not appear to be food for native animals as they stay untouched on the plants for a long period. The root system on old plants is very extensive and goes very deep into rock crevices. Seed germinates with ease and cuttings strike quite well. It makes an ideal plant for a pan, appearing to fruit best when well established and possibly root bound.

Another member of Ericaceae is *Pernettya lanceolata* a creeping shrub spreading by underground shoots to form extensive colonies. I have only recently seen this plant growing in nature and it appears to be rather rare. This colony was growing at 1200 m on a rather dry northern slope near the summit of Drys Bluff which is on the northern side of the central plateau. It was growing in open

Eucalypt forest in association with *Cyathodes parvifolia, Lomatia tinctoria* and low bracken, the soil being gravelly and of volcanic origin.

Members of Liliaceae in Tasmania are neither numerous nor bulbous but several are rather spectacular and are found in alpine zones. The genus Milligania has five species which are all endemic to Tasmania. They all enjoy a deep, peaty, acid soil with abundant moisture and are found on wet moors, around tarns and among boulders on mountain sides. *Milligania densiflora* is the most plentiful. Its flowering scapes reach up to 60 cm and are covered in hairs. The flowers are generally white but occasionally pink variants are found.

Slightly smaller in growth and foliage and with a silver indumentum beneath the leaves is *M. lindoniana*. The flowering scape reaches to 35 cm but more often it is only 10 cm. The white flowers have crimson ovaries which greatly enhance the beauty of the plants.

Now rather rare, since its main habitat was destroyed when Lake Pedder was flooded to form a larger dam for hydro electric power, *M. johnstonii* is the baby of the genus. The short rosettes of foliage hug the ground and the sweetly scented creamy white flowers nestle in among the leaves. The whole plant is only 2 to 5 cm high. It used to grow in the white sand on the shores of Lake Pedder at an altitude of 300 m. It still survives in small colonies in several localities in the south west of the state. Seed of all these species will germinate quite freely but plants are rather slow to develop. Although *M. johnstonii* will divide without too much trouble the other two may sulk and be slow to establish if disturbed.

Of the several species of Blandfordia found in Australia, only one occurs in alpine regions and this is *B. punicea*. It is endemic to Tasmania. It is also variable in colour, the outer surface of the flower displaying orange-red shades while the inside of the corolla is golden yellow. A pure yellow flowering plant can be found at times. Its habitats are numerous and range from coastal plains to high open moorland and rain forest. It grows easily in a sandy peaty medium. Propagation is by division or seed which germinates quickly.

There are several members of Iridaceae that are of interest. One of the most spectacular but also difficult to cultivate is *Isophysis tasmanica* which is classified by Hutchinson under Isophysideae because of the different arrangement of the ovary perianth tube. The colour of the flower does not seem to vary much, although yellow forms have been reported. It is difficult to propagate and slow to grow, resenting disturbance and seldom setting much seed. It is found in south west Tasmania in high rainfall, mountainous country. The only growing medium in this area is almost pure peat and quartzite sand. Seed will germinate quite well if it can be obtained. Dividing old plants is not very successful as they sulk for long periods and separated pieces are slow to re-establish.

Only recently recognised as a separate species, *Diplarrhena latifolia* was long considered to be a form of *D. moraea*. It is endemic to Tasmania and confined to mountainous areas in the south and west of the state. Frequently found growing in peaty soil in between boulders, it forms large clumps. Differing botanically in the perianth, it is visibly quite a distinct plant from *D. moraea*. The flowers are heavily pencilled with purple on the inner perianth parts. The foliage, although variable, is generally stiff and up to 30 cm high. The rhizomatous roots are more spreading in this plant and can be easily detached for propagation. Even pieces with no roots can be placed in sand and these will develop roots quickly.

There is only one member in the plant family Rubiaceae I wish to discuss. It is *Coprosma moorei*, a prostrate plant of limited extent in distribution in Victoria but quite plentiful in Tasmania. Its habitats are very exposed alpine moorland in moist situations and rock crevices, generally on east or south sides exposed to the prevailing cold winds and rain. It differs from most other coprosmas in having bisexual flowers and therefore it can be depended upon to produce a good crop of its shining blue fruits. These appear during summer and can persist right into winter. Cuttings placed in pure sand in autumn will root with ease even without heat. It is a wonderful plant for a pan and grows easily if sited in full or semi-shade.

New Zealand has many aciphyllas, Umbelliferae, some being quite large and spectacular. There are only three species found in Australia—two, *A. glacialis* and *A. simplicifolia*, on the mainland mountains and the third, *A. procumbens*, endemic to Tasmania. The prostrate plant forms clumps. Its emerald green leaves are ferny and quite soft. It makes large colonies in rocky screes near to and on the summits of mountains in the south and south-west of the state. The white inflorescences have both hermaphrodite and unisexual flowers, and individual plants can be either polygamous or dioecious. It cultivates easily in a peaty well drained compost. Sections of the plant can be rooted in pure sand.

There are large forests of Nothofagus, Fagaceae, "Southern Beech" in New Zealand and South America. Australia has only one species which is quite plentiful and is a commercial timber tree. This is *N. cunninghamii* which can attain a height of 50 m. There is another species however which is endemic to Tasmania and, to us, most unique, as it is deciduous; in fact it is our only leaf-shedding native tree. It is *N. gunnii* and it is found in the west of the state and on the central plateau at altitudes of 900–1200 m. At the lower limit of its range, it can reach a height of up to 7 m growing in association with Eucalyptus. However, above the tree line amongst rocks and low shrubs, it is only a small bush and forms dense thickets with its wiry twisted branches, so earning the local name of "Tanglefoot". It is very slow growing and could well be used in the rock garden, as plants in cultivation for ten years are still only 90 cm high. The small, deeply veined, crenate leaves change to deep gold in the autumn. It must have an acid peaty soil and resents feeding. I have tried cuttings on several occasions and at different times of the year without success. I have attempted to graft *N. gunnii* on to stocks of *N. cunninghamii* with complete failure. However seed germinates quite readily if stratified for several months in moist peat at 35°F.

Although there are a great many Australian plants included in Proteaceae most are not found in alpine areas. *Bellendena montana* is monotypic and is endemic to Tasmania. It is widespread on mountains throughout the island and forms a shrub from 20–60 cm high. The terminal racemes of white or white flushed pink flowers appear in mid summer and are followed in autumn by orange-red fruits. These are arranged around and along the stems in a pendulous manner and this gives rise to the common name of "Mountain Rocket". It grows in a variety of soils as long as these are well drained but it is intolerant of phosphates (in common with most

Australian Proteaceae). Cuttings strike with ease in sand if kept on a cold bench for several months and then given bottom heat. Seed must be sown fresh and even then it will take two seasons to germinate.

While mentioning these few larger plants, I should like to draw your attention to a pygmy form of *Eucalyptus vernicosa*, the "Varnish Leaf Gum". This species is endemic to Tasmania and is found at high altitudes in the south-west and on the central plateau. It forms a small tree at the lower extent of its range and a tight shrub of less than 90 cm on the summits. This little plant appeared in a batch of seedlings and when six years old was only 5 cm high. It must be the tiniest Eucalypt in existence but is going to be a most difficult plant to propagate, as Eucalyptus are almost impossible to strike from cuttings.

A Tasmanian endemic, restricted to a number of mountains in the south and west and only then in small colonies, *Geum talbotianum*, Rosaceae, must rank as one of our most beautiful and difficult alpine plants. It grows in between boulders and in crevices on slopes facing west or south, many of these sites never receiving direct sunlight. The large kidney-shaped leaves are wrinkled on the upper surface and a mat of fine hairs covers both upper and lower surfaces. It forms clumps 5 to 8 cm high and will often ascend vertical cracks in rocks for several metres. The flowering scapes are up to 20 cm high and the pure white flowers are produced singly. These may be up to 5 cm in diameter, the outer rows of stamens being reddish-brown and greatly enhancing the flower. It is not an easy plant to cultivate, demanding a southerly aspect in our hemisphere and regular watering in dry weather. It can be divided, even small pieces can be rooted, and seed, if fresh, germinates well although seedlings can be slow to develop.

The group of plants classified as Composites contributes more than any other to the wonderful show in the Australian alpine regions. This is particularly so in the Bogong High Plains in Victoria and on Mount Kosciusko in New South Wales. Celmisia, Brachycome and Craspedia clothe the valleys and mountain slopes for miles in a spectacularly colourful display during January. Australia has only four species of Celmisia compared with 50 plus in New Zealand, but one of these is found in abundance in all the alpine regions. This is *C. asteliifolia.* Up until 1969 it was known as *C. longifolia* but research into Celmisia by Dr D. R. Given, of the D.S.I.R., Christchurch, revealed that the original *C. longifolia,* Cass. discovered in the Blue Mountains in New South Wales, was botanically distinct from all the other Australian populations. From a gardener's point of view, they both look the same but I have found the Tasmanian plant more difficult to cultivate. The foliage of *C. asteliifolia* varies and in most forms may be 3 to 6 cm wide, but in Victoria some may have leaves up to 25 cm in width. One of these broad-leaved forms has been described as var. *latifolia.* I have found that *C. asteliifolia* in all its forms is far easier to grow in our conditions than any of the New Zealand species we have tried. Many but not all spread by rhizomes and propagate easily by division. Detached rosettes root freely if placed in sand. The flowers are white, as with all celmisias but some with deep pink buds and several pink flowered variants have been frequently seen. *Celmisia saxifraga* is endemic to Tasmania and is quite plentiful in high mountain areas. It forms extensive colonies, hugging the ground with its silvery-green foliage. This has a hint of gold which is hard to describe. The flowering scapes are up to 20 cm and carry tiny, 25 mm, white flowers. It will propagate with ease in the same manner as the other celmisias. The final species is *C. sericophylla,* called "Silky Daisy" because of its foliage which is densely coated with silvery hairs. It is endemic to the Bogong High Plains in Victoria and grows along seepages and small mountain streams, forming large cushion-like mounds. The flower is disappointing, being rather weak with irregular petals. In cultivation it grows quite well beside a pool or in a moist position.

Ewartias, closely resembling raoulias, and included within this genus when first described, provide some most interesting foliage. *Ewartia nubigena*, commonly called "Brown Edelweiss" grows on the higher Victorian and New South Wales mountains in exposed positions and is the only species found on the mainland. It prefers a well drained soil with some loose gravel or stones on the surface, to help aerate the foliage which will not tolerate damp conditions. The leaves are silvery-grey and the almost stemless flowers are light brown surrounded by white or pinkish bracts. *Ewartia catipes* which is endemic to Tasmania grows in a similar manner. The foliage is an intense silver. The flowers vary from reddish-brown to crimson surrounded by creamy-white bracts. It is essential to place this plant in full sun in a well drained position and if this is done, it will quickly make a mat up to 50 cm in diameter. Both ewartias will divide easily and small rosettes root quickly in coarse sand. A much tighter growing prostrate species *E. meredithae*, forms hard dense mats on exposed high mountain areas throughout Tasmania. Due to the presence of golden hairs on the leaves the normal silver-grey foliage has a yellowish tint. The solitary flowers are produced on 2 cm stems and are white or occasionally pink. It prefers moist peaty positions and is much harder to please in cultivation. It tends to lose some of its tight habit at lower altitudes and care must be taken not to overwater it for, although liking a moist root run, it resents moisture on the foliage. It will propagate by cuttings and make an interesting specimen plant in a pan.

There are many helichrysums in Australia but most are too large for the rock garden. However the following two are not and are well worth trying. Both are Tasmanian endemics and are found on higher mountains throughout the state. *Helichrysum milliganii* forms clumps up to 20 cm in diameter with its rather fleshy green rosettes often criss-crossed with a light cobwebbing of fine hairs. The 15 cm flowering stems each have a 4 cm pure white flower which is deep crimson in bud. In its native habitat it prefers a moist peaty soil and full exposure to wind and sun. Seed germinates quickly and it can be divided with relative ease. Cultivation can present a challenge, however, but it is no more difficult than a lot of the other less easy plants we grow and is well worth the extra effort. *Helichrysum pumilum* resembles a small Celmisia in foliage, being dull green plastered with white hairs on the reverse side. It forms tight clumps in moist peaty ground or rock crevices. The 2 cm single terminal flowers are held on 10 cm stems and are deep pink in bud, opening to pure white. It will grow quite well in cultivation if kept in a place where it is moist yet well drained, and where there is free air movement. It divides very easily and seed germinates well.

All helipterums are sun lovers and are happy in a well drained, sandy or gritty soil. *Helipterum albicans* is variable, some forms being annual while others are perennial. Several have been given specific recognition and the one I like particularly is *H. albicans* var.

alpinum. Apparently it is endemic to the Bogong High Plains in Victoria between Mount Hotham and Mount Bogong. The intense silvery-white foliage has a dense covering of hairs and the bracts appending the 35 mm white flowers are red on their reverse sides. It is found growing on dry rocky knolls in open plain country in well drained volcanic soil. In cultivation it must have full exposure to sun and air movement. Plants seem to last for only about three years but it is easy to keep them going by taking cuttings every year or two. These strike quickly in pure sand.

Finally the type of country in which the plants I have listed grow is located on Cradle Mountain in the north western central plateau of Tasmania. This is typical of a large part of this area. Plants such as *Nothofagus gunnii, Gaultheria depressa, Milligania densiflora, Blandfordia punicea, Aciphylla procumbens, Bellendena montana, Celmisia saxifraga* and *Helichrysum milliganii* grow here.

Mount Kosciusko in New South Wales is the highest in Australia at 2200 m. *Celmisia asteliifolia* is at its strongest in this area and craspedias, Pentachondra and *Ewartia nubigena* are plentiful.

Pine Lake is situated near the main Lake Highway in the central plateau in Tasmania and is so named because of the *Athrotaxus cupressoides.* It is known locally as "Pencil Pine", and it grows about the shore line. Plants found in this area are *Abrotanella forsterioides, Pterygopappus lawrencei, Trochocarpa thymifolia, Pernettya tasmanica, Diplarrhena moraea* and *Ewartia catipes.*

Finally, Mount Bogong is Victoria's highest mountain and it is just over 1800 m. Celmisias are most prolific in this region and provide a most spectacular display when in bloom.

Cultivation of New Zealand and Tasmanian Plants

BRIAN HALLIWELL

There are a few nurseries, especially in Scotland and the north of England which offer a selection of New Zealand plants. It may be necessary to search more widely to trace stocks of the choicer items since they will be limited. With few exceptions a hunt for species from Tasmania will prove fruitless. Prospective growers would be ill advised to try to import living plants from Australasia as phyto-sanitary regulations pertaining to exporting and importing countries pose a great many problems. The result of this is that nurserymen down-under are reluctant to involve themselves with plant exports and, even if one is found who is obliging and will co-operate, there is a period of up to two years when living plants need special attention. They require particular care to keep them alive until they are adjusted to the change of seasons. Plants raised from seed do not have these problems. Unlike seeds produced by most plants from the mountains of the northern hemisphere, exposure to winter temperatures is not essential for germination for those harvested from plants south of the equator. Where they are subjected to a period of cold for 2–4 weeks, however, germination seems better.

New Zealand alpines only thrive where growing conditions in summer are cool and where there is plenty of moisture in the soil and in the atmosphere. Because of these limitations they are easier to cultivate in Scotland and in the north of England than in the south. Apart from one or two, they prefer a lime-free, gritty soil well supplied with peat. In southern England they are more suited to the peat garden type of environment but if one is not available, a shady part of a rock garden may be chosen. Many New Zealand alpines may be grown in pots in a compost comprised of equal parts of lime-free soil, sand and peat. Plants found in screes respond better where coarse sand or grit or even fine gravel is mixed with the growing medium while a covering of grit or gravel, half an inch in depth on top of the compost, is also helpful. These plants are usually deep rooting and where long tom pots are at hand they should be used.

In the case of many genera, for example Astelia, Coprosma, Aciphylla, Anisotome, Pimelia and Hectorella, male and female flowers are produced on different plants. In addition to these, in some species of Clematis, Cotula, and Bulbinopsis this condition sometimes occurs. If, as in Coprosma, it is the fruits which are the

Raoulia eximia   (*Plate 66*)

Haastia pulvinaris   (*Plate 67*)

Aciphylla dobsonii   (*Plate 68*)

Aciphylla spedenii   (*Plate 69*)

Ranunculus lyallii   (*Plate 70*)

Myosotis macrantha   (*Plate 71*)

Ranunculus haastii   (*Plate 72*)

Clematis marmoraria   (*Plate 73*)

main attraction, then it is important to have plants of both sexes. In any batch of seedlings, plants which are female seem to outnumber those which are male and it is interesting to note that male plants are always the last to flower. Therefore, when raising these dioecious plants from seed, it is important not to separate the young seedlings individually, but to sow the seed very thinly in a number of pots and to plant out the resulting plantlets undisturbed.

In a large number of New Zealand plants, juvenile growth differs markedly from that of the adult. To the uninformed when confronted with these two phases it may seem that one is dealing with two completely different species. So, the lesson is, if seedlings do not appear to be in character, do not be in a hurry to discard them. Plants which seem to be wrongly named may, in fact, simply be displaying juvenile growth.

Jim le Comte showed many plants rare in cultivation. Few are likely to be found in Britain and only some of these have been tried at Kew so I must generalise when dealing with cultivation.

Of the species of Ranunculus shown, the easiest at Kew is *R. insignis*. It grew and flowered freely for many years in a peaty soil at the edge of a woodland garden in light shade. Whilst *R. crithmifolius* var. *crithmifolius* has not been tried, *R. crithmifolius* var. *paucifolius* has been grown successfully as a pot plant and has flowered. Seed took two years to germinate and it may well be that the apparent failure of other species to germinate has been due to the discarding of seed pans too soon. It does seem that seed of New Zealand Ranunculus will germinate within a few weeks if harvested before being fully ripe, just as the achenes are beginning to turn brown. Very much quicker germination can be expected if seed can be stored moist rather than in a dry state. Unfortunately rarely is either of these conditions possible or practical. *Ranunculus lyallii* is the most spectacular of all New Zealand buttercups but it is too large for the average rock garden. It is better treated as a waterside plant where the soil is always moist but never stagnant. Cultivation is not easy out of doors, even in Scotland, although it can be grown successfully and flowered in a pot, but blooms produced are usually only travesties of what they could be like where conditions suit it. The germination of seed can be hastened by placing the packet of seed in a refrigerator for two or three weeks before sowing.

In the genus Aciphylla there is a startling difference between juvenile and adult growth; in the former state which lasts only for a short period leaves are soft and carrot-like. Once juvenility has passed the leaflets and stipules become thick and leathery and their tips can end in sharp points. Many species make large plants quite unsuited to a small rock garden so it is important to know the ultimate size of the species when ordering. Very occasionally male and female flowers may be produced on the same plant but it is more usual for them to be borne on separate plants. The rosettes of some species die after flowering so if a plant seems likely to develop a flowering shoot when it has but a single crown it is advisable to cut this off to encourage the production of secondary rosettes. The smaller kinds have interesting leaves in a variety of shades of green, bronze and gold. They can be grown in pots for use in the alpine house but they are very prone to attack by aphids, mealy bug or scale which infest the crowns where they are difficult to reach with normal insecticides. In the open aciphyllas may suffer from excessive winter wet and, conversely, in summer, dryness of the soil.

Anisotome is related to Aciphylla but has soft finely divided, aromatic leaves. Whilst a safer plant for the rock garden, in that it is not spiny, it has neither the attraction nor the curiosity value of Aciphylla. It seems easier of cultivation and is less vulnerable to winter wet. Lignocarpa was once included in Anisotome but I have no experience with *Lignocarpa carnosula*.

The plant family, Compositae, was well represented on the slides shown and contains a large number of very choice New Zealand alpine plants. Almost all of those found at higher altitudes produce little good seed so that any seed sample which has been wild collected will consist of a mixture of fertile and infertile seed. Feeding by insects may further reduce the amount of good seed available. Even viable seed has a brief life and this can be shortened by poor storage conditions such as too high temperatures and excessive dryness. Seed from commercial sources and from seed exchanges arranged and organised by northern hemisphere plant societies must be a year old, at least, possibly very much older, on receipt, if it is said to be wild collected. It is therefore unlikely to be viable. One may be fortunate in having friends in New Zealand who are prepared to collect seeds in the wild and to despatch them quickly. However if enthusiasts were to join the Canterbury or the Otago Rock Garden Societies and so be eligible to participate in their seed exchange schemes this would increase their chances of obtaining fresh and therefore viable seeds.

Attacks by aphids are a serious problem with many composites. Unless plants are regularly inspected, these pests can become established among the hairy rosettes or in the crowns of the plants. This results in yellowing of the foliage, distortion, weak growth and eventual collapse of the plants. Unfortunately control methods can be as damaging as the pests.

Some mention was made in the lectures of those difficult plants, the "Vegetable Sheep", species of Raoulia and Haastia. There are a number of growers in North Britain who succeed with them and we can admire their efforts at the shows. I also ought to avoid mentioning Celmisia when I know of no better collections anywhere than those found in Scottish gardens. In my experience the smaller leaved kinds are easier to cultivate in the south of England than those which bear large foliage. The latter are the more spectacular although I know that even in Nottingham *C. coriacea*, probably the finest of all species, grows well.

Leucogenes grandiceps, which has the common epithet of "New Zealand Edelweiss", I consider to be vastly superior to the European plant which bears that popular name. It is not so easy in cultivation as *Leontopodium alpinum* but it is easier than many other New Zealand plants. It is more often grown in a pot for display in an alpine house or on a show bench, but it will succeed if planted in a rock garden in a scree mixture. In the south it seems to respond better if placed in light shade rather than in full sun.

Cotula atrata has not proved too difficult when grown in cool conditions. It is not a strong grower and I doubt if it could hold its own in competition with aggressive plants on a scree. *Notothlaspi rosulatum* is a biennial of limestone screes. The difficulty here is to obtain seed which will germinate. Most species of Myosotis require a moist soil and grow better in shade, even in Scotland. None is long lived and they are better treated as annuals or even biennials. Probably the easiest of all plants shown by Jim le Comte was *Hebe haastii*. It can be grown anywhere on a rock garden so long as the soil is free of lime and is never allowed to dry out.

Tasmanian plants, generally, are not reliably hardy out-of-doors in Britain. In nature many mountain plants are sheltered from cold in winter under a covering of snow which, in addition to providing protection for the aerial parts, also reduces frost penetration of the soil. Winter damage is always more serious in Britain when the ground is frozen to any depth. Like New Zealand alpines, those from the mountains of Tasmania are sensitive to high summer temperatures and to low moisture content in the atmosphere and soil. Some species have an altitude range which extends through several thousand feet, and these are often more tolerant of adverse conditions in cultivation than those where the band is narrower. Areas which are amenable to the cultivation of New Zealand species will almost certainly be suitable for the easier Tasmanian plants. Again the best place to grow them is in the peat garden or in a cool and shady part of a rock garden in rather poor soil, devoid of lime. At Kew, so far the results have not been too encouraging when these plants were grown out of doors but with the recent construction of a peat garden with controlled overhead misting, greater success is expected. Up until now plants have been grown in pots and pans in frames, and have been plunged up to their rims in sand which has been kept moist throughout the summer. Many Tasmanian plants have proved to be sensitive to mains water which contains lime. Representatives of the plant families Ericaceae, Epacridaceae, Myrtaceae and Rutaceae have developed chlorotic foliage under these conditions, and so it is advisable to use rain water for all Tasmanian species.

Of the cushion plants shown on slides, *Abrotanella forsterioides* has proved to be the easiest, whether grown as a pot plant under glass, or planted out, in the protection of a frame or glasshouse, or even out of doors. Following the recommendations made by Ken Gillanders it seems as though *Pterygopappus lawrencei*, of which he sent a plant to Kew, may prove to be as easy.

Whereas *Gaultheria depressa*, a species also to be found in New Zealand, is prostrate in habit, *G. hispida*, which is part of the understory of the Eucalyptus forests, can reach 6 ft (2 m). At that height it is too large for most rock gardens but in addition to that it is inclined to be tender and therefore likely to suffer damage in a cold winter.

To suggest growing Eucalyptus on a rock garden will make many a reader smile for they know that most are forest trees. Among them are some of the tallest trees in the world. *Eucalyptus vernicosa* is, however, the smallest and while specimens at the lower part of its elevation range may make small trees up to 10 ft (3 m) in sheltered places, on exposed mountain tops above 4500 ft (1500 m) they are small shrubs rarely ever exceeding 12 in. (300 mm) in height. Seed is often either completely infertile or nearly so, and even good seeds have a short period of viability. Germination will be more even and quicker if, after watering, the seed container is wrapped in a polythene bag and placed in a refrigerator for two or three weeks before being transferred to a house giving gentle heat. Unlike most species which can tolerate drought conditions, this one needs a permanently moist soil.

Nothofagus, the Southern Beech, is another genus comprised mainly of forest trees but the deciduous *N. gunnii* is the smallest species, making a much branched shrub which, although it can reach 6 ft (2 m), is usually seen at half this size. In summer the leaves are pale green, crinkled and oval in shape, turning to a beautiful gold before they fall at the onset of winter. This is a shrub that I should like to see introduced into cultivation but I must confess that although I have sown seeds on numerous occasions, only in one instance did a single seed germinate. The resulting seedling proved to be sickly and did not survive. It is my view that this genus, like its northern counterpart, the beech, Fagus, produces good seed only in some years and that the seed is not viable for long and it needs moist storage. This year I received seeds which had been packed in moist moss so I may have the chance to see if my hypothesis is correct.

Diplarrhena latifolia is a much more desirable plant than *D. moraea*, of which it has long been considered a form, having been known as *D. moraea* var. *alpina* and *D. moraea* (alpine form). It is a much better rock garden plant for it is smaller, with shorter flower stems and larger flowers. It is also hardier in this country and will tolerate drier and warmer summer conditions.

Blandfordia punicea has the common name of "Christmas Bells", (Christmas in the southern hemisphere falls during their summer). It is one of Tasmania's most beautiful flowering plants, occurring over a wide area and from sea level to an altitude of over 4000 ft (1250 m). The size of the plant varies according to its location, being 3 ft (1 m) or more at sea level while at its highest point it may not exceed 6 in. (150mm). It has been in cultivation at Kew for many years where it is grown in a pan for display in the alpine house. Although it is easily raised from seed it does not lend itself to increase by division. Seedlings were planted out in a warm sunny border where the soil can become dry in summer, and flowering took place two years after planting. Plants have remained small, about 9 in. tall (225 mm), and have survived all winters including that of 1979–80, which was particularly severe.

Unlike the New Zealand members of Coprosma, *C. moorei* has flowers of both sexes on the same plant and so, although there may be only one plant, it is possible that purplish-blue berries will be produced. As yet it has not been tried out of doors but I feel it ought to succeed in a peat garden where it could be hardy.

Celmisia asteliifolia is probably better known as *C. longifolia*. Though less spectacular than many of the New Zealand species, it is easier to cultivate. It is hardier and seems to have a longer flowering season, tolerating drier conditions in summer. *Celmisia saxifraga*, which is a much tinier plant, has not been in cultivation long enough to assess its amenability to cultivation in this country, but it is much more demanding that *C. asteliifolia*. *Helichrysum milliganii* and *H. pumilum*, which are of similar size to *Celmisia saxifraga* are somewhat alike in appearance, and have proved to be as difficult to grow.

Helipterum albicans with its everlasting-type flowers has long been grown in the Order Beds at Kew and there it has been treated as an annual. I do not know the form *alpinum* and can find no reference to it. If it sets seed readily in cultivation this is one way in which it may be kept alive, especially if it should prove to be unreliable as a perennial. If it behaves at all in any way like the species I should expect it to be able to tolerate drier conditions.

Tasmanian plants deserve to become better known so that more people will want to grow them. Many are handsome either in flower and/or fruit but additional information is required as to their cultural needs, how hardy they are and their tolerance to drier summer conditions.

And so, finally, for those who are fascinated by the southern hemisphere plant species, the Southern Alps of New Zealand and the High Alpine Plateau of Tasmania are the homes of a wide range of interesting and endemic genera which are capricious, challenging and rewarding.

Plants of the Argentinian Andes

ROLF FIEDLER

Viola canobarbata

In trying to locate South American alpine flowers in any European Rock Garden flower book one might get the impression that those from the southern parts of South America are all from Chile. But of course this is not so. Most of the plants mentioned grow in both Chile and the Argentine. This is not surprising as the two countries share a common mountain chain, the Andes. There are plants which are unique to either the west or east side of the range but these are few compared with the large number which occur in both. This is correct for the southern part of the Andes between latitudes 51°–38° south up to Neuquen Province. The mountains there are lower, not much higher than 2000 m except for the volcanoes, and woods grow on both sides. The whole area has a relatively mild climate and the rain clouds coming in from the Pacific can easily pass over these mountains and precipitate their moisture on the eastern slopes, Argentine, as well as on the west side. Further north, where the mountains rise to 6000 m and higher, these same clouds cannot pass over to the eastern slopes so readily and it is here that the climate becomes much drier. The flora then becomes quite different and more distinct.

The main reason why Chile alone is normally mentioned is that the first book about Andean plants was published in Chile long before anything appeared in the Argentine. The Chilean flora was published in 1845 by Claudio Gay and consists of six volumes. The most recent work is Luisa Eugenia Nava's "Flora de la Cuenca de Santiago". The first volume was published in 1973 and the third appeared in 1979.

In this respect, the Argentine is very far behind. The first important publication was produced in 1943. It was a pretentious work under the direction of R. Descole of the Lillo Institute of Tucuman and was contained in enormous, bulky volumes measuring 35 cm × 50 cm. Done on fine paper, printed and illustrated with whole page plates in the manner of the earlier Herbals, it was also illustrated with beautifully coloured pictures. It should have been seen that such a prestigious work could never be completed. The edition stopped in 1956 after five volumes had appeared.

In 1953 the first useful book was published. It is "Plants of the Surroundings of Buenos Aires" by Angel Cabrera, but as this area is totally flat country and almost at sea level it contains very few alpines. In 1968 the first volumes of "Argentine Flora" appeared. It is a work which has still to be completed in a number of volumes and is edited by I.N.T.A. (Instituto Nacional de Tecnologia Agropecuaria). The first volume is "Flora de Patagonia" and this is the most important part for us since it contains the monocotyledons, except Gramineae, from that part of the country. This includes the Provinces of Neuquen, Rio Negro, Chubut, Santa Cruz, Tierra del Fuego and the Falkland Islands and parts of Antarctica, an area of more than 800,000 square kilometres outwith the antarctic regions. The second volume which came out in 1972 was "Compositae", also written by Angel Cabrera, and the third, which appeared in 1978, is titled "The Gramineae". Patagonia includes the mountains of these provinces and the flatter part further south, down towards the antarctic region, so the plants described from there are, to a great extent, alpines. They are most useful works and very well produced. It is to be hoped that volumes on the other families will follow soon.

In addition to the Patagonia volumes, "The Gramineae of Entre Rios Province" has appeared and the first two parts of "The Flora of Jujuy Province", which also contains a number of alpines. These books are large, 27 cm × 28 cm, but the recently published "Flora of Buenos Aires Province", also written by Angel Cabrera, is of a more practical size. The illustrations are simple but quite well done, except that they are drawn mainly from pressed specimens and not from live material. Therefore there are discrepancies, such as curled petals, whereas in growing plants they are shown to be straighter, and other similar-type inaccuracies which are rather important. Examples are to be found in Compositae. It should not be forgotten, however, that as there were few works of reference to serve as a basis, much original research had to be carried out. In this case it meant that descriptions had to be written from the only source easily available, the herbarium, and this required very great dedication and enthusiasm.

There are, of course, quite a number of short publications, for example the excellent work on Leguminosae by A. Burkart and more recently the "Argentine Astragalus Species" by E. Gomez-Sosa. There have also been a number of papers published by botanists abroad like Dr Sleumer's admirable "Loasaceae", unfortunately not illustrated, and a paper on the subspecies of *Viola maculata* by Bengt Sparre, but it is difficult to get to know of the existence of such separata. The botanical literature of the Argentine, however, is developing in a very encouraging way.

The lack of books and the short botanical tradition in South America often makes the identification of alpine flowers quite a problem. In Europe, of course, the situation is different for quite apart from the larger, comprehensive floras there are in existence a number of excellent, well illustrated pocket size floras which can be easily taken on any mountain excursion. I always take my plant presses with me on my trips and although I have given a number of pressed specimens to a well known botanical institute here, quite a number of them have never been identified. There are also comparatively few botanists in this country and each is more than *just busy* with his own work and publications. The terrain itself is so vast and extensive and difficult of access that these botanists can specialise only in a few plant families. Thus, in general, the flora of the high mountains is less well known.

I have also sent pressed specimens abroad but here again there is the problem of transport or post. In certain instances some plants have been identified from seeds, for example, several calceolarias by Prof. Otto Schwarz of Jena University. In Europe it is also easier to find specialists and to discuss plant identification with those interested in alpine flora. Additionally there are many others living near mountain regions who have expert knowledge of the distribution of plants in the area near where they live, but in this country such people are exceptions and one meets them but rarely. Trees and shrubs are generally accorded much more attention and until recently very little importance has been attached to small plants.

In the first years of my excursions I sent seed by post to their destinations. Fortunately I soon made the discovery that this was unreliable and very precious seed went astray. In view of the very difficult conditions of plant hunting in the Andes this was more than simply discouraging. Not only must one climb and find the seeds when they are ripe, but an added complication is that it must also have been a good seed year and that no insect plagues have fed on the seeds and so on. In the case of rosulate violas there is only the lapse of a day or two between the ripening of the seed capsules and the explosive dispersal of the seeds, so that one oftens finds empty pods. Such seeds are therefore precious and one cannot risk their loss.

Due to a number of circumstances and because the flora of this part of the Andes differs from that of Europe, there seems to be a general impression that alpine plants from the Argentine, or even the whole of South America are not sufficiently resistent to cold to stand the European climate. This point has often been put to me. This generalisation is, of course, wrong. If the plants grow in mountains high enough for cold winters, that is to say with conditions of snow and intense frost, then they certainly are hardy enough for European gardens. Snow, of course, is necessary to protect the plants from lower temperatures. The seeds I have collected are mostly from sufficiently high areas with severe winter conditions but with deep snow to protect the plants from biting, icy winds.

Ourisias, for example, must be able to withstand frost. *Ourisia alpina* grows at an altitude of 1500 m, just above the limits of the woods and sometimes higher. Winter starts in April, sometimes with snowfall and frost, and by May everything is in its grip. This lasts till September or even October and on occasions even later, with temperatures down to −10°C and lower. *Ourisia racemosa* (syn. *O. coccinea*), can be found at elevations of 1800 m but may also occur as far down as 400 m near waterfalls where there is hardly any snow and very little frost. So plants from some provenances must surely be hardy.

I have found *Mutisia decurrens* at about 350 m and also at 1200 m and provided that the base of the plant at least is covered with snow in winter, it should be able to resist frost. What is more to the point is whether British winters are severe enough for quite a number of the Argentine alpines. It is possible that plants might need longer and harder winters with lower temperatures. It is also likely that such plants would need more sun, higher noon temperatures with great fluctuations in summer and often a drier climate as well. There are regions in the high mountains where, even in summer, the temperature falls to several degrees below zero at night and rises to over 30°C at midday. That is a difference of up to 40°C daily, depending of course upon the altitude and latitude of the area in the mountains. As the Argentine Andes stretch from 22° to 55° latitude south there must occur incredible variations in temperature.

To undertake a trip in the Alps or any other range of European mountains is a very different experience from climbing in the Argentine Andes and there can be no comparison. There are very few accessible mountains. Relatively few roads lead up to sufficiently high regions from where excursions can be taken and those that do normally lead over high passes to Chile. Only a small number of mountains are accessible by ski-lift.

Three choices lie before you. You can take one of the ski-lifts, drive up a track in the "zona turistica" or select an unfrequented mountain zone where hardly anybody ever goes, taking care to make some enquiries before you go. In the more northern regions where there are no woods but only arid stony, rocky heights in every direction for as far as the eye can see, it is much easier as one has simply to climb scree slopes and wind-swept, sparse "grass-steppes". But distances up to the higher altitudes are sometimes very great and the effort to get there extremely tiring.

From repeated trips I know the regions from Mendosa to Esquel, a distance of approximately 2200 km, and normal conditions consist of areas in which alpine plants are sparingly scattered over screes. Real grassland or patches of fertile grass as in the "Alms" in the Alps, is more the exception. Where there is increased humidity you may find spots of continuous green dependent upon streams, torrents or swampy parts but usually the vegetation is quite thin. Further south the rainfall increases, especially after latitude 37°–38° where the forests begin, but up north grass, often a species of Stipa, grows not in continuous alms, but more like scree plants in single tufts which, from a distance, resemble dry meadows.

The climate does not allow the growth of soft grass to occur in the Alps, but in the Andes which I know, it is much tougher with narrow or rounded leaves evolved to resist the severe climate and similar to coarse Festuca, much too tough to pick.

There are very few paths and marked ones are rare. Such zones are normally partly sterile and quite isolated with individual plants growing among boulders and volcanic ash. The less stony area is the tufty grass steppe. Vegetation depends solely on water supply and in the small patches where the torrents flow from snowfields and glaciers, the growth is quite lush.

Going south and starting roughly from the northern part of

Neuquen where the wooded region begins, the aspect changes completely. Frequently thick virgin forests and dense impenetrable bamboo thickets (Chusquea) and ñire (*Nothofagus pumilio* and *N. antarctica*) render progress exceedingly difficult, and in order to reach the higher mountain areas where the timber ceases and the alpine flora begins, one has to find and follow the few "sendas" or "picadas", narrow paths hewn through the vegetation by machete, ways that often are recognisable only to the trained eye. On a number of occasions I have missed my way and my direction and have been completely lost struggling through the dense walls of the giant thickets losing hours on the way and becoming exhausted. Everywhere I was seeing nothing but endless bamboo with stems like steel hawsers some 5 cm in diameter while endeavouring to find some gap through which I could squeeze. From far below they appear so harmless, more like small plants, or even moss or grass slopes, but on reaching the thickets one discovers that they are 3 m or more high so that no way out can be seen. One may be completely surrounded by bamboo or ñire. There is often more fallen timber in the woods than upright trees, sometimes this is piled up to 30 m and it is difficult to retain a sense of direction as the sky itself is frequently shut out. In order to find the way back one has to observe very carefully all special and characteristic details. There are occasions on which, especially in the first years of my excursions, I had to give up and return, and very glad indeed I was to be able to do so. Quite often not another single person was encountered. I undertook most of the climbs alone, my only companion being my dog, to whom I was very grateful for his sense of direction. He helped me on several occasions.

Sometimes because of having to cross icy rivers without bridges, and face long stiff climbs through woods, it is simpler to go on horseback and then camp, but even a horse has a tremendous struggle clambering over the fallen giant trees and frequently one has to dismount.

The view from the top above the ñire is greatly rewarding in the vastness and grandeur of the empty spaces spread out before you.

One of the mountains which is now readily accessible and which I know well from many expeditions at flowering and seed collecting-times is Cerro Chapelco near San Martin de los Andes. Because

of the road and ski-lift I have chosen this as a fairly typical representative of an easy climb and worth while for plant collecting. A
number of interesting flowers grow there.

From the old main road that leads south from the town, a side
road ascends rocky slopes through wooded valleys and climbs over
steep hilly parts to the new ski-lift, main station. I used to continue
along the road, now unfortunately closed to the public, which goes
on rising steeply, curving through bamboo and ñire slopes and soon
reaching the lenga woods (*Nothofagus pumilio*) which are similar in
appearance to European beech woods. As the road is not now
used, it is in very bad condition and on the last occasion my car
had to be pulled out of the mud by two obliging oxen before I
could go on.

The less dense woods and the verges of the road are full of
Alstroemeria aurantiaca, incorrectly called Amancay in the Argentine, a blaze of colour and in full bloom from the end of January to
the middle of February. The shrubby ground cover in the lenga
woods is mainly *Berberis pearcei*, with dark, shiny leaves. In open
sunny places grows *Viola maculata* one of the beautiful yellow
violets, a subspecies with heart-shaped, rounded leaves. There is
also quite a lot of *Rubus geoides*, with nice, soft, geum-like foliage
and large, single, strawberry-like white flowers. This is an attractive, low growing sub-shrub which, at the end of March, bears
raspberry-like fruits and with a similar taste. Near the small streams
grows *Lenceria thermarum*, the violet flowers not unlike those of
Mulgedium alpinum from the alps, and in the pebbly stream beds
one can find the beautiful *Mimulus cupreus* growing among the
stones in the midst of the rushing waters. On the banks are *Calceolaria bigibbiflora*, and in patches of grassland nearby is found the
yellow *Geum magellanicum* with long stalked and not very interesting small flowers.

Finally the road ends at the refugio, an old, unused and neglected
blockhouse at about 1400 m almost at the limit of the scattered ñire
bushes. Here and there is a sort of sandy terrace and a little higher
begins a stony-sandy scree with bigger stones and boulders, where
can be found a lot of *Rhodophiala andicola* (Hippeastrum), one of
the showiest plants in the area. The first days of February are the
beginning of its flowering season and the short stemmed flowers

Conference Hall   (*Plate 74*)

Show Hall   (*Plate 75*)

Rhododendron keiskei 'Yaku Fairy'   (*Plate 76*)
(Winner of Farrer/Forrest Award)

Townsendia hookeri   (*Plate 77*)

Leiophyllum buxifolium (*Plate 78*)

Primula kisoana var. alba ☿ (*Plate 80*)

Primula edgeworthii 'Alba' (*Plate 79*)

Primula strumosa   (*Plate 82*)

☿ Gentiana algida   (*Plate 81*)

Trifolium uniflorum 'Album'   (*Plate 83*)

Milligania longifolia   (*Plate 84*)

Dryas octopetala var. minor   (*Plate 85*)

Plant Family Ericaceae, Barry Starling's Exhibit   (*Plate 86*)

Marquee—Ingwersen's Stand   (*Plate 87*)

have a dark purple, nearly violet glow. The later flowers are longer stemmed and of a purple-rose colour, while the last ones at the end of February are dark pink. In this area and also higher up you will find *Perezia fonckii* (syn. *P. pediculatifolia*), which varies from pure white to quite intense bluish-violet. *Perezia bellidifolia* is a slightly smaller species, with glaucous-green entire though wavy-margined leaves, which grows among grassy tufts on another slope and has similar, dark blue flowers. *Perezia pilifera* is completely different. It is often seen with white individual flower heads and very divided, decorative leaves which form nearly flat rosettes.

A nice cushion flower is *Valeriana fonckii* forming dense mats of oval, sturdy leaves, the flowerheads, on 8 cm–12 cm high stems, composed of small pink buds opening to white flowers. A little further on at about 1600 m one can find the very pretty *Loasa nana* with yellow, starry flowers, the curly moss-like leaves making handsome cushions. There is another Loasa growing on Cerro Chapelco mainly among grass tufts on a slope facing south. It has stems around 20 cm–30 cm sometimes slightly bent over or a little twisted and carrying largish, creamy-white flowers. I also found this same Loasa on some slopes of Volcano Lanin. It was said to be *Loasa bergii* but that species usually grows at lower elevations among shrubs and is frequently seen by the roadside trailing and clambering to a height of 1 m and sometimes more. it has brilliant yellow flowers which are smaller than the cream ones and I am far from certain that it is the same species.

The most common plant to be seen is *Armeria magellanica* only being slightly different botanically to the European thrift. It looks just the same while height and colour vary according to altitudes and position. A Sisyrinchium, possibly *S. macrocarpum*, also grows there in a sandy scree. It is a very attractive plant, quite low, about 10 cm and forms dense, broader-leaved tufts with relatively large flowers for a Sisyrinchium which do not exceed the leaves. They are light yellowish-cream with a brownish-purple zone in the centre. This plant has a certain similarity to *S. arenarium* but is considerably lower and sturdier and the flowers are very much bigger while *S. macrocarpum* is usually pure yellow.

Tristagma nivale is a bulbous plant with very curled, nile-green leaves and grows there. It also has greenish, nicely perfumed flowers similar in form to that of a very tender hyacinth. The green becomes darker, depending on the altitude until at around 2000 m it is nearly black. *Viola cotyledon* is plentiful here, the flowers being very pale yet in other locations they may be intense violet. On sandy slopes one can find *Haplopappus marginalis* with slightly hairy leaves and showy yellow flowers.

In wetter spots, in rich black humus and often in grass one finds the beautiful *Ourisia alpina*. Sometimes the flowers are pale pink but stronger coloured forms are found. On volcanic soil and where more exposed to the weather I have found plants bearing nearly mauve-pink blooms. I think they are one of the nicest flowers in this part of the Andes.

Still higher, not far short of the first snow patches and growing in humid spots, I found *Ourisia breviflora* but on Cerro Chapelco it is quite rare. The plants are only half the height or even less than *O. alpina* and the flowers are much paler. In fact they are almost white and only the buds show a truly pink tinge. They have two flowers per stem. The leaves, too, are smaller forming thick mats and often hanging in clumps.

The showy *Ranunculus semiverticillatus* can be found in quite coarse scree. The buds, pinkish on the outsides open into lovely pure white flowers surrounded by mossy leaves.

Of the various Cruciferae, *Heptacera cuneifolia* is the most interesting. The greyish-green leaves form an elongated rosette on top of which are carried small pinkish-white flowers in a long inflorescence.

Of Calyceraceae there are at least two genera on Cerro Chapelco. *Gamocarpha scapigera* is a biennial, forming a rosette of scabious-like, shiny leaves and, in its second year, a mushroom-like inflorescence of peculiar form. The flower heads bear small, greenish flowers and on the sides of the principle one there are several lateral flower clusters. The second, *Moschopsis subandina*, grows in groups or colonies and has greyish basal leaves and loose inflorescences carrying bigger, single, greenish-white flowers.

Some slopes are covered with very colourful *Oxalis enneaphylla* with large flowers and in shades of light to mauve-pink. In the bud stage the colour is more intense and on one occasion I found a form with big, pure white flowers. On calm sunny days the air is heavy with their lovely scent.

In a side valley that leads up to a saddle and by the side of a waterfall and on wet rocks are masses of *Ourisia racemosa* (syn. *O. coccinea*). The tubular flowers are brilliant scarlet, the colour contrasting with the shiny, dark green leaves. This species is also found at lower altitudes but at these elevations they bloom more sparsely and are therefore less decorative. Also growing in rather humid sites among shorter grass tufts one can sometimes see hemispherical cushions of *Anagallis alternifolia* up to 2 cm high. Their pale to shell-pink flowers often cover the entire plant. They have an attractive scent of mossy musk. One can also find them in great profusion at lower levels by the shores of lakes. They are quite common. *Ourisia fragrans* grows among smaller rocks either at their bases or in crevices giving at first glance the impression of a dwarf creamy-white Primula 4 cm–7 cm high. The loose rosettes of glandular, dark green foliage bear few flower heads which often start by being creamy-yellow before turning to creamy-white. They then change to a light mauve before fading. Very rarely plants producing mauvy-purple blooms can be found. Their perfume is very faint.

The genus Adesmia, Leguminosae, is represented by at least four kinds on Cerro Chapelco. *Adesmia axillaris* is an extremely flat sub-shrub, 1 cm–1·5 cm high when not in flower bearing rather large cream-coloured flowers with a few black or dark brown lines and a strange black spot on the standard. The same plant grows on Cerro Catedral, near Bariloche but with violet flowers. Also very dwarf but less flat are cushions of *A. glomerula*, a species with small, silvery green leaves and very tiny yellow flowers. *Adesmia retusa* is a bigger plant altogether. It is more of a herbaceous sub-shrub, if there is such a thing, of about 15 cm, with golden yellow flowers marked with small brown spots and carried in small inflorescences. The nicest of the four is *A. longipes*, about 5 cm tall. Here the beautifully divided oval foliage, the single lemon yellow flowers and the divided seed pods, each segment with a single seed, are all covered with coarse woolly hairs which turn brilliant red, or at least browny-red in March. It occurs in rock crevices but more usually it is found on screes or in sandy soil.

Another plant in the Leguminosae, *Astragalus nivicola*, first only known in the Magellan Straits area, was discovered by me on Cerro Chapelco. It has since been found in several other areas. It is a delicate, beautiful plant with a few light and dark violet flowers, grouped in a sort of head and then carried on thin stems over neat, low cushions. The pods have purple markings.

I have found four kinds of Nassauvia on Cerro Chapelco. *Nassauvia argyrophylla* is located by stony, pebbly streams. It grows in big tufts formed from the greyish-green, prickly leaves and has inflorescences of quite small flower heads. Higher, at about 1700 to 1800 m and in scree, grows *N. lagascae*. This species has greyish sometimes purplish leaves and makes a nice rosette and, in relation to other nassauvias has very short stems and big flower heads. *Nassauvia lagascae* var. *lanata* grows in exposed situations. It is smaller than the species in every way with the undersides of the leaves being more hairy and sometimes forming cushions. The third species, *N. pulcherrima*, always grows at higher altitudes in rather coarse scree often near patches of snow. The rough, stiff, sharply toothed dark green leaves are oval and show prominent lighter veins. The flowers form an oval inflorescence on top of erect stems up to 10 or 14 cm. *Nassauvia pulcherrima* is certainly a plant with a lot of character. The fourth, *N. pygmaea* var. *media*, forms dense mats of low yet erect stems up to 5–12 cm with fine, narrow leaves. It closely resembles the club moss, *Lycopodium selago* or a coarse Polytrichum. It flowers profusely but the individual flower heads are very small. *Nassauvia pygmaea* var. *media* occurs on many mountains usually quite high among the rocks and in coarse scree. The genus is included in the plant family Compositae.

Amid the rocks in this area at around 1800 m grows another species of rosulate viola. The leaves are a little more succulent than those of *V. cotyledon*, are more pointed and really look like sempervivums. The flowers are pure grey, without a vestige of violet, with black markings. Regrettably I do not know its name.

Everywhere in the wet parts and when actually standing among stones in the shallow water of the mountain torrents, one sees the very peculiar double-decker-leaved Andean calthas. They also grow in swampy meadows and round the edges of lagunas, sometimes in great masses. They are mainly *C. sagittata*. The whole plant is much smaller and more compact than *C. palustris* and so is the foliage while the auricles are doubled up and cover part of the leaves. The flowers are greenish-white, quite flat, and not too showy but it is a true alpine plant. Also high up, but not so frequently met with is a second species, *C. appendiculata* which has narrower leaves and sepals. The flower is more star-shaped.

The white flowers of *Euphrasia subexserta* can also be found growing on Cerro Chapelco in meadows and in wet areas. The blooms are bigger than those of the European *E. officinalis* although here they appear to be less interesting than these found growing elsewhere in the Andes.

There are at least two kinds of Calandrinia, one with narrow leaves and pretty pink flowers and said to be *C. linearifolia*. The other, *C. portulacoides*, forms very low Armeria-like tufts of slightly succulent narrow leaves and has big yellowish-orange flowers up to 5 cm across. The specific name fits its flowers exactly.

There is a nice species of Leuceria, *L. millefolium*, growing at 1700–1800 m with pinkish-white flower heads, quite pretty with its pure coloured flowers, which seem to be double with only ligular and no discoid flowers.

The most showy and largest of the many senecios (in Patagonia there are about 200 species), is *S. argyreus* which grows around the boundary of the wood and also a little higher up. It forms bigger herbaceous-like shrubs, 25–45 cm with narrow, grey-green leaves and big, beautiful golden yellow flowers, a plant one must always admire every time one sees it. There is also a remarkable species, *S. subdiscoides*, 10–15 cm with much divided light green foliage and where the stems and involucral bracts of the inclined flower heads are intense purple. It only has tubular florets. There are also dwarf senecios with brilliant flower heads.

I feel I must mention *Chiliotrichum rosmarinifolium*, which belongs to the Compositae. It is a shrub which grows about knee high with rosemary-type foliage and many small marguerite-like flowers. It is found at an altitude of around 1600–1700 m and although quite common it is extremely difficult to get good seed. Usually they are either undeveloped or have been eaten by insects.

Having reached the ridge one has a superb view. To the west and far below stretches of the extensive Lago Lacar can be seen, deep brilliant blue during the day and silvery grey towards late afternoon, and framed in the background by the snowy peaks along the border with Chile. In the north, over the long expanse of green valley of Las Vegas, soars the characteristic form of the outstanding Volcano Lanin, always half covered with snow. This beautifully shaped mountain towers above all the other mountains in the area by 1200 m.

Over all the eastern part, nearly half of the whole view, one looks on to the several peaks of the Chapelco Massif, the main and highest summit which is over 2300 m. A little more to the south rises the impressive rock block called El Castillo (The Castle) with, at its foot, a small laguna surrounded by dense woods, forming another attractive group. Behind are the serrated peaks of the more distant Cordillera Azul and usually they are really blue. All three are strenuous climbs for plant hunting.

The ridge extends to the south and is dominated by one of the main peaks, the towering rocks of the gigantic El Piramide (a sort of rocky step-pyramid) but less high, 2130 m. One has to follow along this ridge and then drop down a little to the left along the immense rock walls. Sheltered from the strong winds that sweep the crest, this area is more humid. Both the rock walls and the scree are full of different plants, all slightly straggly and more green as they grow in the shade of the towering rocks, flowering a little later. There one can find *Ourisia racemosa* and *O. fragrans* and many of the other plants already mentioned. In addition I found *Saxifraga magellanica*, not unlike the European *S. exarata*, with small white flowers growing in round cushions in the vertical rock walls and also the very nice *Calceolaria lagunae-blancae*, 7–12 cm growing in crevices. The single flowers are small but the short inflorescences over a loose rosette of oval leaves bear many flowers. It really has a special charm. In other parts it also grows in sunny scree.

Access to El Piramide is not difficult but, botanically, it is not too interesting. Among the rocks grow a lot of *Phacelia magellanica*, a herbaceous plant with pink, nearly white flowers but up there they are dark violet, smaller and less leafy but quite attractive. The wind-swept rocks of the summit are covered with the shrub lichen, *Usnea melaxantha*.

From the top one can see as far as the high Cordillera Tronador, over 120 km away near Bariloche on the other side of the immense lake Nahuel Huapi out of sight far below. Cordillera Tronador,

3554 m, is also a volcano, beautifully white and glistening with snow. The view is really magnificent.

Thus this typical and easily accessible mountain which I have chosen as representative of alpines in the Argentine Andes, rewards the climber with botanical treasures and magnificent, inspiring and varied scenery. There are, of course, many more Andean alpine plants spread over the vast extent of the Andes but this very abbreviated cross section gives a good idea of some of the plants shown in my talk. As the tourist stream is constantly increasing, let us hope that nature's bounty is not too quickly spoiled and that botanists, enthusiasts and nature lovers can enjoy Cerro Chapelco's flora for many years to come.

Japanese Plants in the Garden

ALFRED EVANS

British plant collectors ranged far and wide in search of plants and in the early days their briefs were invariably to collect plants of horticultural merit or economic importance. In many instances the cost of their journeys was under-written by a combine of estate owners who wanted to embellish their policies with exotic, decorative plants or even by individuals wishing to reap the full benefit from a man's labours in the collecting field. The botanical approach where all manner of plants were collected or classified, although always present to a degree, is a little more recent and the financing of this was and still is met by institutions. Gardeners today, and particularly rock gardeners, often join with others in helping to meet the costs of a collector who indicates that he is going to harvest seeds in an alpine area and many worthwhile plants have been introduced into cultivation through this sort of joint effort.

In general, Japan has never been a country where free access into its hinterland has been possible. For centuries it did not welcome foreigners to its shores and where contact was possible this was usually confined to the areas immediately in the vicinity of the ports of trade. Collecting wild plants or seeds on a large scale was virtually impossible.

A number of interested people, however, whose names are well known to gardeners and botanists did manage to gain admittance to the country and were able to collect to a limited extent. They were mostly working under the protective umbrella of the Dutch East India Company and include Kaempfer (Iris), Thunberg (Astilbe) and Siebold (Magnolia and Primula). Maximowicz was a Russian botanist and is remembered in Lilium. It was not until the middle of the last century that the English names began to appear among those who had introduced plants into our gardens and two who are prominent are James Gould Veitch (Abies) and Robert Fortune (Hosta). Among the Americans at that time were S. W. Williams (Clematis), James Morrow (Carex) and J. Small (Trillium).

Although Japanese botanists have been interested in their own flora for many years and have published a great deal of information on their work, this is largely unintelligible to the European. The reports were in Japanese. One of the first useful publications to appear which helped western gardeners was the "Illustrated Flora of Japan" by T. Makino. It was well implemented with line drawings and had the plant names in Latin. Unfortunately the text was in Japanese but the sketches were informative. In 1953 Dr Ohwi published his comprehensive study of the Japanese flora and thanks to generous sponsors in America an English edition, "Flora of Japan" appeared in 1965. This has a few illustrations but what is particularly valuable is the inclusion of plant identification keys throughout. Suddenly a ready means of obtaining information on the whole of the Japanese flora was opened up to the layman. Since then there have been innumerable publications in Japanese, but many of them contain outstanding colour plates of some of the most garden-worthy or challenging species. A good example is the "Wild Flowers of Hokkaido" by Dr Hideo Hara.

Japan is made up of a group of islands, the main ones being Hokkaido, Honshu, Shikoku and Kyushu. They form a long archipelago within the band of 45 degrees north and 30 degrees north, stretching in an arc from close to the long Sakhalin Island to south of Korea. In general the terrain is mountainous with flat lands in the vicinity of the coast and up river valleys. The weather can be extremely severe especially in the north. The flora is rich and highly decorative and quite a few species are unique (endemic) to certain areas. In fact a name frequently heard on the lips of gardeners is Yakushima, in the form of yakushimanum for Rhododendron and yakusimana for Viola. There are others. Yakushima is a small island of approximately 200 square miles and sits in a cluster of small islands off the most southerly tip of Kyushu. It is noted for the number of dwarf forms of species found growing on it.

Quite apart from the attractive wild plants native to Japan the nurserymen of that country have cultivated, raised and selected particular forms of certain genera and species. This they have done over the centuries, for their interest in things beautiful has resulted in their selecting flowers, flowers which are enjoyed in western gardens today. Notable among plants introduced are the numerous forms of dwarf conifers, the Retinospora, (I wonder how many clones are really in existence?), and the most decorative of all woody plants, the race of dwarf, cut-leaved maples. Primulas, lilies, cherries, Kurume azaleas and hostas are examples of others which have been subjected to intensive selection and propagation. Over the years their value as garden plants has been assessed and tested and today many of those which are highly prized in our gardens can trace their origins to the Japanese islands. By garden plant I mean just that for, while I may have a leaning towards growing plants of wild origin (and I admire the tolerance of some of those very fine species), I am not blind to the beautiful forms which have arisen in cultivation.

Two examples which must be familiar to all are Cydonia, often referred to as Japonica and offered as "Japanese Quince", and of course the Prunus, "Flowering Cherry". They seem to epitomise Japan.

Chaenomeles japonica, (syn. *Cydonia japonica* and *C. maulei*), arrived in this country, Britain, as long ago as 1869. It was then given the name of *Cydonia maulei* in recognition of a Mr Maule of Bristol who was instrumental in its introduction. The flower colour varies although, at the time, it was the orange shade which was considered typical. It forms a sprawling, untidy shrub but when trained as a cordon on a wall it comes into its own. The range of cultivar names seen today refer mostly to the race of hybrids which appeared spontaneously in gardens of which this species is one parent. The other is *C. speciosa*, introduced from China the century before and the grex name given to the progeny is *C.* × *superba*. "Knap Hill Scarlet" is only one. The "Yoshino Cherry", *Prunus* × *yedoensis*, has never been found in the wild. Apparently it is widely planted in Japan, especially in cities. It, too, is said to be a hybrid between two species, *P. speciosa* and *P. subhirtella*, and quite naturally one would expect the seedlings to vary in habit and flower colour. Erect and spreading forms are recorded and the flowers are available in shades from white to pale pink. The attractive spreading white-flowered clone is much sought after and in spring gives the oriental effect so many of us admire.

However, to begin with, I should like to examine a number of low stature plants, the kind of plants which appeal to us as plantsmen and rock gardeners. I hasten to add that they are not all rock garden plants, neither are they alpines but all of them we find fascinating and most of them we should like to see flourishing in our gardens.

If we were to look into one of the more primitive families of flowering plants, Ranunculaceae, we should find many by which we place great store, Adonis, Aquilegia and Eranthis being examples.

The early flowering *Adonis amurensis* is named for Amur, an area in S.E. Asia but it also occurs throughout the Japanese islands. We all seem to favour the double flowered form in this instance but once the bronze and pink shaded kinds become more readily available we may change our loyalty. The aquilegias, too, are not without their admirers and *A. flabellata* must surely be a favourite. It is native to the northern islands and is quite long lived in gardens, having the most perfect flowers. It is variable in height and flower colour and there is a particularly fine form with pure white blooms and glaucous foliage. The familiar yellow *Eranthis hyemalis* is from western Europe but the Japanese *E. pinnatifida* is something different. It is much more delicate. It has tuberous roots and from these arise stems bearing a ruff of pinnate foliage. This surrounds the pure white flowers and against this background the purple-topped stamens are most pronounced. The plant flowers in early spring, February, in an alpine house. I have not tried this species out of doors but I should think it is quite hardy. One requires to have sufficient stock before putting this to the test. Who could deny the lovely *Glaucidium palmatum*? This monotypic genus grows wild in the alpine woodlands of Hokkaido and Honshu. It is a herbaceous perennial of up to three feet in height and carries large, lilac coloured flowers on top of its handsome, palmate leaves. The flowers are of short duration but are so attractive as they unfold their crinkled petals that a sheltered and favoured site is usually chosen for it. The form with pure white flowers is in even greater demand but unfortunately it will always be scarce. Seed from this form does not breed 100% true. Division is possible but the pieces are slow to re-establish. Finally one can hardly over-enthuse about *Paeonia obovata*. It is native to north Japan growing in high altitude woodlands. It appears to be represented solely by the white phase in gardens, and what a good thing, for *P. obovata* var. *alba*, the name by which it is usually recognised, must be examined closely to appreciate the white crystalline globe-forming petals which encase the multitude of yellow stamens which in turn add prominence to the scarlet tipped stigmas. The foliage, too, is attractive, being broad and covered with a grape-like bloom. Please don't spoil it by fingering.

Ericaceae is a plant family which is world wide. It includes forms which are tall trees and others which are lowly creepers. Japan certainly has its share of desirable genera, species and varieties. The circumpolar distribution ensures that *Andromeda polifolia* varies. In nature it creeps and suckers and, being gregarious, it finds company in other woody bog-loving plants. In gardens some forms can be less attractive but the white 'Compacta' and the floriferous 'Grandiflora' are both from Japanese sources. *Arcterica nana*, the "Northern Heath", is rare in the northern islands. It is easy to grow and just requires time to spread and form a solid patch. A batch of seedlings may produce a range of shades in their foliage and calyxes but, on opening, the flowers themselves are described as cream. This tiny evergreen forms a carpet of vegetation barely an inch in height. Of the number of gaultherias listed from Japan, *G. adenothrix* is the one I want to discuss. It has also been known under the generic names Andromeda and Diplycosia. It is a little tender in our northern gardens where it can suffer from cold frosty winds. It has bright red calyxes which partially enclose the pure white orb-shaped flowers, the two colours contrasting well. Although also found in north west America one could hardly ignore the presence of *Harrimanella stelleriana* in Japan. This species is easier to cultivate than the European *H. hypnoides* although one could hardly claim that either species contributes much to the floral display in our gardens. They are plants for the connoisseur and I think they always will be. The phyllodoces are different, they really can put on a colourful show. *Phyllodoce aleutica* is yellow, *P. caerulea* is purplish-pink while *P. nipponica* is white. These dwarf, heath-like shrubs may be admired from a distance for their colour effect or examined more closely where one can appreciate the individual bells. Top dressing with fine peat and attention to watering in dry weather will help to keep the plants in youthful vigour.

Liliaceae is another group of plants on which we as gardeners rely for special effects. It contains one of the most beautiful plants I know, *Lilium japonicum*, the "Bamboo Lily". But how rarely does one see this lovely species in gardens! It is long lived provided it is protected from suppression from other more robustly growing neighbours and is not denied too much light. Just like *L. rubellum*, which has broader leaves and flowers about two weeks earlier, it requires dappled shade in order to preserve the delicate pink tones from being bleached out by strong sunlight. There are fritillaries, too, *F. camschatcensis* being one much sought after by rock gardeners. It has a double form but this does not appeal greatly to me. The dwarf *F. japonica* var. *koidzumiana* is one for the enthusiast. It is rarely ever seen more than six inches tall. Basically the flower colour is white but this is diffused with reddish tones. The flowers are hidden below the top leaves and they are held delicately pendulous. The pencil-like *Chionographes japonica* with its narrow inflorescences requires careful siting. It demands a dark background if it is to produce an effect. It should be noted that the segments of the flowers are of unequal lengths. The pale cream colour of the blooms may be the reason why this plant was at one time listed as *C. lutea. Heloniopsis orientalis* is a meadow plant. It also enjoys plenty of moisture in cultivation. It forms ground-hugging clumps from which arise the four to six inch spikes of pink flowers. If one looks closely at the tips of some of the leaves and where they are in contact with the soil it is just possible that young plantlets will be seen developing from the leaf points. The British Paris is botanically interesting while the Chinese species is decidedly handsome, especially when in fruit, but neither has the white colour pattern of *P. japonica*. This species has had several names applied to it such as Trillium, Trillidium and perhaps the one most often heard, Kinugasa. The tuber-forming root is quite robust and the flower stalk stout, and this will eventually reach 12 inches. *Trillium kamtschaticum*, its close neighbour, is the one we all admire from Japan. Its distribution takes it into Hokkaido. It is typically Trillium but has the distinction of decorating the three ovary tips with a purple spot. It is completely hardy and multiplies satisfactorily. I have reserved to the last in this group *Tricyrtis macrantha*, a plant said to be rare in Shikoku. It is herbaceous and produces long arching stems, and in the axils of the leaves near to the tip large yellow trumpets develop. These are decorated inside with light, chocolate coloured spots. It is slightly tender in Britain and due to its pendulous, arching habit is difficult to site in the garden.

Campanulaceae contributes quite a few worthwhile plants and Adenophora, Campanula (itself) and Platycodon immediately come to mind. *Campanula pilosa* is a species with which we are all familiar and this is a synonym of *chamissonis* or is it *dasyantha*? It all depends on what you wish to name it. I doubt if we will ever get to the bottom of the nomenclature but growers will continue to cultivate that creeping, floriferous plant we know as *C. pilosa* 'Superba'.

Diapensiaceae is but a step from Ericaceae. Naturally it contains Diapensia, that extremely rare Scottish native, *D. lapponica*, although I am quite aware that the species is widespread throughout the northern hemisphere. The form found in Japan, *D. lapponica* var. *obovata* seems to be the one which is *cultivatable* but even that form is seen only infrequently. Young plants should develop into tight clumps, something resembling an upturned bowl, if only one could keep it alive for 100 years. But plants much more diminutive than those of that age are worth having even if the perfect proportions of the creamy-yellow flowers are only seldom seen. There is some confusion in Shortia or is it Schizocodon? Whichever it is does not really matter, for under either name are some of the most desirable plants in our gardens. Although *Shortia uniflora*, with its large singly produced bells in varying shades of pink, will take first prize at most flower shows when seen in its full glory, what does one do about the plant which produces numerous, fringed, thimble-like blooms and is called *Shortia soldanelloides*. The form 'Ilicifolia' is particularly fine but so, too, are well grown specimens of the clone 'Magna'. They all seem to like a peaty soil and in nature favour woodland conditions.

Three members of the poppy family which occur in the northern islands are Pteridophyllum, Hylomecon and Dicentra. The last mentioned must surely foster thoughts of *D. peregrina* var. *pusilla*, that tiny, tricky variety which, according to Ohwi, favours gravelly to sandy slopes on the side of volcanoes. I know it is not necessary to simulate these conditions to the letter to get good results but possibly if a volcano happened to be at the back door the plant would respond better. These dainty "Dutchmen's Breeches", either in white or shades of pink set against blue, filigree foliage, paint their own pictures. *Hylomecon japonicum* is a good perennial. The flowers are composed of large bright yellow petals and although the individual blooms are short lived, the flowering season is still a long one. It seems to go on all summer. The pinnate foliage is

Laguna Epulauquen (*Plate 88*)

Rhodophiala andicola (*Plate 89*)

Ourisia racemosa   (*Plate 90*)

Adonis amurensis 'Flore Pleno'   (*Plate 91*)

Penstemon frutescens   (*Plate 92*)

Tropaeolum polyphyllum (*Plate 93*)

Tropaeolum speciosum (*Plate 94*)

Tropaeolum tricolorum (*Plate 95*)

Mertensia asiatica   (*Plate 96*)

Menziesia ciliicalyx   (*Plate 97*)

in itself most attractive. *Pteridophyllum racemosum* is rare in coniferous woodlands of Honshu. It is also rare in cultivation for, like all poppies, it transplants badly. It can be divided but small pieces, even when potted up, sometimes never grow away. The name is very descriptive. The derivation means that it has leaves like a fern which has a flower spike in the form of a raceme. What it does not say is that the foliage is evergreen, the spike rises to six inches in height and carries small, pure white flowers for most of its length.

Two gentians of the family which bears that name and which are amenable to cultivation in gardens are *G. algida* and *G. triflora*. The first also occurs in North America and is a proudly erect plant with creamy-white flowers and small but strap-shaped foliage. The spike is approximately six inches high. The herbaceous *G. triflora* has attractive, glaucous foliage. The stems could measure twelve inches and its stature is stiff and upright. A cluster of dark blue flowers terminates the shoots and a white form of this species is also available.

One could dwell long on Iridaceae but I think *Iris gracilipes* will suffice to stimulate interest. This species is extremely floriferous, each scape carrying two or three flowers which are pale purple. It blooms in June when stems six inches high are normal.

Mertensia asiatica occurs on sandy shores on Honshu and Hokkaido. How familiar that sounds! Our Oyster plant, *M. maritima*, likes similar conditions, and not surprisingly, for the Japanese species is sometimes considered to be simply a form of that British native. This form is easy to grow in gardens, which is one difference, and is in demand for its foliage effect alone. This is of the brightest, glaucous shade and stems may spread a yard from the central crowns. Self sown seedlings are not uncommon.

Familiar generic names such as Kirengeshoma, Tanakaea, Astilbe and Deinanthe indicate the wealth of plant material in the family Saxifragaceae. All of these are suitable for the rock garden. Parnassia also comes into this group and *P. foliosa* var. *japonica* is one of those fascinating plants which seem to go to great lengths to attract its pollinator. The flowers are pure white but it is the frilliness of the petals which is so delicate. It is found in wet places on Honshu. Our own *P. palustris*, which incidentally is also a Japanese native species, favours similar places, for this moisture is important during the growing season if the plants are to survive in cultivation.

Patrinia belongs to the Valerian family, and *P. triloba* is the one which is considered most garden-worthy. The red stems may reach twelve inches in height, terminating in an umbel of bright yellow flowers. These are numerous and are spurred. The foliage is a delicate shade of bright green, lobed and thinly textured. Flowering in July it protracts the interest in rock gardening into mid-summer.

Penstemons are usually thought of as plants of the North American continent but the genus is represented in Japan by *P. frutescens*. This is a herbaceous perennial, not shrubby like so many of its North American cousins and it dies back to a resting crown each winter. In fact a new generic name, Pennellianthus, has recently been suggested for it. It forms dormant buds and spreads by means of short underground rhizomes. It can reach six inches in height and produces a few lilac coloured to pale purple flowers. It has broad leaves but it is the old fashioned colour of the perianths which is so distinctive. I have seen a transparency of a white form.

Some members of Polygonaceae are just a little on the rampant side for the rock garden but among those which are suitable is the little *Polygonum tenuicaule*. It is a glabrous, creeping perennial which will spread quite slowly. The scape is usually about six inches long and carries a string of small white flowers which closely resemble beads. The leaves are broadish, up to two inches wide, and form an effective ground cover. It is quite hardy but it must have moist soil if it is to remain healthy and vigorous.

Potentilla of course belongs to the rose family, and although there are many good garden plants in this group I feel that the brightly coloured *P. megalantha* should be chosen as Japan's representative. It grows in rocky places in nature and does equally well in similar sites in gardens. It prefers a deep root run so as to support the numerous spreading stems and the large quantity of flowers it can produce. It is hardy and densely pubescent and has divided leaves. The leaflets are very hairy and coarsely toothed while the large yellow flowers up to 1½ inches across are freely produced.

All rock gardeners grow primulas of some sort or another, in fact there are so many to choose from that it is usually difficult to be discriminating in what species to cultivate. It would be very easy to say the less easy ones or those not often seen should be avoided but here I have chosen two as reminders that there is more to Primula than the coarse candelabra, *P. japonica*, or the old conservatory *P. sieboldii* which has been widely grown in its many forms. *Primula hidakana* is a rare plant from Hokkaido where it is said to grow on rocky cliffs and in ravines. It is a good perennial with a rhizomatous rootstock. The leaves are broad and have seven lobes, each of which is irregularly toothed. The scapes are only few flowered but the colour of each bloom is a delicate rose. Also from the northern islands, Hokkaido and Honshu, and found in the higher mountains, is *P. jesoana*. I have grown this for many years in a shady part of the garden and although it has been raised from seed on occasion, it is a good perennial. It has roundish leaves with seven to nine shallow lobes. It has a short, creeping rootstock and although it could be increased by dividing the crowns, it sets seed so regularly and freely that I consider germination the best method of increasing stocks. The flowers are in clusters with usually several flowering stems together.

Ranzania japonica has been known as *Podophyllum japonicum* and is monotypic. It is one of those plants which suddenly erupts through the soil in spring and as it emerges its flowers are already formed and open almost immediately. The stems develop quickly, elongating until very soon the lilac flowers are seen to be pendulous in the crotches between two large leaves. The fruit is a white berry. Although rhizomatous, and this suggests that it can be divided, it is inclined to sulk and take a long time to grow away from pieces separated from the main crown. There is a shortage of fibrous feeding roots on divided plantlets. It belongs to Berberidaceae which apart from the shrubby genera, also includes Caulophyllum, Epimedium, Achlys and Diphylleia.

Sedum seems to be the natural choice to represent Crassulaceae. We all grow some species and it may be that we are lucky in that most of us manage to grow a selection. *Sedum kamtschaticum* is widespread throughout the islands. It is also widespread in gardens, sometimes masquerading as a variety of *S. aizoon* and sometimes under the different name of *S. ellacombianum*. The numerous starry flowers are carried in a broad head. They are yellow and are effectively set off against a background of shiny leaves. It is one of the more easily grown plants in this family.

Viola brevistipulata var. *hidakana* is a small plant with a long name. It represents a race of lowly little violets which often are but fleeting visitors to our gardens. There are a few genera included in Violaceae but Viola is the only one native to Japan. This variety, *hidakana*, is truly alpine and is confined to north Hokkaido. It has a rhizomatous root, is herbaceous and as the growth develops in spring the thickish, coarsely toothed leaves can, at times, display a bronze lustre. The small bright yellow violets are carried on short stems approximately three inches in height. It grows in Edinburgh in a cool sheltered spot.

As the title of my subject is Japanese Plants in the Garden I think it would be misleading if I were to finish here without making some reference to the value of the many woody species and genera native to that country. Up until now we have discussed small attractive species which often blend with others to form a patchwork pattern, or difficult genera which test the skill of the cultivator. The next dozen plants I wish to consider are shrubby, even small trees. By themselves some of these make dominant features and in some instances require little else to create an effect.

Aceraceae is an example and if I mention two maples, *Acer japonicum* and *A. palmatum*, I have immediately introduced the names of plants which appeal to all gardeners. Both are common in nature and both have long been cultivated by the Japanese. This lengthy association with growers·has resulted in numerous good forms being selected and named; forms which may vary very slightly in some instances but be perceptible to the collector's discerning eye. *Acer japonicum* is slow growing but it can eventually attain a height of 20 feet. It varies a great deal and among the forms sought is *A. japonicum* 'Aureum'. This has pale golden-yellow foliage which remains constant for most of the season. One of the advantages of growing a plant because of its lovely foliage is that it is attractive immediately it comes into leaf, even when still young. In fact a fully grown specimen may be too large for the site but small plants can provide a more than adequate return. *Acer palmatum* is a small tree which is very common in the wild. It is offered in many forms. The leaves are usually five pointed although forms with seven, nine and eleven points are quite usual. Those bearing foliage which is much divided are usually classified under the heading

"Dissectum", and 'Dissectum Atropurpureum' simply indicates the colour of the leaves. Both species favour a moist, fairly fertile soil. They look particularly well overhanging a pool and are tolerant enough to be able to grow either in full sun or partial shade.

Actinidia kolomikta is not usually seen as a free standing specimen and gives the best results when trained to a wall. It requires to be tied in as it is a clamberer and has no tendrils or suckers by which it can attach itself. It is deciduous but its leaves in summer are its greatest asset. These develop their fascinating, bi-colour effect and the pink and white leaf tips give an overall brightness to the plant. The leaf changing phenomenon occurs only on old established specimens. Those which are young and vigorous rarely show this and neither do old plants if they are in too much shade. It is most suited to a sunny warm corner. It belongs to Actinidiaceae.

A common plant throughout Japan is *Hydrangea paniculata*, a member of Saxifragaceae. One of its valuable assets is that it blooms in autumn. Furthermore, the faded inflorescences are suitable for using in dried arrangements. The flower trusses contain fertile and sterile flowers but in the case of the clone *H. paniculata* 'Grandiflora' only sterile flowers are present. This gives the inflorescence a solid appearance. The colour tones of the flowers change with age, altering from cream to shades of pink. It was introduced from Japan more than 100 years ago. Severe pruning keeps this form in check and at the same time ensures that large panicles develop. The pruning is done in March and if the loam is moist and fertile vigorous growth and large flower trusses result.

It would not be possible to discuss garden plants from the Orient without mentioning Magnolia, which belongs to the family of that name. I should like to draw attention to two species since they are completely different. They require similar conditions which include an open situation and a soil with high fertility. The first is *M. sieboldii* which is really a large shrub or small tree. It produces long annual growths and these should be left alone. The full glory of this species cannot be fully appreciated until the plants are above head height. The white flowers are pendulous, and seen against a blue sky are breathtakingly beautiful. The blooms are further enhanced by having bright scarlet stamens. This species is not recommended for a limey soil. *Magnolia stellata* is a plant for the rock garden. I say this because it will flower from an early age and while still small. It can reach ten to twelve feet after many years but in the rock garden at Edinburgh there is a specimen in the open which is all of 50 years old and still measures less than four feet in height. It blooms well every year. There is a form with pink flowers but I would hesitate to say that it was an improvement on the species. *Magnolia stellata* is much planted in Japan and, like *M. sieboldii*, is a plant from the mountains.

Ericaceae is well represented in gardens and when considering larger species the family cannot be ignored. *Menziesia ciliicalyx* for example is very popular. This deciduous shrub is most effective in spring. The young leaves and flowers develop together. The foliage is quite glaucous while the wine-coloured flowers, too, have a bloom but when lit up from behind by a low light the corollas glow. The bristly calyxes provide the name and are themselves lovely when seen at close range. Rhododendrons there are in quantity but the one which has received most publicity must surely be *Rh. yakushimanum*. The species varies tremendously and there are all manner of forms but it is the dwarf early flowering clones that are in demand. The foliage is attractive with its buff tomentum on the upper surface and the heavier dressing on the under-sides. This is at first white but changes to rust as the leaves age. Dry plants are unhappy but if cared for these forms will flower well when quite small, even in pots. *Rhododendron* 'Hinomayo', an old but popular cultivar of the ubiquitous Kurume azaleas, has extreme flower power. These Kurumes are considered to be hybrids raised in Japan by intercrossing *Rhododendrons kiusianum, kaempferi* and *obtusum*. They are deciduous but unfortunately they start into growth quite early in the year and so are liable to be damaged by spring frosts. Not all are hardy. They start to flower when quite young and although at their best in an open site they can be effective in partial shade. The site influences their stature and too much shade can result in poor flowering. Wilson introduced 50 clones into the Arnold Arboretum in 1920. He re-christened them and applied English names and while I understand these new names were quickly accepted in the U.S.A. they were never popular in Europe.

A family so far unmentioned, Caprifoliaceae, contains both Viburnum and Weigela. *Viburnum plicatum* includes a number of forms. Two which are popular are *V. plicatum* var. *plicatum*, the "Japanese Snowball Tree" bearing round balls of completely sterile white flowers and *V. plicatum* var. *mariesii* which produces large flat inflorescences, the outer ring of flowers being large and sterile. Fertile flowers occur in the centre. The wild phase is *V. plicatum* var. *tomentosum* which can be grown as a free standing shrub or trained against a wall. *Weigela middendorffiana* grows naturally in thickets on alpine slopes. These occur on Hokkaido and Honshu. In gardens it is not seen as often as it should be for it is one of only two species of Weigela with yellow flowers. It forms a medium sized bush and is not so coarse growing as some of the other more vigorous kinds. It requires a moist, rich soil for the amount of bloom carried is dependent upon the number of strong young growths produced during the previous year.

After describing so much floral beauty, much of it attributable to a country's wild flowers, it is surprising to find a form of gardening favoured by some Japanese growers where flowers play little or no part. One cannot but admire and enjoy the quiet tones in a green garden. One must surely find peace and solace in the beauty of reflections in still waters. The placing of decorative stone lanterns, the graceful yet simple designs of small bridges and other features give a picture of completeness and permanence almost irrespective of season.

While I could not say that I prefer the large, flamboyant, pom-pom Chrysanthemum to the stillness and tranquillity of the green landscape, I must confess that if I lived in Japan my garden would be full of the native wild plants; the plants that give so much pleasure to western plantsmen and add so much beauty to their gardens.

The Conference Show and Awards

BARRY STARLING

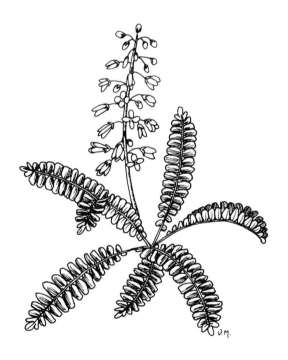

Pteridophyllum racemosum

Perhaps the greatest attribute of an International Rock Garden Plant Conference Show is that it is held only once in ten years. To the keen exhibitor this factor is the spur to produce plants of an even greater degree of excellence than is usual at annual shows, for to be among the prizewinners at such a prestigious show is achievement indeed.

Despite the coquettish behaviour of the weather in the months leading up to the Conference, many and varied were the plants which graced the show benches. As to the period of the show itself, it is rumoured that the Show Director had a prior arrangement with the Almighty to ensure cool enough temperatures to keep blossoms in a state of suspended excellence throughout.

The main competition took place in a large, well illuminated, airy hall which, by the time judging commenced was comfortably filled with colour and interest. There was excitement in the air, too, at the thought of having a chance to see the finest of the world's mountain plants at close quarters. In the first half-dozen classes dwarf shrubs took pride of place, all being well established veterans. *Daphne × napolitana* was a dome of misty rose-purple 40 cm (16 in.) high by 40 cm (16 in.) in diameter, while just along the bench an enormous plant of *Rhododendron valentinianum*, undaunted by spring frosts, had opened unusually rich, yellow corollas. Of completely contrasting shape was the 45 cm (18 in.) diameter, flat, dense mat of *Cassiope lycopodioides* over which danced thousands, yes thousands of tiny glistening white lanterns grasped atop by scarlet-fingered calyxes suspended from hooked, fine, wiry stems 3 cm (1¼ in.) high.

It was good to see *Viola albanica* take a first place. Few rock plants flower for so long or are less demanding than this tough little Viola which provides, from April to July, an abundance of lavender-blue faces with finely etched black lines radiating from creamy-yellow centres.

In assessing the six pan class the judges were faced with the predicament of choosing between two very fine entries. In both the plants were varied, including dwarf shrubs, bulbs, woodlanders and high alpines all in tip-top condition. The prize went to the six which included *Narcissus* 'Hawera', *Omphalodes luciliae*, *Daphne retusa*, *Asperula suberosa*, *Kalmiopsis leachiana* and *Corydalis wilsonii*. Next, the three pan class was won by *Draba mollissima*, a white

Fritillaria meleagris and *Armeria caespitosa* (now more correctly *A. juniperifolia*) but two other plants in this class captured my attention. One was the moss-green cushion 15 cm (16 in.) by 10 cm (4 in.) of *Pygmea pulvinaris* studded with white, five-petalled flowers, the other, *Saxifraga flagellaris* ssp. *sikkimensis*, shorter stemmed than the type and with runners less red than usual, but very eye-catching with cluster heads of bright yellow.

Draba dedeana not only gained first prize in the class for one rock plant in flower but received an Award of Merit when submitted to the Joint Rock Garden Plant Committee. Here was a dense snow flurry of flowers over a 20 cm (8 in.) diameter lush, green cushion. In the same class *Morisia monantha* showed four-petalled, yellow flowers peeping from the centre of a dark green, ferny-foliaged rosette and *Calceolaria fothergillii* dangled square-pouched blooms on 10 cm (4 in.) stems above furry foliage. In the class for one pan Saxifraga, *Saxifraga demnatensis* triumphed. Looking as it does, like a robust, white flowered, mossy saxifrage, one is tempted to underestimate the skill required to keep this plant in good condition.

While *Primula gracilipes* undoubtedly warranted its first prize in the class for one pan Primula, tribute must be paid to Dr Onoe, from Japan, who brought and staged the second-prize winner, *Primula tosaensis* var. *brachycarpa*. His exhibit was shown in a square box of smoothed, natural wood, pegged at the corners and filled with sphagnum moss in which about twenty small plants were encouraged to feel at home after their long journey. Cortusa-like leaves up to 4 cm (1½ in.) diameter were green, beautifully flushed purple on short petioles surrounding the 3 cm (1¼ in.) tall scapes. Each scape bore several lavender-pink, white centred flowers on 1·5 cm (¾ in.) reddish-brown pedicels. For three pans European primulas the well known Pp. 'Linda Pope' and *marginata* 'Hyacintha' combined with a deep violet, white-centred *Primula* × *pubescens* hybrid, 'Mrs Wilson', to make a winning entry. In the next Primula class the large flowered, creamy-white hybrid *P.* 'Harlow Car' won; also in this class, making its début on the show bench was Beverly Reid's hybrid 'Kathleen Dryden', raised in 1975. This bore dainty yellow clusters reminiscent of the Cowslip, over auricula-like leaves.

Androsace vandellii found the 1981 spring to its liking and performed magnificently for several exhibitors. It combined with an *Androsace muscoidea* collected in Kashmir in 1977 and the blush pink, red-eyed *A. lehmannii* from Nepal, which was flowering profusely over a cushion of green needle-like leaves, to win the class for three pans Androsace over stiff competition from two other excellent entries. *Androsace muscoidea*, notoriously difficult to keep in good condition, won the next class as a 15 cm (6 in.) mound liberally studded with white, pentagonal flowers. This plant also received an Award of Merit and its exhibitor a Cultural Commendation. In the next class *A. vandellii* triumphed again over *A. villosa* 'Taurica' and a coarser form of *A. vandellii*. And then again in the class for one pan Primulaceae this same species, 15 cm (6 in.) in diameter and enhanced by a surround of shales of grey slate won the prize for the best plant in the Open Section.

The Lewisia class in the Open Section was won by *L. tweedyi* with 50 open flowers and many buds. Impressive in this class was the *L. cotyledon* hybrid, 'Harold Judd', a bright yellow with orange-gold centre stripe to the petal. The five rosettes produced a total of over 30 flowering stems.

Two Narcissi from the Atlas Mountains along with *Iris bucharica* won the class for three pans bulbs. These were the tiny, white *N. watieri* and a very good form of *N. bulbocodium*. That fine Cyclamen from S. Greece, *C. repandum* 'Peloponnese' was represented by a 40 cm (16 in.) diameter plant bearing a forest of slender stems topped with smoky-pink flowers over silver-speckled leaves. Contained in one of Dr Onoe's boxes from Japan, apparently growing through the moss, were several dainty, 8 cm (3 in.) high Japanese "Slipper Orchids", *Cypripedium debile*. From twin leaves emerged slender stems supporting pale mauve pouches under lanceolate, green "donkey's ears". The stigma of each flower was framed by a deep violet-black horseshoe. Again from Japan came the attractive and rarely seen *Eranthis pinnatifida* with papery-white flowers and finely dissected leaves. For one pan Trillium perhaps the best Trillium species of all dominated the class, *T. grandiflorum*, quite 45 cm (18 in.) in diameter and bearing 33 huge, snowy-white flowers in pristine condition.

The three pans Ericaceae class included in the winning three a profusely flowered, compact, 10 cm (14 in.) high by 25 cm (10 in.) wide plant of *Phyllodoce caerulea* while in the next class, two plants in particular attracted my attention. First was a robust *Cassiope fastigiata*, luxuriant in growth, without the usual browning of lower stems and with a mass of buds and flowers. The other *Epigaea* 'Aurora' was a most welcome sight, especially as the raiser of this interesting hybrid between *E. asiatica* and *E. repens*, Mr C. Marchant, had told me 15 years ago that he believed the hybrid was no longer in existence. In the class specifically for cassiopes a very well flowered plant of *C. wardii*, with less bristly foliage than usual, stood 25 cm (10 in.) high and almost as much across. Two ericaceous shrubs, *Phyllodoce caerulea* and *Cassiope lycopodioides* were joined in the class for dwarf shrubs by a well-flowered *Daphne collina*, while in a class for one dwarf shrub two seldom seen plants took first and second prizes. First was the prostrate *Rosmarinus lavandulaceus*, sprawling gracefully and bearing soft, blue flowers towards the tips. Though not considered hardy, winter wet is possibly more damaging to this plant than low temperatures, so that the protection of an alpine house is usually sufficient to ensure survival. The second shrublet was the white form of the well known *Daphne cneorum*, a plant which has probably remained scarce due to the fact that it is less easy to propagate than the type.

The class for three pans dwarf conifers must have been a tough one for the judges, for here were six entries—all excellent veterans in good health and character. The winning entry comprised three different genera in the shape of *Cedrus libani* 'Nana', *Chamaecyparis obtusa* 'Juniperoides' and *Picea abies* 'Gregoryana'. It was a form of this last mentioned dwarf spruce, *P. abies* 'Veitchii', that won the single specimen class; here was a tightly compacted, 30 cm (12 in.) high, 40 cm (16 in.) diameter, round-topped pyramid clothed in the emerald-green of emerging new growth. Where dwarf pines are exhibited *Pinus sylvestris* 'Beuvronensis' is always a hot favourite, all the characteristics of the rugged Scots Pine being scaled down to a miniature of perfect proportions. The winning entry was a broad-topped specimen some 60 cm (24 in.) high, with no trace of wear and tear to the over-wintered foliage.

Dwarf Salix were much in evidence, the show occurring at optimum "catkin" time. A fine male plant of *Salix reticulata* intrigued visitors, not only by its conspicuous catkins but also the gnarled and prostrate habit of the older branches and finely etched filigree of veins on firm oval green leaves which were silver beneath. This plant received an Award of Merit.

Three winning pans of Diapensiaceae were in fact three shallow baskets containing *Diapensia lapponica*, sadly not in flower, and two shortias, *S. uniflora* and the handsome-leaved *S. soldanelloides* 'Ilicifolia'. However it was the single pan of *Shortia* 'Wimborne' in the next class that contributed one of the most spectacular exhibits of the show. This hybrid between the Japanese *S. uniflora* and N. American *S. galacifolia* bore nearly 40 pale pink, frilled-edged corollas on 12 cm (5 in.) stems, framed and enhanced by round, glossy, red-margined leaves. As well as winning its class, *S.* 'Wimborne' was awarded a First Class Certificate by the Joint Rock Garden Plant Committee.

An interesting group of N. American plants included the rare *Lewisia stebbinsii* and even rarer, tiny *L. sierrae* with white, star-shaped flowers striped on each petal deep pink, together with *Dodecatheon frenchii* from western N. America. Winning the class, however were two fine and difficult cushion plants, *Kelseya uniflora*, well flowered, and a bright green dome of *Lepidium nanum*, combined with *Primula ellisiae* from New Mexico. Next, two more plants from the N. American continent distinguished themselves. *Lupinus lepidus* var. *lobbii* (better known as *L. lyalli*) owes its dwarf stature and silvered foliage to its high mountain environment and it is very difficult to retain these characteristics on cultivated plants. The plant shown came very close to achieving this, being merely 15 cm (6 in.) in height and having silver-edged leaves which provided the ideal foil for the five stubby spikes of clear blue flowers. In second place *Aquilegia saximontana* danced little blue and white ballerinas over a ferny haze of foliage.

New Zealand plants were represented by three pans of aciphyllas, *A. simplex* being in flower, and in the next class by an effectively staged perfect green dome of *Pygmea pulvinaris* surrounded by grey slate.

From the rich and varied Japanese flora came *Rhododendron keiskei* 'Yaku Fairy', *Arisaema ringens* and the curious *A. thunbergii* with inverted "two-tailed mice" in place of flowers. Appropriately a first prize for one Japanese plant went to a Japanese exhibitor, the plant being a white form of *Primula kisoana* var. *shikokiana*. Above rosettes of Cortusa-like leaves, white, green-eyed flowers, 2 cm (¾ in.) in diameter were held in dainty umbels of from five to ten. Effective, though unplaced, was *Arisaema amurense* with light green leaves and spathe erupting from a carpet of dark green moss. Plants collected by Dr George Smith in Nepal were much in evidence in the section for Himalayan plants and included two forms of *Saxifraga georgei* as green domes studded with sturdy little 3 mm (⅛ in.) diameter white flowers and also the deep violet, green-eyed *Androsace muscoidea* var. *longiscapa* with furry green rosettes in prime condition. Sometimes called "Queen of the Himalayas", *Paraquilegia grandiflora* nodded deep blue, golden-anthered "poppy-like" flowers on slender stems over blue-green, ferny foliage.

To stage a collection of twelve plants of one genus or family is something of a challenge, especially when hardy orchids are the choice. Noteworthy they all were but particularly eye-catching were flamboyant *Orchis papilionacea*, *Ophrys lutea* var. *lutea* with black tongue on yellow lips and *Orchis provincialis* displaying creamy flowers over spotted leaves.

The effectiveness of *Ophiopogon planiscapus* 'Nigrescens' as a foliage plant was well demonstrated by its inclusion in no less than five of the entries for three pans coloured foliage. The winning entry also included the variegated *Arabis ferdinandi-coburgii* and N. American *Sedum spathulifolium* with succulent rosettes of leaves covered in grey "bloom".

In the second half of the Open Section where pan size was limited to 16·5 cm (6½ in.), two unusual plants made me pause and look again. One was *Geum pentapetalum* 'Plenum' displaying double, cream, 2·5 cm (1 in.) pom-poms on wiry stems above ferny-green leaves—the quaintly shaped Japanese terra-cotta pot in which the Geum grew was as desirable as the plant! *Saxifraga hypostoma*, with each of the five, round-lobed, white petals distinctly separate and around the conspicuous green centre, held my attention. Even out of flower the brilliant green cushion of foliage must be most effective.

Then followed a feast of primulas and androsaces. Noteworthy among these was an entry of three small species, the British native *P. scotica*, a white *P. rubra* (syn. *P. hirsuta*) *exscapa* and a deep rose-lilac *P. frondosa*. Of several *Androsace vandellii* it was a plant flowering to its absolute maximum that received the accolade of best plant in the Open Section.

Many bulbous plants were already over so that two classes for these were poorly supported. A charming little Narcissus of close affinity to *N. rupicola* was worthy of its prize. Representing Orchid-aceae was *Aceras anthropophorum*—a spike of vegetation from which hung numerous tiny brown men with large green hoods. Pleiones had two classes to themselves and it was the much ac-claimed, bright yellow *P. forrestii*, fielding several blooms, that won the single pan class. With the current vogue for fritillaries it is not surprising that their two classes were well supported. Though the sombre green and brown lanterned *F. kurdica* received top honours, for sheer grace and warmth of colour the flared orange trumpets of that tantalising western N. American species, *Fritillaria recurva*, had the greater appeal.

And so the tremendous variety of plants which we choose to grow under the heading of alpines, continued to unfold; the intense blue of *Gentiana brachyphylla* and whiter than white *Cassiope lycopodioides* 'Beatrice Lilley'; the myriad of creamy droplets dan-gling from whipcord stems of *Cassiope selaginoides* L & S 13284 watched by the upturned pea-like flowers of creeping *Polygala chamaebuxus* var. *purpurea*; the superb black-green orb of *Cham-aecyparis obtusa* 'Hypnoides' spangled with lively bright green tips, and the gnarled shrublet of Kingdon Ward's "Pink Baby", *Rhodo-dendron pumilum*, ringing in the spring with tiny pink bells. Both these shrubs were of considerable age despite their diminutive size. Demonstrating considerable skill in cultivation were the six pans of New Zealanders representing two three pan entries which were judged equal firsts. Three 8 cm (3 in.) diameter grey domes of *Raoulia bryoides*, *Haastia pulvinaris*, and *Raoulia mammillaris* made up one very uniform exhibit, while the other again included *Haastia pulvinaris*, but in this instance was joined by *Raoulia rubra* and *R. × loganii*.

Classes for plants new or rare in cultivation are often exciting, giving the enthusiastic plantsman that extra incentive to seek out the new and take up the challenge of growing it. Certainly the Himalayan *Androsace muscoidea* var. *longiscapa* (Dolpo Form), grown and staged as an alluring confection of lavender-pink, must have gladdened the heart of its skilled cultivator. On much the same theme one can claim success and satisfaction when one has completed the life cycle of a difficult plant by raising it from seed to flowering. How much more rewarding when one has raised such an Orchid as *Ophrys speculum* from seed to flowering size, and then placed it proudly and with clear conscience on the show bench knowing that it has not been torn from a precious wild colony. If only this technique could be mastered by others! Also skilfully raised from seed was the winning entry in the next class, all three plants originating from the Middle East. From western Caucasus came the rare *Gentiana oschtenica*, resembling a large, clear yellow flowered *G. verna*, while from the Varzob Valley of the Pamir Ali came the oval-leaved, green rosetted *Dionysia involucrata* with heads of white buds. Thirdly there was another Dionysia, *D. diapensifolia* grown from seed from Iran. As a single plant raised from seed *Androsace vandellii* triumphed yet again but it was another exhibit, much easier to grow from seed, that I found most striking. This was *Aquilegia viridiflora* with slender stems arching to bear blooms fashioned in graceful curves. Above a goblet of olive-green and black extended five snake-like spurs at first gently curving outwards and then reversing direction almost to meet at the tips. From the mouth of the goblet erupted a fuzz of yellow stamens.

In section B, for members who had won less than twenty-five first prizes, the high standard of cultivation and interesting variety of plants was just as evident with exhibits, for instance, of *Primula deuteronana* from high altitudes in Nepal, with large, soft lavender flowers set in a rosette of crisp, crinkled, dark green leaves; from N. America, *Townsendia exscapa* bearing large, white daisies amongst the slightly silky leaves; a New Zealand Ranunculus, *R. insignis*, holding aloft eight-petalled buttercups above rounded, crenate leaves and then back to Asia again for another Primula, *P. irregularis* with its crowded umbel of bluish-purple flowers held in a tight posy by a robust rosette of foliage.

Judged the best plant in this section was that most garden-worthy hybrid Cassiope, *C.* 'Randle Cooke' with its green "pile" of shoots almost totally hidden by white bells dangling on red pedicels at the tips of the shoots. In the same class it was astounding to see *Gaultheria procumbens* with cherry-sized fruits and *Pernettya tasmanica* massed with red berries still intact in April. In my garden the fruits of these are barely allowed to colour before being devoured by blackbirds. Rhododendrons were represented by *R. pemakoense* flowering prolifically as ever, to beat narrowly *R. fletcherianum* and the none too easy *R. imperator.*

Lewisia tweedyi 'Rosea' pushed out exquisite salmon-rose wagon wheels on strong axles from amongst succulent leaves, while a double white *Anemone nemorosa* displayed 4 cm (1½ in.) diameter flowers of six large elliptical petals framing a central white pom-pom.

Novice exhibitors, often reticent about entering at major shows, supported this Conference Show well, there being thirteen entries in the three pan classes alone. It was the very difficult *Androsace muscoidea* in its white form that proved to be the best plant in this section—a challenging plant if ever there was, resenting even a little moisture on its tiny, furry rosettes.

Winner of the three pans Primulaceae was an exhibit of three distinct genera from different lands. Difficult to please, rosy-red flowered *Douglasia montana* from western N. America was joined by the Japanese *Primula modesta* var. *alba* and yet another excellent *Androsace vandellii* representing Europe. Magnificent in the Asiatic Primula class was *P. petiolaris*, a complete dome of lavender, 15 cm (6 in.) in diameter, each flower with an inner white zone and green eye.

In the Orchid class beautiful *Ophrys tenthredinifera* expanded broad satiny-pink sepals, pale green through the centre, above a furry brown, large lower lobe. The central red-brown area of the lip was outlined in bright blue. The shade loving *Epigaea repens* in its white form won the Ericaceae class whilst that tiniest of dwarf shrubs, *Kelseya uniflora* won its class sporting a sprinkling of pink dots which pass for flowers, over the silvery-green, close mat of foliage. From seed collected by Watson and MacPhail in Turkey, *Alkanna aucheriana* added a touch of brilliant and intense blue with Anchusa-like flowers in the final class of the competitive section.

Occupying the small hall were a number of non-competitive exhibits staged by private individuals. These, besides being informative and interesting, often showed a high degree of skilful cultivation. Foremost among these was an exhibit by Kath Dryden who, besides shouldering the responsibility for the entire Conference Show, managed to find time to grow and display 110 plants, and among them, the plant judged "Best in Show". Too many facts and figures can be bewildering but the following data relative to Mrs Dryden's exhibit is well worth recording. Included were 31 distinct genera; of these 25 were different fritillarias, 10 trilliums, 13 lewisias, 8 cyclamen, 8 primulas, 3 orchids, 4 dodecatheons and 7 distinct forms of *Ranunculus asiaticus* as well as a diverse range of genera represented by only one or two species. A veteran specimen of the Tasmanian *Trochocarpa thymifolia* caused much comment while to flower and exhibit *Calypso bulbosa*, perfectly at home in a setting of moss, was no mean achievement. However, from the centre of the exhibit, glowing like a great, soft-yellow, full moon, was the 35 cm (14 in.) disc of prostrate *Rhododendron keiskei* 'Yaku Fairy'. Undoubtedly the plant had leaves but these were completely obscured by the hundreds of 3 cm (1¼ in.) wide corollas. The timing was perfect—the buds opening wide for the first day of the Conference and remaining, in the coolness of the hall, at perfection to the last day. Thus *R. keiskei* 'Yaku Fairy' was given the Farrer and Forrest medals, awarded jointly for the "Best Plant in the Show".

For Fritillaria enthusiasts, Dr Jack Elliott's display of 50 different forms provided a marvellous opportunity to study the relative merits of the species and geographical forms. As one of the uninitiated I found the beautiful orange *F. recurva* from California and pale green lanterns of *F. pontica* quite fascinating.

Of considerable interest and educational value was the exhibit by Miss E. Liquorish devoted to ferns. This comprised books and excellent botanical drawings together with pressed specimens. The life cycle of the male fern was illustrated showing the complicated process of fertilization leading to the production of a new seedling, or sporling.

Dr D. J. Harberd's work with pleiones resulting in the production of the 'Shantung' race of hybrids, incorporating the yellow of the still rare *P. forrestii*, is already known to some members. It was interesting to see how they were derived in a comprehensive display of Pleione species and hybrids together with some excellent photographs.

Margaret and Henry Taylor used a huge map of Europe to illustrate the distribution of Primula species over that continent. Strings from distribution centres on the map carried one's eye to living species in pots. Altogether some 50 species and hybrids were included. Not content with one genus Mr A. R. Woodliffe staged impressive exhibits of both Salix and Pinus, including 33 different willows and 34 dwarf forms of *Pinus sylvestris*. The diversity of the willows was well illustrated by graceful or quaint stems bearing yellow, pink, red or silver catkins. Perhaps the most rare of all was the small-leaved, totally prostrate *Salix reticulata* var. *prostrata*, a particularly choice form of a well known dwarf willow. Outstanding among the pines were a 25-year-old specimen of *P. sylvestris* 'Compacta Compressa', and a cone-bearing form introduced by Laurence Walker 20 years ago as *P. sylvestris* 'Hesley Hall'. The rare *P. sylvestris* 'Nisbett's Gem' and *P. sylvestris* var. *brevifolia* were both represented, while a six-year-old, 15 cm (6 in.) high *P. sylvestris* 'Longmoor' formed a perfectly-shaped miniature Scots Pine.

The Artistic Section gave overseas participants a chance to exhibit and was well supported by members from both home and abroad. This section also gave delegates a chance to see, even if not "in the flesh", plants which do not appear on the show bench. Two such plants were included in the winning entry for three colour photographs, one being the "Bear Grass", *Xerophyllum tenax*, and the other the parasitic but beautiful *Pedicularis rostrata*. In another entry *Diapensia lapponica* at home on Mount Washington, was to be seen flowering as it very rarely does in cultivation. North American plants featured again in three monochrome photographs. The diversity of habit and form of the three plants ranged from a twiggy shrub with clustered white flower heads, *Ledum glandulosum*, to the little woodland ground orchid with outsize flowers, *Calypso bulbosa*, and light and airy white stars of *Trientalis latifolia*.

Three winning colour photographs of plants in cultivation brought out the effect of contrasting colours in *Potentilla nitida* and *Edraianthus pumilio* and the clean, clear lines of *Aquilegia flabellata* 'Nana'. Best entry in the following class for three black and white photographs depicted *Saxifraga* × *apiculata, Primula bhutanica* and *Draba aizoides*, all as well cultivated specimens.

Four painting classes followed, the first two showing plants in their natural environment with just enough of the habitat in evidence to enhance the alpine characteristics of the plants depicted. *Papaver rhaeticum, Ranunculus glacialis* and *Pulsatilla halleri* formed the winning entry in the first class with tantalizing *Eritrichium nanum* in rugged surroundings winning the second class. Lifelike paintings of *Narcissus bulbocodium* subsp. *romieuxii,* a Tulip and a Crocus species combined botanical accuracy with pleasing design and while a species of Ornithogalum and "Bee Orchid" took first and second places for paintings of individual plants, a very beautiful, though less diagramatic, pink *Ranunculus asiaticus* was aesthetically most pleasing.

Line drawings are not only easy on the eye but are most helpful in identification. The winning entry of three drawings showed in intricate detail the complex structure of the flowers of three species of Iris, *I. latifolia, I. reichenbachii* and *I. planifolia,* while in the final class, by the same exhibitor, the unusual *Haplophyllum biossierianum* was finely drawn. Excellent non-competitive exhibits were staged by Mrs Todd, Professor Pontecorvo and, from Vancouver, Geoff. Williams.

Around the perimeter of the huge lecture hall Rock Garden Plant Societies and individuals displaying crafts and hobbies featuring alpines, staged exhibits which captured the theme of the Conference and provided an interesting area in which to muse quietly during intervals between lectures. The two "patron saints" of the Conference sponsoring societies were represented by exhibits which must have involved much painstaking research. Arranged around a photograph of George Forrest, Dr Burbidge, Royal Botanic Garden, Edinburgh had unearthed, prepared, printed and put on display sepia prints of plants and scenery taken by Forrest on plant collecting trips in Burma and Yunnan and associated these with large coloured pictures of plants in the garden. A huge colour transparency of *Gentiana sino-ornata,* back lit, provided an added impact. While this exhibit occupied one corner of the hall, another commemorating Reginald Farrer dominated the opposite corner. Harry Ward, of Nottingham, had Farrer's original manuscripts and field notes, articles, catalogues of Farrer's Craven Nursery and books all displayed beneath five of Farrer's paintings of Chinese plants, all executed in the high mountains during his most fruitful expeditions. Also of interest was a plan showing the area of Clapham in Yorkshire, in which Farrer had his home.

A well deserved Gold Medal was awarded to Jean Wilson for an exhibit of alpine embroidery in which she had by exquisite needlework depicted in life-like manner such gems as *Cypripedium calceolus* and species of Gentian. Mrs Wilson also raised several superb prize winning plants in the show and while most of us will get no further than recording our successes on colour transparencies, no doubt the image of some of Jean's plants will be preserved in colourful embroidery.

An unusual exhibit was one of hundreds of postage stamps from all parts of the world with one common theme—alpines. It was staggering to see just how many well known and rare wild mountain plants have been featured in this way. Close by, another exhibit reminded us that this was the Year of the Disabled with illustrations of the work being done by the Disabled Trust to provide gardens. For many of the physically handicapped, alpine gardening in the form of troughs or raised beds in which a wide variety of small plants can be tended from a wheelchair, can open up a whole new sphere of interest. A first class exhibition of original paintings of garden plants, the work of Lawrence Greenwood, was very much admired.

One of the most enjoyable regular features of the American Rock Garden Society bulletin are those beautifully executed line drawings of alpines, particularly N. American native plants, by its editor Laura Louis Foster. A collection of these focused much interest on the A.R.G.S. stand. Line drawings of native plants of N.W. America executed by various artists were displayed. These formed an attractive feature in the publication of the North-West Horticultural Society, which has its base in Seattle and prints this informative yet very readable journal and annual seed list. Just over the Canadian border in Vancouver, B.C. are the headquarters of the Alpine Club of British Columbia whose stand displayed colour photographs of alpines in rugged mountain and in montane-woodland settings.

The newly formed Japanese Alpine Rock Garden Society, which incidentally issues an excellent and extensive bulletin with articles in Japanese and English, also displayed photographs of their native alpines, setting the scene with spectacular shots of Japanese mountains. A relief map was a great help to those of us familiar with the names of areas of floral richness in Japan but unaware of geographical locations. The Alpine Garden Society of Sweden incorporated paintings, photographs, posters and magazines in its display, all emphasising Swedish native plants and scenery.

In a huge marquee, adjacent to the Conference centre, exhibits were staged by botanic gardens and members of the trade. On entering the marquee one's attention was immediately drawn to the Royal Horticultural Society's Wisley Garden's exhibit which occupied about one quarter of the tented area. Here the various methods of growing alpines were demonstrated and included the facets of alpine house, rock garden, sink garden, sleeper beds, alpine lawn, scree, peat terrace and an impressive raised bed contained within huge oblong blocks of sandstone. A central hexagonal raised stand comprised six sections, of which four featured the various materials used by the rock gardener in pursuit of his interests, such as tufa, peat, a variety of stones and soils and a fifth section illustrated methods of propagation. The sixth highlighted the work of the National Council for the Conservation of Plants and Gardens, in maintaining in cultivation old fashioned plants such as gold-laced Polyanthus, green Primroses and the graceful *Uvularia grandiflora*. At one corner of the Wisley exhibit, R.H.S. Publications had arranged a most impressive choice of books from easily digested handbooks for beginners to such learned publications as the Royal Botanic Garden, Edinburgh's publication on the new classification of the genus Rhododendron.

Kew's exhibit of southern hemisphere plants in cultivation included many less familiar to rock gardeners. It demonstrated not only how different in appearance and structure many of these are to our northern hemisphere mountain plants but also made one realise and appreciate the expertise with which these little known plants are grown at Kew. That outrider of the genus Primula, *P. decipiens*, from the Falkland Islands bloomed well alongside *Bolax* (syn. *Azorella) gummifera* the little cushion-forming umbellifer from the same location. From New Zealand came *Fuchsia procumbens*, interesting in flower and later decorative when bearing its red plum-like fruits; the flora of Western Australia contributed *Isotoma petraea* while S.E. Australia was represented by the heath-like *Epacris serpyllifolia* bearing short leafy clusters of white flowers. *Blechnum procera* from Tasmania sported handsome bronze fronds and from Chile, *Leucocoryne coquimbensis* displayed graceful, long-stemmed, blue flowers.

On a small stand next to Kew's exhibit, Sally Walker had come all the way from Arizona to offer seeds of N. American native plants. In the lecture hall an impressive display of photographs graphically illustrated her wares. Next, from Yorkshire, was Hartside Nursery with magnificent plants of *Primula aureata, P. deschmannii,* (syn. *P. × vochinensis*), *P. forsteri,* (syn. *P × steinii* (forsteri form)), and *P. sonchifolia* looking quite at home amidst mossy logs. Broadleigh Gardens emphasised monocotyledons with a wide range of Narcissus, erythroniums, pleiones, fritillarias, trilliums and tulips but apart from those producing swollen roots, there were included several well grown pans of *Viola pedata*.

The Scottish Rock Garden Club took the next bay with mouth-watering photographs of Scottish native plants such as the rare *Diapensia lapponica* and *Loiseleuria procumbens.* On the stand arranged by Holden Clough Nursery the dainty white *Primula modesta* caught my eye together with a compact *Salix repens* cultivar called 'Voorthuizen', while Highgate Alpines were offering plants of the rare biscuit-yellow flowered gesneriad, *Briggsia muscicola*, with handsome, furry, yellow-green leaves, together with other rarities, On a central table, Mrs Parker-Jervis had staged a mainly green and white display giving a cool airiness enhanced by long stems and catkins of three species of willow. *Dodecatheon dentata* figured prominently here. Contrasting with the restrained effect of Mrs Parker-Jervis's exhibit, the fiery colours of *Lewisia cotyledon* (Sunset Strain) drew one from afar to Jack Drake's stand where the light delicacy of the grey-leaved, white "lockets" of *Dicentra cucullaria* held one entranced. Also eye-catching were five species of Aciphylla and the green ferny-leaved, white flowered *Pteridophyllum racemosum*. Dominating the centre of The Linn Nurseries exhibit was a large flowering branch of the huge-trussed, waxy-yellow flowered, Himalayan *Rhododendron macabeanum* surrounded by an array of interesting and unusual trees and shrubs.

Paul Christian's collections of Fritillaria, Narcissus and Muscari were large and varied and included many rare and difficult species. Being as yet uncertain about the world of monocotyledons, it was with heathen-like curiosity that I approached the curly-headed *Fritillaria verticillata* with greeny-yellow flowers, and then fell for a dicotyledon, *Anemone gortschakovii*, with large, soft golden flowers tinged green on the backs of the petals.

At least for the moment John Watson has come to rest from his world-wide wanderings in search of plants and under the heading of Four Seasons Nursery is raising for sale unusual plants including several of his own introductions. Prominent among these was the now well known, easily grown *Mimulus* 'Andean Nymph', rewarding in its profusion of salmony-pink and cream flowers throughout summer. Another traveller come to rest is Jim Archibald of Buckshaw Gardens, now expertly propagating many of those tempting little cushion plants which so personify the alpine scene. *Androsace pubescens, A. vandellii, Veronica bombycina, Trachelium asperuloides*, quaint *Calceolaria darwinii* and the new and entrancing hybrid *Campanula* 'Joe Elliott', were amongst his wares but by far the largest demand was for species of Dionysia, a genus for which Jim Archibald has done much to introduce into cultivation.

Coming late into the marquee, Ingwersen's, old hands at exhibiting, in no time transformed a large blank area into a spectacular table of delights. These included pleiones, among them the rare *P. forrestii*, trilliums, the rich blue *Anchusa caespitosa*, the rare Tasmanian conifer *Microcachrys tetragona*, and a large collection of well grown European primulas.

Ramparts Nursery, famous for silver and grey foliage plants, illustrated the value of these plants, not only in their own right but in enhancing a range of pastel coloured pulsatillas. Small but no less conspicuous was a drift of the tiny *Primula scandinavica* while close by *Calceolaria* 'Walter Shrimpton', with all the appeal of *C. darwinii* but much easier to grow, made a golden splash of colour against the silvers. Asiatic primulas were given prominence in Edrom Nursery's display; beautifully grown and abundantly flowered *Primula boothii* and *P. petiolaris*, Sherriff's form of *P.*

bhutanica and the minor form of *P. gracilipes* were offered. So, too, were excellent little plants of *Shortia soldanelloides* and *Epigaea asiatica.*

Finally, my own stand composed entirely of ericaceous plants in a peat garden setting provided a colourful corner close to the entrance. Free-flowering dwarf Rhododendron hybrids clothed one side in pink, crimson and gold while facing front, two plants of *Rhododendron keiskei* 'Yaku Fairy' at different levels spilled moonlight from one to the other. Kalmias, cassiopes, Kalmiopsis, Zenobia, etc. had been coaxed into flower ahead of their normal season solely to illustrate the diversity of colour and form within the plant family Ericaceae. On one corner a group of seven or eight different bigeneric hybrids made a talking point both among the botanically and horticulturally orientated members.

For many months before the Conference, frenzied and at times frantic industry had been the order of the day both among organizers and exhibitors. At times prior to the show I am sure others allowed themselves to think, as I did, "Is it all worth it?". As the grand parade of the world's best alpines got under way there could be little doubt as to the answer. It was worth it on many counts—not least of all for the camaraderie, for the team spirit of all concerned to make this show memorable. It was worth it for the comments overheard from visitors to the show; worth it for the stimulating conversations about plants; for the old friends met and new friends made; worth it, above all else, to have taken part.

The Premier Award, the Farrer and Forrest Medals awarded jointly for the best plant in the show, went to Mrs Kathleen Dryden for *Rhododendron keiskei* 'Yaku Fairy'. In the Open Section the plant grown in a 12 inch pan and judged to be best went to Geoff Rollinson for *Androsace vandellii* and in a 6½ inch pan to David Mowle, also for *Androsace vandellii*. In Section B the best plant was judged to be *Cassiope* 'Randle Cooke' shown by Frank Walker and in Section C, *Androsace muscoidea* shown by Jonathan Davis.

The highest aggregate of points in the Open Section went to Mrs Jean Wilson, in Section B to Brian A Scowen, in C to Mrs Pat Lowe.

Other major awards in the form of Gold Medals for specific displays went to Mrs Kathleen Dryden (Alpine Plants), Jack Elliott (Fritillarias), D. J. Harberd (Pleiones), Henry and Margaret Taylor

(European Primulas), Ray Woodliffe (Dwarf Salix and Conifers), Norman Woodward (Alpine Flower Stamps), Mrs Jean Wilson (Embroideries), Lawrence Greenwood (Paintings), Royal Horticultural Society, Wisley (Alpine Gardening), Royal Botanic Gardens, Kew (Southern Hemisphere Alpine Plants), Hartside Nursery (Rock Plants), W. E. Th. Ingwersen, Ltd, (Alpines), Barry Starling (Ericaceous Plants), Paul Christian (Rare Bulbs), Harry Ward (A Tribute to Reginald Farrer).

Silver Medals went to Miss E. M. Liquorish (Ferns), F. E. Turner (Pleiones), Norman Woodward (Alpine Plant Prints), Ramparts Nursery (Silver Foliage), Inshriach Alpine Plant Nursery (Alpines), Royal Botanic Garden, Edinburgh (George Forrest Display).

Bronze Medals were awarded to Sally Walker (Photographic Display of south western U.S.A. native plants), Broadleigh Gardens (Bulbs), Holden Clough Nursery (Rock Plants).

The following exhibitors won first prizes in classes requiring three entries and more. The Class numbers are given. S. E. Lilley and Mr and Mrs M. Shrimpton, jointly, (8. six pans, Rock Plants); P. Semple (9. Rock Plants); E. G. Watson (19. Androsaces, 70. Himalayan Plants, 108. New Zealand Plants, 114. Plants from Seed); B. Russ (29. Sempervivums); Mrs Sheila Maule (33. Bulbs); A. Chambers (37. Cyclamen, 82. Saxifragas); Mr and Mrs H. Taylor (43. Ranunculaceae, 66. New Zealand Rock Plants, 88. Primulas); Miss I. M. Welfare (49. Ericaceae); Mrs Jean Wilson (51. Rhododendrons, 64. North American Rock Plants, 77. 6 vases cut alpine flowers, 79. six pans Rock Plants); Mrs Mary Randall (54. Dwarf Shrubs, 68. Japanese Rock Plants); D. Carter (56. Dwarf Conifers); J. B. Saxton (59. Salix); K. Onoe (61. Diapensiaceae); T. Norman (72. twelve pans Hardy Orchids); Mr and Mrs C. Norton (73. Rock Plants for Foliage, 74. Silver Foliage); S. D. Taylor (80. Rock Plants, 84. Primulas, 109. New or Rare Rock Plants); Frank Tindall (86. Primulas); P. Marsh (94. Bulbs); Mrs J. Wilder (96. Orchidaceae); Geoff Rollinson and Eric Watson jointly (108. New Zealand Plants); Brian A. Scowen (116. six pans Rock Plants, 144. Plants from Seed); David Mowle (100. Fritillarias, 112. Bulbs); R. G. Rolfe (117. Rock Plants); A. J. Richards (119. Rock Plants from one country, 140. Silver-Grey Foliage); I. Raynor (134.

Bulbs); B. A. Rushton (139. Rock Plants for Foliage); Miss E. M. Liquorish (142. Rock Plants); Mrs Pam Lowe (148. Rock Plants, 150. Primulaceae).

Artistic Section. Mrs M. D. Walkley (1A. Colour Photographs, 3A. Colour Photographs); F. E. B. Ferns (2A. Monochrome Photographs); M. A. Beswick (4A. Monochrome Photographs); Mrs M. Todd (5A. Paintings of Alpine Plants); Miss S. D. Aitchison (7A. Paintings of Alpine Plants); Lionel Bacon (9A. Line Drawings of Alpine Plants).

Reginald Farrer Exhibit

HARRY D. WARD

The display was compiled as a tribute to the memory of Reginald Farrer, 1880-1920, and to his achievements in the quest for alpine plants. It consisted of an upright unit with two side wings. Two separate tables extended at an angle of 30° from the back of the display. These units were linked by a raised half-moon shaped display space which gave an overall area of 120 square feet. On the back units were mounted the main title, paintings, photographs, maps, etc.

The left hand wing panel showed Farrer's birthplace under the heading of "It began in the hills of Ingleborough, Yorkshire". It comprised an illustrated map of Clapham, the village where Farrer was born and lived. Mounted around this map were coloured postcards, guides, etc., giving a comprehensive picture of the beautiful areas around Ingleborough where Farrer first discovered the charm of alpine plants.

It was originally planned to tour the Ingleborough area to photograph the landscape and things of interest but, unfortunately, on the day of the visit, it poured with rain and this made photography impossible. Luck changed with a call at Clapham Post Office where a good selection of guides, maps and postcards of this attractive area of Yorkshire was purchased.

The centre board was used to exhibit possibly the most interesting part of the project, this being five original watercolour sketches painted by Farrer in the fields of Kansu and Thibet in the years 1914–15.

The paintings were:

F 93	*Stellera chamaejasme*	1914
F137	*Trollius pumilus* and *Geranium* sp.	1914
F255	*Meconopsis psilonomma*	1914
F509	*Incarvillea grandiflora*	1915
F560	*Primula farreri*	1915

Also mounted in this section were Farrer's portrait and a reference to the fact that an exhibit of 101 watercolours painted by Reginald Farrer was held at the Fine Art Galleries in 1917.

The right hand wing panel was used to show the travels of Farrer under the title "Into the High Lands". This was mounted in the form of a map of Kansu, China, when Farrer's companion was

William Purdom of whom Farrer wrote "I had the very rare luck of happening on an absolutely perfect friend and helper in Mr Purdom". He dedicated both "On the Eaves of the World" and "The Rainbow Bridge" to Purdom. These two books are a record of their journey to China in 1914–15.

The second map was of Upper Burma which was the location of a trip taken in 1919–20 with E. H. M. Cox with whom he spent the first year. It was on this journey that Farrer died in October 1920. Mounted around these maps were illustrations of the mountain areas of China and Burma.

On show on the tables were all the books written by Farrer with the exception of four works which are difficult to obtain. Farrer wrote twenty books of which eleven were on gardening and his travels. In addition he made numerous contributions to periodicals over a number of years. Also to be seen were copies of "The Gardener's Chronicle" for 1920–21 which contained reports of his journeys in Burma and an essay on "Some British Alpines" which appeared in "The Flora and Silva" edited by W. Robinson, 1905. Included were books by E. H. M. Cox who has possibly written more about Farrer than any other author. The titles on show were "Farrer's Last Journey" and "The Plant Introductions of Reginald Farrer". Among this collection of books and manuscripts could be found a number of real gems.

Two 56-page catalogues of the Craven Nursery, Clapham, were exhibited, one issued in 1902. The other was undated but it had a very interesting cover which was embossed with the Flora Medal issued by the Royal Horticultural Society and stamped in silver and gold. This catalogue is also full of marginal notes which indicates it may have been used in the preparation of copy for the publication of a new edition. These notes appear to be written in Farrer's own hand.

The Alpine Garden Society received four original letters written in manuscript which were published in the A.G.S. Bulletin, June 1966. These were correspondence with Mrs S. K. Garnett-Botfield while Farrer was in Kansu in 1914–15. An interesting point about these letters is that there were three original envelopes and stamps covered with frank marks (a real find for the philatelist). This correspondence is an insight into Farrer's character. To quote from a letter dated 25th July, 1915 "Your two delightful letters arrived together yesterday by means of our only link with the outside world—an old gentleman of Sining, so unhappily married that to escape from Madame he is only too glad to come trailing over mountains with our mail".

Hand-written field notes were on view under the title of "Manuscript Records and Fieldnotes of Plant and Seed collected in Thibet and Kansu, 1914–15—Reginald Farrer, W. Purdom". These included collections made by Farrer and Purdom. There was also a brief summary of ferns, etc., sent home from the 1919–20 expedition to Burma and additional notes enclosed with consignments of plants giving general instructions to George Redman who was Farrer's manager at Craven Nursery. These records make fascinating reading. To quote:

> "F556 Ribes sp. Wolvesden Coppice June 9—11,000—a hideous dingy flowered affair.
>
> F539 Euphorbia sp. About Tien Tang Ssu—Brought in by a monk.
>
> F531 *Primula urticifolia.* Confined to deep shady gullies of the limestone in damp crannies. 9–12,000. June.
> A little beauty suggesting minima × bella. Painting and photograph. In the combes above Wolvesden Pass it grows freely in the earthy slopes under the cliffs at 13–14,000. Seed early September. Seed and plants.
>
> F671 Leguminosae sp. Wolvesden 10,000 August. An ugly graceless great yellow thing."

Also to be seen was a copy of The Journal of Botany, November 1894 which was the magazine that first found Farrer in print at the age of 14 years with an item on *Arenaria gothica,* a plant he discovered at the foot of Ingleborough.

I am happy to acknowledge the assistance and encouragement I received from many friends in assembling this exhibit and the Alpine Garden Society for the loan of paintings, field notes, letters and catalogues.

Paeonia obovata   (*Plate 98*)

Ranzania japonica   (*Plate 99*)

Primula hidakana   (*Plate 100*)

Eranthis pinnatifida   (*Plate 101*)

Gentiana acaulis   (*Plate 102*)

Raoulia australis   (*Plate 103*)

Primula sonchifolia   (*Plate 104*)

Ramonda myconi   (*Plate 105*)

George Forrest Exhibit

BRINSLEY BURBIDGE

In purely commercial terms the selling of alpine and rock garden plants has never been big business whereas trees and shrubs, when sold in quantity to large estates and to Government or Local Authority buyers can make large sums of money for the nurseryman. A consequence of this is that plant collectors have always been encouraged to bring back decorative trees and shrubs: plants for the smaller garden and the specialist grower have been forced into second place.

This commercial emphasis on larger plants has resulted in many collectors, including George Forrest, concentrating on trees and shrubs and in Forrest's case being known mainly as the "greatest ever collector of rhododendrons". More than one in ten of his gatherings were, in fact, rhododendrons and from these over three hundred new species were to be described, but what of the other nine out of the ten? Some were trees: Abies, Magnolia, Sorbus and so on but the majority fall into the category of rock garden and alpine house plants.

In sheer numbers, primulas rank second to rhododendrons with over forty new species still recognised (and another forty names now reduced to synonymy). Rather strangely few of his primulas still survive in cultivation. *Primula helodoxa, P. bulleyana, P. beesiana* and their hybrids are frequently grown in marshy garden areas but only *P. denticulata* and its many variants could be said to be commonly grown (it was originally introduced by Dr Royle). *Primula malacoides* has had outstanding success as a "florist's primula" but only the rare *Primula forresti* is occasionally encountered as an alpine house treasure.

Other genera contribute more prolifically to the smaller garden with Gentiana coming out top of the list in sheer numbers of plants. Forrest's collection no. 408 made during his first expedition in 1904 was named *Gentiana sino-ornata*. Introduced into cultivation by Forrest in 1910 it must rank as one of his supreme additions to our garden flora both as the species and for its influence as a parent of many hybrids. The gentian which bears Forrest's forename, *G. georgei* (not regarded by all authorities as a species in its own right) is unhappily no longer in cultivation. From Forrest's descriptions, photographs and herbarium specimens (the flower has a deep purple trumpet with a green base and broad green stripes on the exterior) it is an astonishingly beautiful plant. A photograph of it was shown in the exhibit.

From the genus Meconopsis Forrest gave us *M. delavayi* (a rarity), *M. horridula* and *M. integrifolia* among others, all excellent plants. Among his irises the yellow *I. forrestii* and the beautifully marked *I. chrysographes* with golden markings on almost-black velvety falls take pride of place. *Paraquilegia grandiflora* stands out as one of the great challenges to the alpine house enthusiast and *Roscoea humeana* is the best species in its genus for beauty and for comparative ease of cultivation and hardiness.

So the list continues through Nomocharis, Pieris, Omphalogramma, Pleione, Lilium, Delphinium, Daphne and many, many others. The exhibit aimed at showing just a few of Forrest's smaller introductions and something of the country and conditions in which they were collected.

Post-Conference Tour

ELIZABETH IVEY

After an amusing time spent in watching the drivers trying to accommodate all the luggage and plants which had accrued during the Pre-Conference Tour and the Conference itself, four coaches left Nottingham for the north on the morning of 17th April slightly behind schedule.

We were blessed with a fine morning and everyone set off in happy anticipation of what was to come. Our first stop was at Harrogate, to visit the Northern Horticultural Society's Garden at Harlow Car, where Mr Philip Swindells, the Garden Superintendent, was on hand to answer all our questions. Most people gravitated towards the rock garden and peat terraced areas to see the early spring display. The primulas were looking superb, especially the drifts of European species and hybrids. Inevitably we all congregated in the vicinity of the alpine house and raised beds. Among the delights in the alpine house were the lewisias and many dwarf bulbs, particularly irises and fritillaries. The troughs and raised beds contained a wonderful selection of silver foliage plants and bulbs which, in cultivation, require very sharp drainage.

After lunch at Harrogate the coaches continued north into Scotland where the participants were based in various hotels in Edinburgh for the duration of the tour.

Saturday was spent in visiting Mr and Mrs Masterton's garden at Cluny, Aberfeldy and the Inshriach Alpine Plant Nursery at Aviemore.

Spring was typified by the marvellous drifts of golden daffodils cascading down the grassy bank at the rear of Cluny House. We were also treated to a wonderful display of *Primula sonchifolia* in full bloom in various parts of the woodland garden. Our American friends must have enjoyed seeing many of their native trilliums and erythroniums growing so happily in the woodland setting. The ever popular *Primula denticulata* in its varying colour forms and sited on a sunny bank was a sight to behold. Lovers of woodland plants were in their element admiring the numerous hybrid hellebores scattered around the slopes. We saw a box of *Primula aureata* in the porch which had been displayed for our enjoyment and in another area a particularly rich ruby-purple *P. calderiana,* raised from seed sent home by the late Len Beer, was much admired.

After lunch at Pitlochry, and with good weather remaining with us, the drive north through the centre of Scotland to Aviemore was really beautiful. To see the Scottish scenery in all its grandeur, coupled with brilliant sunshine was unbelievable, certainly not typical of the climate we can too often experience in a late spring in Scotland.

Inshriach Alpine Plant Nursery is Mecca to alpine gardeners. John Lawson has taken over the reins from Jack Drake very successfully, but Jack is an enthusiast and just cannot resist working with plants! They were both there to greet us and were kept busy fetching and carrying all the plants they could handle in the time allotted for the visit. The nursery garden was very colourful, and as the Inshriach soil is peaty the ericaceous plants grow to perfection. Most cameras were at some time focused on *Corydalis ambigua* in full bloom—how interesting it was to see it in reality after viewing Brian Mathew's beautiful slides at Nottingham on this particular genus. Another plant which caught the eye was *Polygala chamaebuxus* 'Rhodoptera' planted on top of a retaining wall alongside the frames containing many New Zealand treasures which also grow happily under Inshriach conditions.

It was an extremely tired' but happy group which returned to Edinburgh that evening. It was a long day but a memorable one both for plants and scenery.

On Sunday we played "musical coaches" round three notable gardens in the Carse of Gowrie. They were Branklyn Garden now owned by the National Trust for Scotland but formerly the home of Mr and Mrs John Renton who were recognised plant authorities, Mr and Mrs Peter Cox's garden at Glendoick and the garden belonging to Lt-Col and Mrs J. D. C. Anderson at Invergowrie.

The schedule was tight and we had to rely on our coach drivers to keep us up to time. This they achieved with precision, greatly admired by all, especially me, as I had been responsible for arranging the itineraries which everyone said could not be done! Thanks to the co-operation of the drivers everything worked out perfectly.

Branklyn Garden looked well and over the years several areas had been redesigned. To those who were familiar with the garden it was obvious that a great deal of time and effort had been put into making new peat beds and walls in which to accommodate ericaceous genera. The scree was in the process of being completely refurbished. Larger rocks had been introduced and there were many new plantings. The past winter had been kind to the early spring flowering plants and, as no severe frosts had occurred prior to our visit, the rhododendrons were resplendent. Many cassiopes were to be seen in the peat area and, in particular, several hybrids of *Cassiope wardii* were outstanding.

Colonel and Mrs Anderson's large garden shows the hands of true plantsmen. It is maintained entirely by this knowledgeable and far travelled couple. Many of the larger specimens had been received as cuttings when they were laying out their garden but, with skill in cultivation and foresight in siting and taking advantage of screening trees, those scions are now mature flowering plants and are enjoyed by all who visit the garden. The overall effect can be best viewed from the front of the house. The terraced area is for rock garden type plants and dwarf bulbs, a burn runs through the garden allowing moisture-loving primulas, soldanellas, omphalogrammas and ourisias to be cultivated, on the high sunny banks are displayed many of the rarer and more difficult bulbs, and an area round the perimeter contains many trees, shrubs, rhododendrons, Meconopsis and liliums. Mention must be made of the *Paraquilegia grandiflora* flowering magnificently in a large trough. It had the cameras clicking! On this occasion our thanks are also due to members of the Angus Group of the S.R.G.C. for their industry in assembling a beautiful and comprehensive collection of plants in the garage. Many of these had been on display at Nottingham.

To complete the day we visited the garden of Mr and Mrs Peter Cox at Glendoick, famous for its rhododendrons and shrubs for specialists. Those who were at the garden in the morning were fortunate in meeting Peter himself, for by the afternoon he had to prepare for going off on a plant collecting trip to western China. However, his nephew, Mr Peter Milne, ably substituted for him. Dry sunny weather made the walk up through the "Den" very pleasant as conditions underfoot were ideal. The Den area is kept as natural as possible, and wild flowers are encouraged to an extent. To many of us it was breath-taking to see so many Rhododendron species magnificently grown in conditions ideally suited to their height and spread. Many of them were names in catalogues to some of us. The smaller rhododendrons and ericaceous species are grown in an area to the west of the dwelling house. It would be unjust to the others to single out particular plants as they were all equally beautiful and I feel it is sufficient to say that Peter and Tricia Cox are doing a grand job in keeping in cultivation many of the rare and more difficult shrubby species which many of us would love to have in our own gardens if space, soil and climate permitted.

Monday was given over to the St Andrews University Botanic Garden. We were welcomed at the gate and were provided with a list of plants recorded in flower at this time during the previous year and a map of the layout of the garden. These proved to be very useful. The weather was warm and sunny and the gentle stroll round the rock garden, down the scree and over to the peat and woodland areas was delightful. The alpine house was especially interesting where *Primula scotica*, the dionysias and androsaces were in full bloom. This is a relatively new botanic garden, at least the site is new, and Bob Mitchell, the curator, is putting his own particular stamp on the layout. Dwarf bulbs were very much in evidence in the rock garden, especially Narcissus, and the scree housed some well known treasures such as *Iberis pygmaea* and *Androsace microphylla* grown to perfection. I saw numerous people so busily photographing *Gentiana dinarica* that they missed *Iris bucharica*; the yellow of the iris, alas, took second place to the blue of the gentian. Trilliums, hellebores, phyllodoces and cassiopes featured prominently in the peat areas were too numerous to mention specifically. Great credit is due to the staff for the work being put into this new garden which in time, I'm sure, will rank amongst the finest in Britain.

A private garden visited near Edinburgh was that belonging to Sheila and John Maule at Balerno. This garden is unique—it has been developed in an old quarry and every particle of soil had to be imported and the rock garden built up in the form of raised beds from the quarry floor. Sheila is one of the top growers and exhibitors at S.R.G.C. Shows and, naturally, we were all eager to see the alpine houses and frames where she keeps her "potted treasures".

Her expertise is renowned and in particular her ability to grow dwarf bulbs from seed. She is well known abroad for, as Overseas Liaison Secretary, she corresponds with many overseas enthusiasts exchanging seeds and know-how. Many troughs have been collected over the years and these contain specimens of the more compact and slower growing plants from all over the alpine world. It is obvious that Sheila and John love New Zealand plants, particularly celmisias, as several different types were dotted around the garden. The Maules have travelled far and wide to see and examine plants growing in the wild and have assembled and established a fine selection of plant material over the years.

Because of the demand for places due to the popularity of this tour it was decided that other gardens should be added to the list originally published. The object was not only to relieve the pressure on some smaller gardens but to increase the variety on the itineraries. So some participants were fortunate in spending an afternoon at Keillour Castle, the home of Mrs Mary Knox Finlay. The garden at Keillour is famous for many plants, Lilium and Nomocharis being prime examples, but primulas and Meconopsis and a host of Himalayan species flourish there. A very well flowered *Magnolia campbellii* with deep pink flowers was much admired, rhododendrons were blooming in profusion, the many spathes of *Lysichiton americanum, L. camtschatcense* and the vigorous cream-coloured hybrid were spectacular, erythroniums were everywhere while the range of colours and forms displayed by the hybrid swarm of *Helleborus × heyderi* were examined at great length. One of the largest plants seen of *Orphanidesia gaultherioides* filled a sheltered corner and some very fine examples of the *Primula griffithii* hybrid 'Fantail' came in for much discussion.

The small garden tended by Henry and Margaret Taylor must be one of the most densely planted. It contains collections of all manner of alpine plants prominent among them being the European primulas. A comprehensive group of these had already been on display at the Conference Show. The beds and borders outside were filled with well-tended ericaceous genera, rhododendrons and cassiopes being especially fine while celmisias, sempervivums, saxifragas, androsaces and a wide selection of dwarf and slow growing conifers were minutely examined. The small alpine house was packed with a wide range of interesting and rare species, *Paraquilegia grandiflora,* campanulas, androsaces, primulas and *Viola cazorlensis* receiving attention, while one or two rosulate violas were critically viewed. A slight deviation was made and this involved clambering over a dividing fence into the garden next door. This belongs to Mr and Mrs F. Hunt, fairly new members of the S.R.G.C., where a remarkably fine collection of plants had been mustered. Peat-loving plants were flourishing and the display of dwarf rhododendrons, small conifers and fine clumps of celmisias, etc., suggested a close liaison between neighbours.

On the way to St Andrews the coach stopped at the tiny garden belonging to Mr and Mrs Jim Christie at Guardbridge. Prominent among the many fine specimens admired were ancient individual plants of *Salix × boydii* and *Juniperus communis* 'Compressa'. The scent from mats of Raoulia species pervaded the atmosphere on entering the garden. The amazing number of plants which can be well grown in a small alpine house was demonstrated here for the collection embraced androsaces, saxifragas, drabas, primulas, campanulas, etc. A technical feature which drew comment was Jim's ingenious method of utilising a capillary-type irrigation system, using sand, to keep his seed pans moist.

The climax of the tour was the visit to the Royal Botanic Garden, Edinburgh, on the Tuesday. We assembled in the lecture theatre where we were welcomed by the Regius Keeper, Mr D. M. Henderson. He explained the origin of the garden and listed all the facilities which would be made available to us that day. We were honoured to be permitted to see behind the scenes, and staff were on hand in the Herbarium and Library to deal with our questions.

The general layout of the garden was also explained to us and members of the gardening staff guided small groups to several areas which were of topical interest before we were let loose to wander at will and view at our own pace this world-famous garden.

It would be difficult to describe the R.B.G., as it is affectionately called, and its plants in a few words. It could be sufficient to say that the rock garden extends to over 2½ acres, that the peat garden covers a fairly extensive area and that the relatively new feature, the alpine house complex, caters for a very large number of interesting species and varieties, but that would provide hardly any information at all.

From the start it was obvious that the accent is on wild occurring species. Large collections of all manner of fascinating genera were on display. Alpine rhododendrons, cassiopes, phyllodoces, gaultherias, and vacciniums were planted in quantity. Hundreds of dwarf rhododendrons were planted as a heath and carpeting the spaces between these were thousands of autumn-flowering Asiatic gentians. This must be a wonderful sight during August and September. Numerous species of Meconopsis were to be seen and trilliums, a genus of particular interest at the time, were present in quantity and variety. Primulas, too, were much in evidence.

The potted alpines, androsaces, drabas, primulas, dionysias, raoulias, lewisias, saxifragas, sempervivums, etc., were objects of much discussion while desirable individuals like Jankaea, Kelseya, Pteridophyllum, Gypsophila and others too numerous to list brought forth favourable comments. Alpine enthusiasts can pay a visit to this botanic garden at any time of year and still find a lot to interest them.

A reception arranged and sponsored by the Edinburgh Group of the S.R.G.C. was held in the Royal Society's Rooms in George Street. These are beautiful rooms and they certainly added grandeur and an ambience to the affair and to the stay in the capital city. The reception, which was held on the last evening of the tour, gave the hosts and invited guests an opportunity to renew contacts with overseas friends made at Nottingham and, at the same time, to wish the visitors a safe return home.

In conclusion I should like to record my thanks to all the garden owners for their hospitality, co-operation and willingness in allowing so many delegates to view their gardens, all those who donated gifts and supplied literature for the 169 participants, and the volunteer couriers who did a grand job.

Index